T0120324

A
LITTLE BOOK
ON FORM

PROSE

Twentieth Century Pleasures

Now and Then: The Poet's Choice Columns

What Light Can Do

EDITOR

Rock and Hawk: The Shorter Poems of Robinson Jeffers

Tomas Transtromer: Selected Poems 1954–1986

Into the Garden: A Wedding Anthology
(with Stephen Mitchell)

Poet's Choice: Poems for Everyday Life

The Addison Street Anthology
(with Jessica Fisher)

Walt Whitman: Song of Myself, A Lexicon

Modernist Women Poets
(with Paul Ebencamp)

OTHER

A Poetic Species:
Robert Hass and E. O. Wilson in Conversation

A
LITTLE BOOK
ON FORM

*An Exploration into
the Formal Imagination of Poetry*

ROBERT HASS

ecco
An Imprint of HarperCollinsPublishers

Pages 433–446 serve as a continuation of the copyright page.

A LITTLE BOOK ON FORM. Copyright © 2017 by Robert Hass. All rights reserved. Printed in the United States of America. No part of this book may be used or reproduced in any manner whatsoever without written permission except in the case of brief quotations embodied in critical articles and reviews. For information address HarperCollins Publishers, 195 Broadway, New York, NY 10007.

HarperCollins books may be purchased for educational, business, or sales promotional use. For information please e-mail the Special Markets Department at SPsales@harpercollins.com.

A hardcover edition of this book was published in 2017 by Ecco, an imprint of HarperCollins Publishers.

FIRST ECCO PAPERBACK EDITION PUBLISHED 2018.

Designed by Suet Yee Chong

Library of Congress Cataloging-in-Publication Data has been applied for.

ISBN 978-0-06-233243-1

HB 07.10.2024

To Connie Brothers

CONTENTS

A

LITTLE BOOK
ON FORM

INTRODUCTION

This is a book about the formal imagination in poetry.

It began as a series of notes and reading lists for a seminar I was invited to teach at the University of Iowa Writers Workshop in the winter of 1995. The invitation was to teach a class on forms. When I looked at books on the subject, I saw that they mostly took form to mean traditional rules previous to composition—rules for the formation of the sonnet, for example, or the villanelle, and while the information in them was quite useful, it didn't seem to me to have too much to do with the way the formal imagination actually operates in poetry. It does not, for starters, address the formal principles, or impulses, that underlie the great majority of poetry in English and American literatures not written in these conventional forms.

It seemed possible to construct notes toward a notion of form that would more accurately reflect the openness and the instinctiveness of formal creation by starting with one line as the basic gesture of a poem, and then looking at two lines and their relation to each other as a form or a proposition of form, and then three lines as another, and four lines—two sets of two—as still another, inside an idea that from these basic forms all the others could be generated. The sonnet is two quatrains and two triplets if it is Italian, three quatrains and a couplet if it is English, and so on. As for genre, our sense of it in English has been increasingly restless since the middle of the eighteenth century. Nineteenth-century poets wrote metrical verse with great facility, but—except for the romantic odes—were not inclined to think inside classical ideas of genre. Twentieth-century poets were attracted, some of them, to gaming forms—the sestina, the pantoum—for interesting reasons, but they were not inclined to write eclogues or odes or formal satires. Still, the essential expressive gestures inside those forms, forms that have held traditional shapes of grief, rage, longing, spite, adoration, have persisted, and it seemed that there could be ways of understanding the persistence of those shapes of thought and feeling. These were the impulses with which I began these notes, these and the feeling that we do not have a very good language for the ways in which it seems most interesting to think about form. I've revised the notes slightly and added to them on subsequent visits to the workshop and updated the readings when a new book or essay appeared on some subject—the ghazal or the sestina, for example. The notes are intended to be suggestive, not comprehensive. I'm very much aware that they come from what I happen to have read or be reading and that other readers will bring other lists and perhaps better example drawn from other traditions to the issues of craft discussed here.

Two books in particular to be recommended that appeared in these years: Annie Finch, *An Exaltation of Forms*; Mark Strand and Eavan Boland, *The Making of a Poem*.

(I should also say that the notes were intended for mostly young poets entering a two-year period of intense reading and writing that was to give them a chance to develop their art, so it didn't seem unreasonable to propose that they might do a quick read through the history of the sonnet or of Harlem Renaissance experiments with the blues form. The class was three hours on an afternoon. For the second half of the class, I asked each student to make a presentation on an idea of form in some discipline or craft other than poetry. They approached this task in many ways, and their informal talks entered the conversation alongside the readings proposed here. One student taught the class to waltz. One played a recording of and analyzed the structure of a raga. One, working part-time as a dessert chef in a local restaurant, demonstrated the construction of an apple galette. There were talks on the formal ordering of 1970s disco albums, form in the photographs of Cartier-Bresson, the building of a wooden canoe, and of a computer program, the plots of films noir, and the architectural design of mosques.)

So we might begin with definitions:

* One meaning of form that has currency has the meaning "traditional form," which usually means the use of rhyme and meter.
* Another meaning is that it refers to one of a number of traditional kinds of poems that apply particular rules of composition. As in "the sonnet is a form."
* Another meaning is "external shape."
* Another is "the arrangement and relationship of basic elements in a work of art, through which it produces a coherent whole."

All four of these usages are common, useful, and none of them capture the nature of the formal imagination—the intuitions that shape a work of art—or the pleasure form gives to writer and reader. Closer might be:

* The way the poem embodies the energy of the gesture of its making.

This is near to the idea of form implied by the aesthetic of abstract expressionist painting—the idea that what's on the canvas is what the painter did to it, using the materials he or she was using.

* * *

Further considerations from four thinkers, one fictional:

1. The energy of the gesture of its making: not far from the aesthetic James Joyce has Stephen Dedalus propound in *Portrait of the Artist.* Here, for example:

> -To finish what I was saying about beauty, said Stephen, the most satisfying relations of the sensible must therefore correspond to the necessary phases of artistic apprehension. Find these and you find the qualities of universal beauty. Aquinas says: *Ad pulcritudinem tria requiruntur, integritas, consonantia, claritas.* I translate it so: *Three things are needed for beauty, wholeness, harmony, and radiance.* Do these correspond to the phases of apprehension? Are you following?
>
> -Of course, I am, said Lynch. If you think I have an excrementitious intelligence run after Donovan and ask him to listen to you.
>
> -Look at that basket, he said.
>
> -I see it, said Lynch.
>
> -In order to see that basket, said Stephen, your mind first of all separates the basket from the rest of the visible universe which is not the basket. The first phase of apprehension is a bounding line drawn about the object to be apprehended. An esthetic image is presented to us either in space or time. What is audible is presented in time, what is visible is presented in space. But temporal or spatial, the esthetic image is first luminously apprehended as self-bounded and self-contained upon the immeasurable background of space or time which is not it. You apprehend it as one thing. You see it as *one* whole. You apprehend its wholeness. That is *integritas.*
>
> -Bull's eye! said Lynch, laughing. Go on.

-Then, said Stephen, you pass from point to point, led by its formal lines; you apprehend it as balanced part against part within its limits; you feel the rhythm of its structure. In other words, the synthesis of immediate perception is followed by the analysis of apprehension. Having first felt that it is *one* thing you feel now that it is a *thing*. You apprehend it as complex, multiple, divisible, separable, made up of its parts, the result of its parts and their sum, harmonious. That is *consonantia*.

-Bull's eye again! said Lynch wittily. Tell me now what is *claritas* and you win the cigar.

-The connotation of the word, Stephen said, is rather vague. Aquinas uses a term which seems to be inexact. It baffled me for a long time. It would lead you to believe he had in mind symbolism or idealism, the supreme quality of beauty being a light from some other world, the idea of which the matter was but a shadow, the reality of which it was but a symbol. I thought he might mean the *claritas* was the artistic discovery and representation of the divine purpose in anything or a force of generalization which would make the esthetic image a universal one, make it outshine its proper conditions. But that is literary talk. I understand it so. When you have apprehended that basket as one thing and have then analyzed it according to its form and apprehended it as a thing you make the only synthesis which is logically and esthetically permissible. You see that it is that thing which it is and no other thing. The radiance of which he speaks is the scholastic *quidditas*, the *whatness* of a thing. This supreme quality is felt by the artist when the esthetic image is first conceived in his imagination. The mind in that mysterious instant Shelley likened beautifully to a fading coal. The instant wherein that supreme quality of beauty, the clear radiance of the esthetic image, is apprehended luminously by the mind which has been arrested by its wholeness and fascinated by its harmony is the luminous silent stasis of

esthetic pleasure, a spiritual state very like to that cardiac condition which the Italian physiologist Luigi Galvani, using a
phrase almost as beautiful as Shelley's, called the enchantment
of the heart.

Stephen paused and, though his companion did not speak,
felt that his words had called up around them a thought-
enchanted silence.

2. To gloss this, here is Terry Eagleton on Thomas Aquinas's notion of form. So, two thinkers, in fact, after the fictitious one, one
alive, one dead though lively:

> Aquinas believed in the soul, as Daniel Dennett and Rich-
> ard Dawkins do not; but one reason he did so was because he
> thought it yielded the richest possible understanding of the
> lump of matter known as the body. As Wittgenstein once re-
> marked: if you want an image of the soul, look at the body.
> The soul for Thomas is not some ghostly extra, as it was for
> the platonizing Christians of his time; it is not to be seen as a
> spiritual kidney or spectral pancreas. The question "Where-
> abouts in the body is the soul?" would to his mind involve a
> category mistake, as though one were to ask how close to the
> left armpit one's envy was located. For Aquinas, the soul is
> everywhere in the body precisely because it is what he calls,
> after Aristotle, the "form" of it, meaning the way in which it
> is uniquely organized to be expressive of meaning. The soul
> is not some sort of thing, but the distinctive way in which a
> particular piece of matter is alive. It is quite as visible as a club
> foot. To claim that a spider has a different sort of soul from a
> human being is in Thomas's view simply to say that it has a
> different form of life. What distinguishes an animal body from
> a hat or a hosepipe is the fact that it is signifying, communica-
> tive, self-transformative stuff, in contrast to the meaninglessly

dumb matter of so much contemporary materialism. It is, in Turner's phrase, "matter articulate."

3. Joyce's Dedalus's Aquinas gets wonderfully, I think, the resonances we experience in—I'm not sure what adjective to use—a well-made thing, a passionately made thing, a thing made from a full commitment to the art it instances, captures the way it expresses both energy and stillness. We experience the formal effects of a work of art along a spectrum between stillness and terrific movement, as some works of art come from depth and silence and others from adrenaline and vigor. Dedalus is especially good on the stillness end of that spectrum—emanations like the ones John Keats renders in the first line of his ode on the Greek vase: "Thou still unravaged bride of quietness!" or that some haiku have, even in translation, like this by Yosa Buson:

> Spring evening—
> the sound of the bell
> as it leaves the bell.

4. In one of her essays, "The Rejection of Closure," Lyn Hejinian catches the sense of fountaining energy at the other end of the spectrum: "Writing's forms are not merely shapes, but forces; formal questions are about dynamics—they ask how, where, and why the writing moves, what are the types, direction, number, and velocities of a work's motion."

ONE

1. A single line is a naked thing. It is both light and heavy. It is, obviously, the basic unit of all lyric forms. Two of them make a couplet or, in Bantu song, a combination, three of them a blues lyric or a stanza of Dante's terza rima, four a hymn stanza or a ballad stanza or a Chinese quatrain. Five in Japanese make a tanka, and so on.

By itself it is identical with itself, if it is syntactically complete.

2. Robert Lowell: "It's much easier to write a good poem than a good line."

Robert Duncan:

> By stress and syllable
> by change rhyme and contour
> we let the long line pace even awkward to its period.
> The short line
> we refine,
> and keep for candor.

This is the Yulelog that warms December.
This is new grass that springs from the ground.

3 . The first formal fact about the single line is that it is either identical with itself or not, matches a completed or partially completed grammatical sense—

April is the cruellest month,

Or does not—

April is the cruellest month, breeding
Lilacs out of the dead land, mixing
Memory and desire, stirring

and from this fact the energy and movement of verse—the word means "a turning"—derives.

4 . If it makes a completed sense, the line is heir and hostage to the structure of English grammar in which (noun-verb-object) something happens to something:

All things that love the sun are out of doors.

And worms will try your long-preserved virginity.

I have done it again.

Or has the quality of something:

The art of losing isn't hard to master.

Unless it chooses not to be, as in this line from Clark Coolidge:

Ink of this Egyptian knock over night.

(Even to a line like this the ghost of syntax sings. We want to read "knock over" as an adjective.)

5. The hidden paradigm of the single line is the completed sentence, without which idea there would be no enjambment.

The sentence imitates insight. It is the mode of individuation, the thought that separates us from others and gives us a self. To say it another way, the sentence is being, enjambment is excess of being, or being in process, reaching toward itself. Which is its basic characteristic. Excess and instability and movement and change. The sentence moves and it arrests movement.

The sentence is also an action, an event in time. In one way of thinking, being is stasis; in another it is movement, that is, the only being we have is becoming, and the self is movement (we are not things but processes). However, the sentence is the instrument through which the self-as-a-process mimics being-as-a-process, at the same time that it arrests it. A sentence, unlike actions in the world, is a proposition of finitude; it has a beginning and an end. The tension in the sentence between its action and its stillness is a source of endless paradox.

In another way of thinking, being is movement, but the self is not movement. There are two ways of saying this, quite different from each other, and they bear on what we think both the sentence and the line are for.

One way to say it is the currently out of favor "essentialist" position, that the self is, and can be accurately represented as, the still point from which movement is perceived. The existentialist version of this is to say that the self wants to be (and can never altogether be) the still point from which movement is perceived, and that is the energy and the torment (or the dance) of this desire that constitutes it. And is the problem inherent in representing the way perception happens, since something happens to something in the English language and both somethings are moving targets.

The other way to say that the self is not movement is to say that it is nothing. Looked at, it's nothing. And this fact—experience, really—has been a traditional way out of instability and change. For some the impersonality of form echoes an emptiness because it's not personal. Form feels different from subjectivity. It feels like it belongs to other, larger rhythms. This is the reason some Buddhist artist/thinkers like John Cage have been attracted to the most arbitrary forms.

And in this way there are perhaps three basic attitudes toward form. First, that it is being, or mimics it, elaborated to a fullness. Second, that it is the emptiness against which being plays, through which it courses. Third, that it is made thing, the work of man the maker constructing a world out of the paradoxical movement and stillness of the sentence:

These fragments I have shored against my ruin

And there is a fourth idea, associated with Oulipo and other experimental practice, that it is, like everything else, a throw of the dice (or of the device) and so the more arbitrary the formal principle that generates it, the better.

6. Greek mathematicians did not think one was a number because the concept *one* did not involve number. To them, two was the first number. And the hybrid marriage of one, which was not a number, and two, which was, begot three, the second number. And from one, two, and three, all other numbers proceeded, so that all odd num-

bers had in them an element that was not number. This is why Plato said that the leap from one to two was the leap to rationality.

Leonard Bernstein, speaking of music, said that two was a rhythm of the body and three was a rhythm of the mind. This has been contested by people who say that three is a rhythm of the body and two a rhythm of the mind. Not everyone has weighed in on this subject. But it seems intuitively right, doesn't it? To say that there is a groundedness in the symmetry of twos, off which threes seem to play, seem airier.

7. Some memorable one-sentence lines:

> I sought my death and found it in my womb (1586)
> Sweet Thames, run softly, till I end my song (1596)
> Shall I compare thee to a summer's day? (1598)
> Those are pearls that were his eyes (1611)
> My sin was too much hope of thee, loved boy (1621)
> For God's sake, hold your tongue and let me love (1633)
> I am a little world made cunningly (1635)
> Is all good structure in a winding stair? (1638)

(Collect your own.) A hundred lines by other people arranged by you is a cento. A cento can be arranged so that the lines from different sources and context make continuous sense. Or not. See John Ashbery, "The Dong with the Luminous Nose."

8. *The one-line poem in Japanese:* As far as I know, there is only one such form in wide use and it is a mixed case, the haiku. It has, of course, a three-part prosodic structure, five syllables–seven syllables–five syllables. But, as written in Japanese, it is usually represented in a single line and there is a long controversy about

whether it should be translated as a one-line or a three-line poem. Hiroaki Sato is probably the best one-line translator of haiku. His versions can be found in *From the Country of Eight Islands: An Anthology of Japanese Poetry*. You will notice, however, that the haiku, a one-line form with a three-part prosodic structure, usually consists of two images. And so you'll also notice that inside what is apparently a single line, there is a play of one, two, or three elements, balanced or unbalanced in various ways that are expressive in relation to what the poem is saying.

Ten by Matsuo Bashō:

Old pond: frog's jumping's water-sound.

Crow just settled on a bare branch—autumn evening.

Snowy morning, by myself, eating salmon jerky.

As for the hibiscus on the roadside, my horse ate it.

The bee staggers out of the peony.

First snow falling on a half-finished bridge.

End of fall and we're parting, clamshells on the beach

Spring going, birds weeping, tears in the eyes of fish

Walked past a man with a swollen face in the winter wind.

What's cool? the clean lines of the pine.

Ten by Buson:

I go, you stay, two autumns.

Coolness: the sound of the bell as it leaves the bell.

Green leaves, white water, the barley yellowing.

Plum petals burning on the clods of horseshit.

Apprentice's day off: hops over kite string, keeps going.

Straw sandal half sunk in an old pond in sleety snow.

Yellow of spring, no whale in sight, the sea darkening.

Mad girl in the boat at midday: spring currents.

Farmer goes out to check his scarecrow and comes back.

Short night: bubbles of crab froth in the river reeds.

Ten by Kobayashi Issa:

Goes out, comes back: love life of a cat.

The man pulling radishes points my way with a radish.

Deer licking first frost from one another's coats.

This world: hell's top's flower-gazing.

Even with insects, some can sing, some can't.

Wren: here, there—you lose something?

Icicles hanging from the nose of the Buddha on the moor.

Washing saucepans: moon glowing on her hands in the
    shallow river.

Not very anxious to bloom, my plum tree.

Not knowing it's in a kitchen, the fish cooling in a tub.

9. *The one-line poem in English:* They hardly exist, of course. But there have been experiments. I'm not sure whether to think of John Ashbery's "37 Haiku" as thirty-seven poems or one poem called "37 Haiku," in which case it is not an example of the one-line poem but of the one-line stanza.

A few examples, in the event that they are individual poems:

> Too low for nettles but it is exactly the way people think and
>   feel
> You have original artworks hanging on the wall oh I said edit
> Pirates imitate the ways of ordinary people myself for instance
> Planted over and over that land has a bitter aftertaste
> What trees, tools, why ponder sox on the premises
> In winter sometimes you see those things and also in summer
> A child must go down it must stand and last
> I lost my ridiculous accent without acquiring another
> In Buffalo, Buffalo she was praying, the night sticks together
>   like pages in an old book
> Did you say, hearing the schooner overhead, we turned back
>   to the weir?

Allen Ginsberg had the idea that the image in a blues refrain was the American haiku. He recalled W. C. Handy writing that the first blues he ever heard, played by a black man in a train station in Tutwiler, Mississippi, had this lyric: "I'm goin' where the Southern cross the Dog." First, here are some refrains from blues lyrics to be reconsidered as haiku:

> I hate to see that evening sun go down.
> Wild women don't worry, right there that's the news.
> Uh oh, black snake crawling in my room.
> Blues come from Texas loping like a mule.

Good morning, blues. Blues, how do you do?
If you don't like ocean, don't fish my sea.
See see rider see what you have done.
Thirty days in jail with my back turned to the wall.
Think someone else's mule is kicking in my stall.
Ain't no use to wandering neither to strutting around.
Get full of good liquor, walk the streets all night.
Just make me a pallet on your floor.
He comes around but the mill done broke.
Blood red river and a rocker chair.

Ginsberg called his adaptations, one-line poems that he thought of as fusing the haiku and the blues line, "American Sentences." Here are a few examples:

Tompkins Square Lower East Side NY
Four skinheads stand in the streetlight rain chatting under an
    umbrella.

Approaching Seoul by Bus in Heavy Rain
Get used to your body, forget you were born, suddenly you
    got to get out!

Put on my tie in a taxi, short of breath, rushing to meditate.
—*November 1991, New York*

Rainy night on Union Square, full moon. Want more poems?
    Wait till I'm dead

The use of title and dates may be thought to violate the pure proposition of a one-line poem. Well, so what? Many of the haiku poets gave their poems brief superscriptions that function like Ginsberg's titles to create a context. And a recent book by Carol Snow, *Breath As* (Em Press), contains both titled and untitled one-line poems:

For K.
Then Kathy—"Is that mine?"—ran out to the crying in the yard.

In Brief
"—necessitated, you know, by his impairments—"

At the Beach
But kept "—then threw back the shell."

Elegy
And now that I can no longer . . . —no longer have to—visit him . . .

Breath As
tidal—ardor . . . fervor . . . horror . . . as moon . . . —

What comfort?

10. *One-line poems in other languages:* I don't know too much about this subject. Here is my memory of an anecdote about the Russian futurist poet Valery Bryusov. In the first issue of an image-centered manifesto in a new literary magazine he published a one-line poem. (I am improvising on my memory of the translation):

Oh! her thighs on the bicycle like fish in the brilliant river
    leaping!

And then he revised and republished it in the second issue:

Oh! her thighs and fish in the brilliant river!

And, aiming for greater purity and concentration, published this version in the fourth and last issue:

> Oh! her thighs!

Czesław Miłosz has published a handful of titled one-line poems, if his "Notes" is many poems rather than one. Here are some samples:

> *On the need to draw boundaries*
> Wretched and dishonest was the sea.

> *Landscape*
> Unending forest flowing with the honey of wild bees.

> *Language*
> Cosmos, i.e., pain raved in me with a diabolic tongue

> *Supplication*
> From galactic silence protect us.

> *Aim in Life*
> Oh to cover my shame in regal attire

11. *One-line stanzas and free verse:* The one-line stanza shows up quite often in free verse poems with irregular stanzaic patterns where it has the heaviness and lightness I mentioned at the outset and gets used in the middle or at the end of a poem for emphasis. The one-line stanza as a uniform pattern, unlike the poem in two- or three-line stanzas, is relatively rare because its expressive effect is usually of—depending on the spacing between stanzas—a slow or rapid series of discrete sentences, resistant to or disruptive of time and relation, which enjambment, the turning of verse, essentially expresses. This suggests the

way in which two of the impulses of poetry, to condense and to render in language the mind stilled or the mind's experience of the world's movement in time, are at odds. The form, I suppose, can express a slow piece-by-piece consecutivity. Ashbery's "37 Haiku" may be an instance of the slow series of discrete but consecutive statements.

12 . One form, implying a kind of consecutiveness, imitates the notebook or book of pensées. Some of Wallace Stevens's "Adagia" can be thought of as an instance. John Cage's "Themes & Variations" is another. Here is a sample from Cage:

> Move from zero.
> All audible phenomena = material for music.
> Spring, Summer, Fall, Winter (Creation, Preservation,
>   Destruction, Quiescence).
> Possibility of helping by doing nothing.
> Music is not music until it is heard.
> Music and dance together (and then other togethers).
> Men are men; mountains are mountains before studying
>   Zen. While studying Zen, things become confused. After
>   studying Zen, men are men; mountain are mountains.
>   What is the difference between before and after? No
>   difference. Just the feet are a little off the ground.
>   (Suzuki)
> If structure, rhythmic structure.
> Boredom plus attention = getting interested
> Principle underlying all of the solutions = question we ask
> Activity, not communication.
> The nine permanent emotions (the heroic; the mirthful; the
>   wondrous; the erotic; tranquility; sorrow; fear; anger; the
>   odious).

In other cases, like Michael Palmer's "Notes for Echo Lake 10," the stanzas are both more and less continuous. Here is a bit of it:

> He would live against sentences.
> Trees here broad of leaf the several speakers.
> Tiered objects of her talking and the water below.
> Trees of sound to broaden shadow.
> Damp walls will quiet things.
> Ahab or Alcibiades.
> He-she before the figure before the mirror.
> This order or Orient is the eighth part and a dislocation,
>   emerald rock to emerald rock.
> Rain hanging and endless plain.
> As water below thought below object.
> I want to see them yesterday.
> Reflects gardens of horizon leaning against an arm of neutral
>   shore.
> Reflects the ardent eye or Alcibiades.

13 . *The strophe and the one-line stanza:* (Webster: "In modern poetry, any separate section or extended movement in a poem, distinguished from a stanza in that it does not follow a regularly repeated pattern") is usually based on the principle of the one-line stanza, but the line is considered one long breath, or pulse, sometimes of several sentences, followed by a pause. It has the effect of merging the idea of line, sentence, and stanza. Palmer's "Notes from Echo Lake 2" is an instance. Here's the beginning:

> He would assume a seeing into the word, whoever was there
>   to look. Would care to look. A coming and going in smoke.
>
> A part and apart.

Voices through a wall. They are there because we hear them what do we hear. The pitch rises toward the end to indicate a question.

What's growing in the garden.

To be at a loss for words. How does the mind move there, walking beside the bank of what had been a river. How does the light.

And rhythm as an arm, rhythm as the arm extended, he turns and turns remembering the song. What did she recall.

It can also be used consecutively as in this section of Miłosz's "City Without a Name"—he's writing about Wilno, the city of his childhood, Wilno in Polish, Vilnius in Lithuanian:

> Why should that city, defenseless, pure as the wedding
>   necklace of some forgotten tribe, keep offering itself to me?
> Like blue and redbrown seeds in Tuzigoot in the coppery
>   desert seven centuries ago.
> Where ocher rubbed into stone still waits for the brow and
>   cheekbones it would adorn, previous to Arizona, though
>   for all that time no one has shown up.
> What evil in me, what pity, makes me deserve this offering?
> It stands before me now, ready, not even the smoke from one
>   chimney is lacking, not one echo, when I step into the
>   river that separates us.
> Perhaps Anna and Dora Duzyno have called to me, three
>   hundred miles inside the Sonora Desert, because except for
>   me no one else knows they ever lived.
> They trot before me down Embankment Street, two gently
>   born parakeets from Samogitia, and at night they unravel
>   their spinster tresses of gray hair.

It is also possible to enjamb a strophe and sustain the measure, I think. See my "Spring Rain":

> Now the rain is falling, freshly, in the intervals between sunlight,
>
> a Pacific squall started no one knows where, drawn east as the drifts of warm air make a channel;
>
> it moves its one way, like water or the mind,
>
> and spill this rain passing over. The Sierras will catch it as last snow flurries before summer, observed only by the wakened marmots at ten thousand feet,
>
> and we will come across it again as larkspur and penstemon sprouting along a creekside above Sonora Pass next August.

14 . *The one-line stanza and chant:* The incantatory structure of chant usually involves a series of end-stopped lines in rapid succession. Think, for example, of Christopher Smart's cat, or of Ginsberg's "Howl":

> who were expelled from the academies for crazy & publishing obscene odes on the windows of the skull,
>
> who cowered in unshaven rooms in underwear, burning their money in wastebaskets and listening to the Terror through the wall,
>
> who got busted in their pubic beards returning through Laredo with a belt of marijuana for New York,
>
> who ate fire in paint hotels or drank turpentine in Paradise alley, death or purgatoried their torsos night after night,

and this method picked up by Anne Waldman, in "Makeup on Empty Space," for example:

> I am putting makeup on empty space
> All patinas convening on empty space
> Rouge blushing on empty space
> I am putting makeup on empty space
> putting eyelashes on empty space
> painting the eyebrows on empty space
> piling creams on empty space
> painting the phenomenal world
> I am hanging ornaments on empty space
> gold clips, lacquer combs, plastic hairpins on empty space
> I am sticking wire pins into empty space

15 . *A predominant sense of the single line in the lyric:* There are poems made from a succession of single lines, not distinctly disjunctive and not marked off as separate stanzas, but kept separate, one sentence per line. What is the expressive effect? Michael Palmer again:

A Dream Called "The House of Jews"

> Many gathered many friends maybe everyone
> Many now and then may have entered
> The ivory teeth fell from her mouth
> The typewriter keys
> Many fell at the entrance
> Many held them
> Many fell forward and aware
> Various friends gathered at the entrance
> Some held back
> The room contains a question

Many said now before then this then that
The room contains a question to be named
He said *I will tell the book the dream the words tell me*
The room is not the place or the name

16 . *Complex forms built largely but not entirely on the single line:* This
usually depends on lineation and spacing to set off the line as a unit
of energy and temporary residence of it. See Robert Duncan's "The
Torso: Passages 18":

> I have been waiting for you, he said:
>   I know what you desire
>
>   you do not yet know   but through me .
>
> And I am with you everywhere.   In your falling
>
> I have fallen from a high place.   I have raised myself
>
>   from darkness in your   rising
>
>   wherever you are
>
>   my hand in your hand   seeking   the locks, the keys

The visual spacing can be indicated in oral performance or not, I
suppose. My experience of Duncan reading is that you did hear the
pauses. Perhaps these are not single lines at all, but the visual and
aural appearance of them, a scattering, to remind us, as in another
Duncan poem, that the line is a seed it is Psyche's task together.

TWO

1. Two, from Old English *twa;* Latin, *duo;* Greek, *dyo*. One line is a form in the sense that any gesture is a form. Two lines introduce the idea of form as the energy of relation.

2. The first question is what formal devices give a pair of lines twoness. There are two basic formal devices in English poetry. The first is aural, rhyme. The second is visual, stanza patterning. There are others, more subtle. The two lines can share the same meter or grammatical structure, or they can make a logical or grammatical unit, or share some other element—first word, last word. The usual term for a pair of lines joined by some device is a couplet, in Greek a *distich*.

TWO-LINE POEMS

3. The best-known, probably the best, two-line poem in the European tradition is this one by Catullus:

Odi et amo, quare id faciam, fortasse requiris?
nescio, sed fieri, sentio et excrucior.

Horace Gregory's translation:

I hate and I love. You may well ask why.
I don't know, but I feel it and I suffer.

Frank Bidart's version:

I hate *and* love. Ignorant fish, who even
wants the fly while writhing.

4 . So it would seem that one of the natural forms of the two-line poem is based on a human pattern of exchange: question-and-answer, call-and-response. This was one of the basic forms in West African folk culture and both the work song and the spiritual evolved from it:

Who is it knows the trouble I've seen?
Nobody knows but Jesus.

Who's that sitting on the tree of life?
We hear the Jordan roll.

One of Wallace Stevens's not numerous two-line poems has this structure:

Why nag at the ideas of Hercules, Don Don?
Widen your sense. All things in the sun are sun.

And there is this by the Slovene poet Tomaž Šalamun, in Charles Simic's translation:

> Emptiness, my bride!
> Who whistles? who listens?

In this form, twoness cuts both ways. In the fields, the foreman calls out, the crew responds; in a religious ceremony, the celebrant calls out, the community responds. It is a kind of social binding. In a poem it can express splitness, or doubleness, and the desire to be whole: two trying to make one.

Wallace Stevens again:

> A man and a woman are one.
> A man and a woman and a blackbird are one.

This is, if it is a two-line poem, a two-line poem that is also like a syllogism. The parallelism makes it one line expanded. One line about two expanded to two lines about a (haunting, haunted) three.

5. *Bantu combinations:* In *Technicians of the Sacred,* Jerome Rothenberg reproduces some work songs of the Bantu people of southern Africa, transcribed by a French Jesuit missionary, Father Henri Junod. They are based on a very subtle version of the call-and-response form. The first singer produces an image; the second supplies another. The two are supposed to be related to each other by an internal comparison, so there is an element of the riddle in them. The connection is explicitly not narrative. The first speaker, in one instance, says or sings:

> *The elephant was killed by a small arrow.*

The second replies:

> *A lake dries up at the edges.*

The first element of the comparison is the diminution of a great thing by a small. The second is that the dry mud at the edge of a lake looks like the skin of an elephant. Here are some others:

> All day I carved the ironwood stick.
> I kept thinking what to say to him.

> A crawfish tugging on the line.
> I think I see someone in the distance.

> Crack of a tusk.
> Voice of an angry man.

> The roof of the old reed hut collapsing.
> Debt, and more debt.

This is basically the principle on which many haiku are based:

> Mad girl in a boat
> at midday—
> and the fast spring river.

And it is, as we'll see, the basis of the couplets in the Persian ghazal.

6 . *Roman epigram:* It's interesting to think about what makes two-ness in the Roman epigram.

There are six two-line poems in the work of Catullus and they are all written in an elegiac meter—a hexameter first line and a pentameter second line. The effect has been described as a fountaining out and a falling back. In English translation, other things about the way he worked become apparent. In *Odi et amo* a couple of things are at work, one is the use of a kind of cross-stitching, what the Greek grammarians called *chiasmus,* and the other is the use of question and answer, call and response.

> *Odi et amo, quare id faciam, fortasse requiris?*
> *Nescio, sed fieri sentio et excrucior.*

> I hate and love, you may ask why?
> I don't know but I feel it and I suffer.

The grammatical structure is balanced contraries:

> statement of feeling   question
> answer   statement of feeling

Very elegant. Another of his couplets that is often quoted is a little different:

> *Nil nimium studeo, Caesar, tibi uelle placer,*
> *nec scire utrum sis albus an ater homo.*

> I have no great desire to please you, Caesar,
> Nor do I care whether you're black or white.

The effect is doubling down. Say it, then say it more intensely. Or make the general statement in A, and then get specific in B. And there is also the balance of syntactical parallelism. I have no desire, pause, to do this; nor do I care, pause, about that.

   (The poem says literally "whether you're a dark- or fair-skinned man." Some translators have chosen to avoid what might seem like introducing modern ideas about race into the poem. Charles Martin imitates the meter of Catullus:

> I am not too terribly anxious to please you, Caesar,
> nor even to learn the first thing about you.

Peter Whigham, who constructed a brilliant Catullus in a prosody like that of William Carlos Williams, renders it like this:

> Utter indifference to your welfare, Caesar,
> Is matched only by my ignorance of who you are.)

Martial, two generations after Catullus, was the epigrammatist whom generations of English schoolboys were set to translate. He wrote a dozen two-line poems in the elgaic couplet form. This is his best-known poem:

> *Non amo te, Sabidi, nec possum dicere quare,*
> *Hoc tantum possum dicere: non amo te.*

> I don't like you, Sabidius. Hard to say why,
> But not hard to say it: I don't like you.

This is the poem that received a well-known eighteenth-century English translation into the quatrain form:

> I do not like thee, Dr. Fell.
> The reason why I cannot tell,
> But this I know, and know full well,
> I do not like thee, Dr. Fell.

Martial's poem seems to take its structure directly from Catullus, and it's interesting to compare the two poems. They both do the same cross-stitching. They both begin with a statement of feeling and end with a statement of feeling. And the difference in tone has to do with the difference in the way the poems separate thought from feeling.

Nescio, I don't know, Catullus's speaker says. But I feel it—literally, *fieri sentio, I am made to feel it,* and I suffer. And it makes one understand the passivity of suffering. Martial's speaker is in control. *Hoc tantum possum dicere. This I can definitely say. I don't like you.* And if that inflicts pain? Well, sorry, can't help it. The difference between lyric and satire.

Martial—snide, captious, witty—was the master of the form. Here are some samples in James Michie's versions (which I've slightly modified to get rid of the rhyme; there is none in Latin):

> Why the applause in the baths?
> Maro has just exposed his tool.

> Those are my poems you're reading, Fidentius.
> But the way you garble them, they're all your own.

Horace Gregory, same poem:

> They're mine, but when I hear you read them aloud,
> Fidentius, I'm quite willing to relinquish copyright.

Back to Martial:

> On each of the tombs of her seven husbands,
> A simple inscription: ERECTED BY CHLOE.
>   ⋆
> Why do I go to the country, Linus asks.
> And I answer: To get away, Linus, from you.
>   ⋆
> Pushing sixty, he's still "a promising poet."
> More "missing" than "prom" at this point, though.
>   ⋆
> Malvinus is so lewd he keeps his trunks on
> When he's cruising the nude beach.

7. *The English couplet:* Rhyme, of course, has been the main couplet-forging device in English poetry. It reaches back. One of the earliest couplet poems—1069—was said to have been composed as a death-bed curse by the monk Aldred against a Baron Urse who built his castle too near a monastery—

> Hatest thu Urse
> Have thu Godes kurs.

And a hundred years later there are the fragments of St. Godric, who died in 1170. They are probably the remains of devotional songs and some of the music survives, though the notation isn't intelligible. One of them is a couplet—

> Crist and Sainte Marie swa on scamel me iledde
> That ic on this erde ne silde with min vare fote itrede.

And there is this thirteenth-century quatrain made from a pair of short couplets:

> Nou goth sonne under wode—
> Me reweth, Marie, thi faire rode.
> Nou goth sonne under tre—
> Me reweth, Marie, thi son and the.

Two make four because the poem is really a single couplet re-peated with a slight variation. And they are linked by pun. "Wode" is also the cross, as is "tre." And "sonne" rhymes with "son."

8. *The English epigram:* The English Renaissance poets who were taught Martial by their Latin masters had a hand at the form but pro-duced nothing amazing. John Donne did fairly well with the witty insult poem:

If in his study Hammon hath such care
T'hang all old strange things, let his wife beware.

And Ben Jonson wrote many, none very memorable:

Thy praise or dispraise is to me alike:
One doth not stroke me, nor the other strike.

   *

Pray thee, take care, that tak'st my book in hand,
To read it well: that is, to understand.

One of the most famous—John Harrington (1615)—has the question-and-answer form:

Treason doth never prosper. What's the reason?
For if it prosper, none dare call it treason.

The sharpest of the political epigrams is, of course, by Sir Walter Raleigh:

Here lies a noble statesman who never served the state.
Here lies the Lord of Leicester whom all the world did hate.

And there is an admirable one by Henry Wotton (1651):

He first deceased; she for a little tried
To live without him, liked it not, and died.

William Blake wrote an epigram based on the epigram:

Her whole life is an epigram: smack, smooth & neatly penned,
Platted quite neat to catch applause, with a sliding noose at the
   end.

And he wrote one wonderful poem by doubling the question-and-answer form:

> What is it men in women do require?
> The lineaments of Gratified Desire.
> What is it women do in men require?
> The lineaments of Gratified Desire.

And, to be done with this subject, Samuel Taylor Coleridge diagnosed the form:

> What is an epigram? A dwarfish whole.
> Its body brevity, and wit for soul.

9. *Some American poems:* The epigram appealed to New England during the days of newspaper verse. Henry Thoreau wrote moral couplets for a newspaper:

> You must not only aim aright,
> But draw the bow with all your might.

But he also tried to undermine the form:

> The wind that blows
> Is all that anybody knows.
>   *
> Where I have been
> There was none seen.
>   *
> The chickadee
> Hopped near to me.

Walt Whitman experimented with the form in his unrhymed verse:

> Stranger, if you passing meet me and desire to speak to me,
>   why should you not speak to me?
> And why should I not speak to you?
>   ★
>
> I last winter observed the snow on a spree with the northwest
>   wind
> And it put me out of conceit of fences and imaginary lines.
>   ★
>
> Of recognition—Come, I will no more trouble myself about
>   recognition—
> I will no longer look what things are rated to be, but what they
>   really are to me.
>
> *(written in his late sixties)*
>   ★
>
> I see the sleeping babe nestling the breast of its mother,
> The sleeping babe and mother—hush'd, I study them long
>   and long.

Emily Dickinson wrote a dozen or so poems of two lines, or what may have been jottings of lines on the run and not thought of as two-line poems. Some of them slip the noose of wit:

> Lest they short come—is all my fear
> When sweet incarcerated here.
>   ★
>
> Trust adjusts her "Peradventure"—
> Phantoms entered "and not you."
>   ★
>
> Soft as the massacre of Suns
> By Evening's Sabres slain

                *

Is immortality above
That men are so oppressed
    *

Brother of Ingots—Ah Peru—
Empty the Hearts that purchased you—
    *

All things swept sole away
This—is immensity—

There aren't really very many imagist poems this short. Ezra Pound's is, of course, the most famous:

In a Station of the Metro
The apparition of these faces in the crowd:
Petals on a wet black bough.

It's based, like the haiku, on internal comparison. So is, more explicitly, this one:

Pagani's, November 8
Suddenly seeing in the eyes of the very beautiful Normande
    cocotte
The eyes of the very learned British museum assistant.

And there are the third and twelfth of Wallace Stevens's "Thirteen Ways of Looking at a Blackbird":

(III)
The blackbird whirled in the autumn winds.
It was a small part of the pantomime.

(XII)
The river is moving.
The blackbird must be flying.

They don't depend on comparison, but something like a syllogism with a suppressed middle term. They return the form to the
riddle. Stevens also tried something like Whitman's manner:

In my room, the world is beyond my understanding.
But when I walk I see that it consists of three or four hills and
    a cloud.

10 . *Recently:* Here are some two-line poems by Carol Snow:

Family
Not just S. but all of us, wanting
and exchanging wanting—the 'strong force'—

By the Pond: Reading
by the pond, the immediate—
breath—and then the text, and then the pond.

By the Pond: Quiet breaths
in a still place. "Each next"
taking up a little of the spill.

By the Pond: Watching the goldfish
(why?)—the body passive,
small eye movements (as though in a dream).

There was a moment
of blessing, calm.
Though it was a pause, a hiatus.

And a couple of Brenda Hillman's:

(That's good, you got there; can we
make it part of the record?)

Sarajevo ceasefire
—/children sledding
after a couple days—

and two of mine:

Sad
Often we are sad animals.
Bored dogs, monkeys getting rained on.

So
They walked along the dry gully.
Cottonwoods. So the river must be underground.

And two by Michael Palmer:

Poem
We will not go out to hear the 'mysterious and private'
sounds because of this storm

Notes for Echo Lake 12/8
But tell me who these acrobats finally are
reappearing in the shape of the letter D?

THE TWO-LINE STANZA

11. *The ghazal:* The ghazal is one of the central forms in Arabic poetry. It originated in Persia and flourished in Urdu. The poetry of the
Middle East developed genres similar to those in Europe. There was
the *nazm,* or narrative poem, the *ruba'i,* a quatrain written in specific
meters something like the ballad stanza, the *qita',* a kind of verse
of four or more lines; the *qasida,* an ode or praise poem; and the
marsiya, a lament or threnody. The *quasida* in early Arabian poetry
usually had an erotic prelude called a *nasib.* The ghazal developed
from the *nasib.* Rudaki (858–941), a Persian poet, is said to have first
separated the prelude from the ode and turned it into an independent form. In India, Amir Khusro (1253–1325) laid the foundations of
the ghazal. Its first great practitioner was Kabir (1440–1518). Others
whom you might know of are Hafiz, Mirabai, and Ghalib. Ghazals
were and are usually sung or are singable. Their musical accompaniment is a kind of raga. For our purposes, the main fact about this
kind of poem is that it is one of the great lyric forms based on the
couplet. It developed as a kind of ecstatic sonnet.

In its classical form it consists of a minimum of five and a maxi-
mum of seventeen couplets. In Urdu (in which it is as easy to rhyme
as in Italian) both lines of the first couplet, the *matla',* end with the
same word or phrase, and each couplet thereafter, or one line in each
couplet, rhymes with the first. In contemporary practice there are
unrhymed ghazals. Usually in the last couplet, the *maqta',* the poet
introduces his or her name. The effect is imitated in Allen Ginsberg's
homage to the Bengali devotional poet Lalon:

> I had my chance and lost it,
> many chances & didn't
>   take them seriously enuf.
> Oh yes I was impressed, almost
>   went mad with fear

I'd lose the immortal chance.
   One lost it.
Allen Ginsberg warns you
   don't follow my path
   to extinction.

The ghazal was intricately metrical in ways that we don't need to go into. Its main difference from European poetry is that each couplet is independent of the preceding and succeeding ones grammatically. As one scholar puts it, "every couplet is in itself a complete story. Every two lines present a complete picture, expressing a feeling, an emotion, or a thought." In practice, though the couplets are discrete, they are linked by theme, and the subtlest of them proceed almost like a set of Bantu combinations, linked line by line, couplet by couplet, through internal comparison. (An awful lot of the ghazals available in translation, however, read like a lot of the English sonnets, a string of clichés about the lover's eyes, lips, etc., connected by the supposed ardor of the speaker.) And, as in the English sonnet, the ghazal passed from an erotic into a devotional form—Mirabai's ghazals are addressed to her lover, the dark one, Shiva.

Goethe wrote and translated ghazals, but the form came into use in American poetry when a scholar of Urdu invited several American poets to collaborate on translations of the Urdu poet Ghalib. Ghalib wrote, they say, a literary, Persianized Urdu, the principal language of northern India. (He lived from 1797 to 1869, so he has the additional interest of being the poet of Delhi in a critical historical moment. "The British conquest of India was completed in those decades, the fabric of the entire civilization came loose, and the city of Delhi became a major focal point for countless traumatic crises," writes Aijaz Ahmad, the editor of *Ghazals of Ghalib*.)

Here, to get the feel of it, is my version of one of Ahmad's literal translations:

The happiness of a drop of water is to die into a river.
When pain is unbearable, pain becomes the medicine.

We are so weak our tears become a mild sighing.
Now we really believe that water can turn into air.

When the spring sky clears after a heavy rain,
It's as if it had wept itself to death.

So that you may begin to understand the miracle of the wind,
Notice the mirror becoming green in the spring.

Ghalib, the rose wants to be looked at.
Whatever the color and condition of things, open your eyes.

The original, of course, is rhymed and metrical. Here is another:

In the dark of the night they have given me a morning.
They have lit the candle so that dawn lives in eternity like
    imagination.

See that face: shut your babbling lips.
They have ravished your heart and opened your eyes.

Fire burned the fire-temple down.
You are the clamorous lamentation of its gong.

They have plucked jewels from the banner of Ajamian kings.
They have given you a pen to scatter treasure with.

They have carried away the crowns of the Turks.
And your speech has the splendor of the court at Kayan.

The pearls in the crowns were plucked out and fastened to
    wisdom.
Whatever they steal, they secretly give it back.

Whatever they have plundered from the wealth of Persia
They have given to you as a tongue to moan with.

O Ghalib, you are in very great trouble.
Your sun in is Sagittarius, your moon is in Cancer.

Very shortly after the publication of this book, American poets began to experiment with the form. Some lines by way of example:

Adrienne Rich, "The Blue Ghazals" (1971). In one poem she begins by varying the placement of the repeated phrase:

Violently asleep in the old house.
A clock stays awake all night ticking.

Turning, turning their bruised leaves
the trees stay awake all night in the wood.

Jim Harrison, *Outlyer and Ghazals*, comments on the ghazal in his practice: "The couplets are not related by reason or logic and their only continuity is made by metaphorical jump." A bit of one of his:

I fell into the hidden mine shaft in Keweenaw, emerging
In a year with teeth and eyes of burnished copper, black skin.

What will become of her, what will become of her now that
She's sold into slavery to an Air Force lieutenant?

I spent the night prophesying to the huge black rock
In the river around which the current boiled and slid

Galway Kinnell, *Imperfect Thirst*, 1994. One, entitled "Passing the Cemetery," begins:

Desire and act were a combination known as sin.
The noise of a fingernail on a blackboard frightened our bones.

The stairwell on the way up to the dentist's smelled of the fire
  inside teeth.
Passing the cemetery, I wondered if the bones of the dead become
  brittle and crumbly, or if they last.

By 2000 the Kashmiri-American poet Agha Shahid Ali had ob-
jected to these freehanded appropriations of the classic form and
published, by way of protest, an anthology of poems, *Ravishing
Disunities: Real Ghazals in English,* which follow the rhyme scheme
and something like the meter of the classic Muslim form. He had
decided, he said, that "those writing ghazals in English had got
it quite wrong, far from the letter and farther from the spirit. Of
course I was exercising a Muslim snobbery, of the Shiite elan, but
the ghazal floating from so many monthlies and quarterlies was
nothing of the kind."

A couple of the beginnings of examples of the "real ghazal" in
English as he proposed it:

Craig Arnold, "Ghazal for Garcia Lorca":

> Still you came back knowing you must die in Granada,
> Intricate, tricky, disapproving, prying Granada.
>
> One hand grips the collar, the other sounds the pocket.
> They make no room for the shameless or the shy in Granada.

Forrest Gander, "Sensations Upon Arriving":

> The swallows fold themselves into sheets of solid air. In silent
>   films
> dust lifts from the field. Light crackles everywhere as it does
>   in silent films.
>
> From black peat-bricks in the fireplace, a concentrated odor—
> like a dog's footpads—wafts clean and rare in silent films.

Heather McHugh, "Ghazal of the Better-Unbegun":

Too volatile, am I? too voluble? Too much a word person?
I blame the soup. I'm a primordially stirred person.

Two pronouns and a vehicle was Icarus with wings.
The apparatus of his selves made an absurd person.

So the form is available in at least these separate ways. Probably
the demands of rhyme in the classic version will always risk making
it seem an exercise in ingenuity in English, but in Ali's "Ghazal," he
demonstrates that the obsessive and repetitive nature of the form,
like that in the sestina and the villanelle, can be quite powerful:

The only language of loss left in the world is Arabic.
These words were said to me in a language not Arabic.

Ancestors, you've left me a plot in the family graveyard—
Why must I look, in your eyes, for prayers in Arabic.

Majnoon, his clothes ripped, still weeps for Laila.
O, this is the madness of the desert, his crazy Arabic.

Who listens to Ishmael? Even now he cries out:
Abraham, throw away your knives, recite a psalm in Arabic.

From exile Mahmoud Darwish writes to the world:
You'll all pass between the fleeting words of Arabic.

The sky is stunned, it's become a ceiling of stone.
I tell you it must weep. So kneel, pray for rain in Arabic.

At an exhibition of miniatures, such delicate calligraphy:
Kashmiri paisleys tied into the golden hair of Arabic.

The Koran prophesied a fire of men and stones.
Well, it's all now come true, as it was said in Arabic.

You will find the whole poem and other ghazals in Ali's *The Country Without a Post Office*.

12 . *The English couplet:* It was in place by the time of Geoffrey Chaucer in the 1370s:

> Whan that April with his showres soote
> The drought of March hath perced to the roote.
> And bathed every veine in swich licour,
> Of which vertu engendred is the flowr;

And the distinction would be made between *closed couplets*, which make a completed statement, and *open couplets*, which are enjambed. In the Renaissance the form is everywhere—trimeter, tetrameter, pentameter couplets, open and closed—and in the seventeenth century there is a kind of war between the closed pentameter couplet, completing its sense every two lines, and the open one, which doesn't. George Saintsbury, the great late Victorian scholar of prosody, describes the poets of the open couplet as thinking "no more of 'the end of the line' than if they were writing prose, except that it is a place where you have to provide a rhyme." This practice, he says, "supplies a sort of *obbligato* accompaniment to the rhythm . . . a sort of low guitarish accompaniment of rhyme-music." In the eighteenth century, of course, the closed pentameter couplet, the *heroic couplet*, came to be the form of choice.

Here's a reading list that will give you some sense of the development of it:

John Donne: "Good Friday, Riding Westward"
Ben Jonson: "Inviting a Friend to Supper"
Andrew Marvell: "The Mower against Gardens"
John Dryden: "To the Memory of Mr. Oldham"
    The Aeneid (translation)

Anne Finch: "A Nocturnal Reverie"
Jonathan Swift: "A Description of a City Shower"
Alexander Pope: "An Essay on Criticism"
  "The Rape of the Lock"
  "Epistle to Dr. Arbuthnot"
  The Iliad
  The Odyssey
James Thomson: "Winter, A Poem" from *The Season*
Samuel Johnson: "The Vanity of Human Wishes"
Oliver Goldsmith: "The Deserted Village"
William Cowper: *The Task*
George Crabbe: "Peter Grimes"
John Clare: "Badger"
Robert Browning: "My Last Duchess"

The one development of the form in the twentieth century was the open rhymed pentameter couplet, furiously enjambed. It's typical of the early work of Robert Lowell, like these lines from "After the Surprising Conversions." The speaker is supposedly Jonathan Edwards:

> *September twenty-second,* Sir: today
> I answer. In the latter part of May,
> Hard on Our Lord's Ascension, it began
> To be more sensible. A gentleman
> Of more than common understanding, strict
> In morals, pious in behavior, kicked
> Against our goad. A man of some renown,
> A useful, honored person in the town,
> He came of melancholy parents; prone
> To secret spells, for years he kept alone—
> His uncle, I believe, was killed of it.

The way to this goes from Robert Browning through Robert Frost.

13 . *Modernism and the two-line stanza:* The best way to study it is to look at what the modernists did with it. The most distinguished example is late, H.D.'s short-lined couplet stanzas in *Trilogy:*

> Take me home
> where canals
>
> flow
> between iris-banks:
>
> where the heron
> has her nest:
>
> where the mantis
> prays on the river-reed:
>
> where the grasshopper says
> *Amen, Amen, Amen.*

William Carlos Williams experimented with it early, in long lines—see "The Flower"—and, more characteristically, short ones. Here's a partial list of poems in the couplet stanza from *Spring and All:*

> "The Right of Way"
> "Shoot It, Jimmy!"
> "The Red Wheelbarrow"
> "Quietness"
> "Rigamarole"
> "The Avenue of Poplars"
> "At the Ball Game"

He also used it in the 1930s for small poems that dole out the perceptions in a way that creates the effect of a snapshot. Another list:

"Proletarian Portrait"
"To"
"In the 'Sconset Bus"
"Sluggishly"
"Between Walls"

Later, Robert Creeley, following Williams, would use the short-lined couplets for a sort of analytic fracturing of the flow of a sentence:

> The kids come
> by on bicycles, the little,
>
> Increasingly large
> people, in the rain.

It was most important for Wallace Stevens who wrote a few two-line poems and many poems with two-line stanzas, mostly for the expressive orderliness of it. See:

"Invective Against Swans"
"Bantams in Pine Woods"
"New England Verses" (a collection of epigrammatic couplets)
"The Surprises of the Superhuman"
"Ghosts as Cocoons"
"The Sun This March"
"Gallant Chateau" (about his mind as a gallant chateau . . .)

Here's an excerpt from "Gallant Chateau":

> There might have been the immense solitude
> Of the wind upon the curtains.

Pitiless verse? A few words tuned
and tuned and tuned and tuned.

It is good. The bed is empty,
The curtains are stiff and prim and still.

"The Man with the Blue Guitar" (tetrameter couplets, rhyme)
"The Dwarf"
"The Candle a Saint"
"A Dish of Peaches in Russia"
"Contrary Theses (I)"
"Phosphor Reading by His Own Light"
"Holiday in Reality"
"Debris of Life and Mind"
"Long and Sluggish Lines" (the title in case you were wonder-
ing, how conscious Stevens was of craft); the poem begins:

It makes so little difference, at so much more
Than seventy, where one looks, one has been there before.

"The Poem That Took the Place of a Mountain"
"The Woman in Sunshine"
"An Old Man Asleep"

It's been said that Stevens acquired a taste for aphorism from the
Pennsylvania Dutch culture he grew up in in Reading. Watching
him move among two- and three- and four-line free verse and metrical stanzas is an education in craft.

THREE

1. Old English, *threo*, var. of *thrio*, fem., neuter of *thri(e)*; Greek, *treis*; Latin, *tres*; Sanskrit, *tri*, *trayas*. Two often regarded as an aspect of one, so that with three number as such, the many, begins. And is infinite. Oddness. Not divisible. So that—trinity, for example—mystery begins here.

THREE-LINE STANZAS

2. *Triplets:* There is something of imbalance and excess in threes. Especially where rhyme is concerned. About two-based forms something hovers of natural complementarities: binary systems, the bilateral symmetries in nature, male and female, lover and beloved. Hence the closing down of two-based rhyme. It seems to secure a completion and emphasizes at once the orderliness of rhyme and its root in sex, in coupling. Ralph Waldo Emerson:

> The animals are sick with love,
> Love-sick with rhyme.

Rhymes in threes—triplets, the prosodists call them—express too much, overflow, play, as in the move from the two-step to the polka. One of the early three-rhyme lyrics from Middle English, very French and courtly in mode, has a startling sweetness:

The Rose Entwined

"I love a floure of swete odour."
"Margerome gentill, or lavendour?"
"Columbyne, goldis of swete flavour?"   (goldis = marigold)
"Nay, nay, let be!
Is none of them
That lyketh me."

"There is a floure, where so he be,
And shall not yet be named for me."
"Primrose, violett, or fresh daysy?"
"He pass them all
In his degree,
That lyketh me."

"One that I love more enterly."
"Gillyflower gentill, or rosemary?"
"Chamomyle, borage, or savory?"
"Nay, certenly,
Here is not he
That pleseth me."

"I chose a floure fresshist of face."
"What is his name that thou chosen hast?
"The rose, I suppose? Thine hart unbrace!"
"That same is he,
In hart so fre,
That best lyketh me."

"The rose it is a royall floure."
"The red or the white? Show his colour!"
"Both be full swete & of lyke savour:
All on they be,
That day to see,
It lyketh well me."

"I love the rose both red & whyte."
"Is that your pure perfite appetite?"
"To here talk of them is my delite!"
"Ioyed may we be,
Our prince to see,
And roses three."

(The subtext is the War of the Roses: Londoners were notorious fence-sitters, so there is also a slyness in the song; it was composed for three voices.)

And, here, later, is Robert Herrick:

Upon Julia's Clothes

Whenas in silks my Julia goes
Then, then, methinks, how sweetly flows
That liquefaction of her clothes.

Next, when I cast mine eyes, and see
That brave vibration, each way free,
O, how that glittering taketh me.

But this triplet stanza is mostly an oddity in English. Probably because, as is so often said, it's not a rhyme-rich language. The poems composed in it all have an air of being curiosities, like Robert Browning's "A Toccata of Galuppi's":

As for Venice and her people, merely born to bloom and drop,
Here on earth they bore their fruitage, mirth and folly were
    the crop.
What of soul was left, I wonder, when the kissing had to stop?

And Thomas Hardy's "The Convergence of the Twain":

Over the mirrors meant
To glass the opulent
The sea worm crawls—grotesque, slimed, dumb, indifferent.

And Robert Frost's "Provide, Provide":

Better to go down dignified
With boughten friendship at your side
Than none at all. Provide, provide!

3 . *Terza rima:* Terza rima is the other three-line rhymed stanza in
English. Borrowed from the Italian, it is, of course, the one Dante used
in the *Commedia.* It is even more demanding, in terms of rhyme, than
the triplet stanza—the pattern is aba bcb cdc, and so on. It is a braiding or weaving form. Osip Mandelstam—see his essay on Dante—has
argued that it grew up in Tuscany with the art of fine weaving. There's
not a lot of it in English, but what there is is impressive. The best-
known example of it is Percy Bysshe Shelley's "Ode to the West Wind":

O wild West Wind, thou breath of Autumn's being,
Thou, from whose unseen presence the leaves dead
Are driven, like ghosts from an enchanter fleeing,

Yellow, and black, and pale, and hectic red,
Pestilence-stricken multitudes: O thou,
Who chariotest to their dark, wintry bed

The winged seeds, where they lie cold and low
Each like a corpse within its grave, until
Thine azure sister of the Spring shall blow

Her clarion o'er the dreaming earth, and fill
(Driving sweet buds like flocks to feed in air)
With living hues and odors plain and hill:

See also Shelley's "The Triumph of Life." W. B. Yeats used the form in "Cuchulain Comforted." It was the second-to-last poem he wrote and returns to the figure from Irish myth who had so preoccupied him and it evokes the *Inferno:*

A man that had six mortal wounds, a man
Violent and famous, strode among the dead;
Eyes stared out of the branches and were gone.

Then certain Shrouds that muttered head to head
Came and were gone. He leant upon a tree
As though to meditate on wounds and blood.

A Shroud that seemed to have authority
Among those bird-like things came, and let fall
A bundle of linen. Shrouds by two and three

Came creeping up because the man was still.
And thereupon that linen-carrier said:
'Your life will grow much sweeter if you will

'Obey our ancient rule and make a shroud;
Mainly because of what we only know
The rattle of those arms makes us afraid.

'We thread the needles' eye and all we do
All must together do.' That done, the man
Took up the nearest and began to sew.

'Now must we sing and sing the best we can
But first you must be told our character:
Convicted cowards all by kindred slain

'Or driven from home, and left to die in fear.'
They sang but had nor human tunes nor words,
Though all was done in common as before,

They had changed their throats and had the throats of birds.

Frost's beautiful "Acquainted with the Night" makes a sonnet out
of it, as a few Renaissance poets had done:

I have been one acquainted with the night.
I have walked out in rain—and back in rain.
I have outwalked the furthest city light.

I have looked down the saddest city lane.
I have passed by the watchman on his beat
And dropped my eyes, unwilling to explain.

I have stood still and stopped the sound of feet
When far away an interrupted cry
Came over fences from another street,

But not to call me back or say good-by;
And further still at an unearthly height,
One luminary clock against the sky

Proclaimed the time was neither wrong nor right.
I have been one acquainted with the night.

And T. S. Eliot evokes, without imitating, both Dante's and Shelley's terza rima in the second section of "Little Gidding," in which,

during a blackout of the London blitz, the ghost figure of Yeats appears to the narrator:

> In the uncertain hour before the morning
> Near the ending of interminable night
> At the recurrent end of the unending
> After the dark dove with the flickering tongue
> Had passed below the horizon of his homing
> While the dead leaves still rattle on like tin
> Over the asphalt where no sound was
> Between three districts whence the smoke arose
> I met one walking, loitering and hurried
> As if blown toward me like the metal leaves
> Before the urban dawn wind unresisting.
> And, as I fixed upon the down-turned face
> That pointed scrutiny with which we challenge
> The first-met stranger in the waning dusk
> I caught the sudden look of some dead master
> I had known . . .

And Seamus Heaney, in his turn, evokes both Dante and Eliot, in the twelfth section of "Station Island," in which James Joyce appears to him. The limitation of the stanza in English has been, of course, the incessant rhyme. Look what Heaney has done with it.

> Like a convalescent, I took the hand
> stretched down from the jetty, sense again
> an alien comfort as I stepped on ground
>
> to find the helping hand still gripping mine,
> fish-cold and bony, but whether to guide
> or to be guided I could not be certain

for the tall man in step at my side
seemed blind, though he walked straight as a rush
upon his ash plant, his eyes fixed straight ahead.

Then I knew him in the flesh
out there on the tarmac among the cars,
wintered hard and sharp as a blackthorn bush.

His voice eddying with the vowels of all rivers
came back to me, though he did not speak yet,
a voice like a prosecutor's or a singer's,

cunning, narcotic, mimic, definite—

Finally, compare these to Robert Pinsky's translation of the passage in Canto 2 of the *Inferno* in which Dante gets his first glimpse of
the souls in hell:

As winter starlings riding on their wings
Form crowded flocks, so spirits dip and veer
Foundering in the wind's rough buffetings,

Upward or downward, driven here or there
With never ease from pain nor hope of rest.
As chanting cranes will form a line in air,

So I saw souls come uttering cries—wind-tossed
And lofted by the storm. "Master," I cried,
"Who are these people by black air oppressed?"

And imagine sustaining it for 3,300 or so lines.

4 . *The tercet in free verse:* One of the great surprises of the prosody
of Walt Whitman's "Song of Myself" is the strength and delicacy and

suppleness with which he manages an almost-independent three-line stanza among the different stanza shapes. Freed from rhyme, it looks like something altogether new.

Here are some stanzas from "Song of Myself":

I celebrate myself, and sing myself,
And what I assume you shall assume,
For every atom belonging to me as good belongs to you.
    *

Houses and rooms are full of perfumes, the shelves are
    crowded with perfumes,
I breathe the fragrance myself and know it and like it,
The distillation would intoxicate me also, but I shall not let it.
    *

Have you reckon'd a thousand acres much? Have you
    reckoned the earth much?
Have you practis'd so long to learn to read?
Have you felt so proud to get at the meaning of poems?
    *

Sure as the most certain sure, plumb in the uprights, well
    entretied, braced in the beams,
Stout as a horse, affectionate, haughty, electrical,
I and this mystery, here we stand.
    *

. . . Loafe with me on the grass, loose the stop from your throat,
Not words, not music or rhyme I want, not custom or lecture,
    not even the best,
Only the lull I like, the hum of your valved voice.
    *

. . . I am not an earth nor an adjunct of an earth,
I am the mate and companion of people, all just as immortal
    and fathomless as myself,
(They do not know how immortal, but I know.)

... The boatmen and clam-diggers arose early and stopt for me,
I tuck'd my trouser-ends in my boots and went and had a
     good time,
You should have been with us that day round the chowder-kettle.

          *

... Sit a while dear son,
Here are biscuits to eat and here is milk to drink,
But as soon as you sleep and renew yourself in sweet clothes,
     I kiss you with a good-bye kiss and open the gate for your
     egress hence.

          *

... And as to you Corpse I think you are good manure, but
     that does not offend me,
I smell the white roses sweet-scented and growing,
I reach to the leafy lips, I reach to the polish'd breasts of melons.

          *

... The last scud of day holds back for me,
It flings my likeness after the rest and true as any on the shadow'd
     wilds,
It coaxes me to the vapor and the dusk.

It's worth looking at these stanzas for a moment to notice that
threes are a lot more complex than twos. In the first stanza above
Whitman uses a basic three-part structure from formal logic, the
syllogism. The syllogism, like the metaphor, effects a category shift.
Yeats:

     Love is a lion's tooth.

But logic is slower; it begins with a proposition involving a particular: Aristotle is a man. Subsumes it to a general proposition: All

men are mortal. And reorganizes the particular: Aristotle is mortal. A three-step dance. (It is probably not incidental that the classical instance demonstrating how the mind achieves certitude has death as its subject.) Whitman rearranges the order: the last line is his middle term.

Formally, you can get to three at least three ways: 1 + 1 + 1 (as in the third of Whitman's stanzas); 1 + 2 (as in the second and last of the stanzas—an image, then two related statements); 2 + 1 (as in the fourth and sixth stanzas). These patterns are easy to see in the haiku, with its 5-7-5 syllabic structure—I won't try to keep the syllable count:

1 + 1 + 1:

> Noon—
> orioles singing,
> the river flows in silence.

Three images, one per line, though one might describe this as 1 + 2, because "Noon" is the *kigo*, the set-up season phrase, and the next two lines are joined by strong contrast, the birds singing, the river silent.

2 + 1:

> On a bare branch
> a crow just settled—
> autumn evening.

1 + 2:

> Coolness—
> the sound of the bell
> as it leaves the bell.

5. *In modernism:* The tercet turns out, freed from the constraint of rhyme, to be such a supple instrument, less orderly looking than the couplet, less final than the quatrain, that it is not surprising that it turned out to be a favored form of the modernists when they began to experiment with free verse. Again the best way to study it is to look at instances. Williams used it in with very short lines, lines of middle length, and long lines. From "Porous":

> Cattail fluff
> blows in
> at the bank door.

Listening to Williams read on old recordings, you'll notice that he doesn't register a pause at line end, or no more pause than each of the three phrases might receive in ordinary speech. Here, as in most instances, three is a weaving form, but you also hear strongly the two beats per line—"cattail fluff," "blows in," "bank door." A play of twos and threes. So that you sense whenever he writes about the crafts, he is thinking about his own craft, as in "Fine Work with Pitch and Copper":

> Now they are resting
> in the fleckless light
> separately in unison
>
> like the sacks
> of sifted stone stacked
> regularly by twos

In free verse stanza, patterning is partly visual, but it's also partly aural. "Now they are resting"—a two stress line; "in the fleckless light"—another. Also with more syllables muting the effect— "separately in unison." The three two stress lines invite enough of a sense of patterning to make one hear a stress on "like" in "like the stacks." And to hear the stresses stacked up in "of sifted stone stacked." And a return to the two stress order on "regularly by twos." This play of visual and aural elements, the patterning of accents in relation to lines—especially when the lines are mostly end-stopped by natural pauses—seems to have been exactly the way the work of formal imagination operates in all of Williams's abundant experimenting with free verse. Famously, he came at the end of his life to flowing triplet stanzas, as in "The Ivy Crown":

> The whole process is a lie
>   unless,
>   crowned by excess,
>   it breaks forcefully,
>   one way or another,
>   from its confinement

and in "Asphodel." The "variable foot," he called it, in which the accentual patterning is more complex, the enjambments more unpredictable.

Stevens, experimenting alongside Williams for forty years or more, wrote three-line epigrammatic poems, free verse tercets, rhymed and unrhymed metrical tercets, and the three-line stanza became the favored form for his long poems like "Notes Toward a Supreme Fiction," "The Auroras of Autumn," and "An Ordinary Evening in New Haven." Early, in *Harmonium*, his short-line tercets have a quick gaiety of movement, compared to Williams's in which the lines measure out perception. See, for example, the lovely movement of two- and three-line stanzas in "The Load of Sugar-Cane" and the use it makes of repetition and rhyme, which gives a slight poem, a sort of watercolor, serious magic. In the longer line he weaves. Take a look again at the one long sentence from which "The Snow Man" is made. The most spectacular tercets early, and the ones nearest to terza rima, are in "Sea Surface Full of Clouds" in which the use of repetition gives each section of the poem something of the feel of a sestina. The rhyme in the first stanza suggests that he had the terza rima in his ear:

> In that November off Tehuantepec,
> The slopping of the sea grew still one night
> And in the morning summer hued the deck.

In the late short poems, it is a fascination to watch his mind and ear move from the measure couplets give him—"The Desire to Make Love in a Pagoda," "Nuns Painting Water-Lilies," "Dinner Bell in the Woods," "Reality Is an Activity of the Most August Imagination"—to the poems in three-line stanzas, the long lines of "The Sick Man," for example, which feel like Stevens near to Whitman and almost delirious:

> Bands of black men seem to be drifting in the air,
> In the south bands of thousands of black men,
> Playing mouth-organs in the night or, now, guitars.

(The psychology of race in his poems: subject for another time.) Also the long line in "The Course of a Particular." And the shorter lines in "A Child Asleep in Its Own Life" (which also moves from a tetrameter stanza to a free verse stanza and back to a tetrameter stanza) and the poem that seems like a summation of his art, "Of Mere Being."

H.D. seems not to have been drawn to the three-line stanza in her early experiments with free verse. In the 1940s, in those violent years, she experimented with short-line free verse stanzas, sometimes rhymed, as in "Ecco Sponsus":

The lonely heart,
the broken vow
have no place now—

And "Archer":

Fall the deep curtains,
delicate the weave,
fair the thread:

clear the colours,
apple-leaf green,
ox-heart blood-red:

For another echo of Dante's underworld, notice how H.D. uses the three-line stanza in the opening section of "The Walls Do Not Fall," which describes the bombing of London in World War II.

6. *Variations:* The three six-line stanzas of John Berryman's "Dream Songs" are built up from pairs of tercets. The scheme is a pair of rough pentameter lines, then a dimeter or trimeter line, and then the same again, with irregular rhyme. Look at #14:

Life, friends, is boring. We must not say so.
After all, the sky flashes, the great sea yearns,
we ourselves flash and yearn,
and moreover my mother told me as a boy
(repeatingly) 'Ever to confess you're bored
means you have no

Inner Resources.' I conclude now I have no
inner resources, because I am heavy bored.

Peoples bore me,
literature bores me, especially great literature,
Henry bores me, with his plights & gripes
as bad as achilles,

who loves people and valiant art, which bores me.
And the tranquil hills, & gin, look like a drag
and somehow a dog
has taken itself & its tail considerably away
into mountains or sea or sky, leaving
behind: me, wag.

And there is the six-line stanza of modified tercets so characteristic of Jorie Graham's *Erosion*. Look at the beginning of "Masaccio's
Expulsion":

Is this really the failure
of silence,
or eternity, where these two
suffer entrance
into the picture
plane,

a man and a woman
so hollowed
by grief they cover
their eyes
in order not to see
the inexhaustible grammar

before them—labor, judgement,
saints and peddlers—
the daylight hopelessly even
upon them,

and our eyes. But this too
is a garden

I'd say, with its architecture
of grief,
its dark and light
in the folds
of clothing, and oranges
for sale

among the shadows
of oranges . . .

It is a ghost of terza rima passed through the modernist stanza.

7. *The blues stanza:* If there is a classic American folk form, this is
it. The standard blues stanza is a couplet in which the first line is
repeated, presumably to give the singer time to improvise a third,
which rhymes with it. It emerges at the beginning of the twentieth
century, or even earlier, though there is no evidence that it reaches
back to slavery times. Its seedbed was Jim Crow, the ferocious terror
and repression unleashed against emancipated African Americans
that began after the brief openings of Reconstruction and lasted at
least until the civil rights movement in the '50s and '60s. Scholars
think the form probably came from the field holler and from the call-
and-response pattern of slave work songs.

Of course, it is more complex than its verbal form. Musically, the
traditional blues is a three-line, twelve-bar sequence. The form is a
dialogue between music and voice—and, as in all transcriptions of
song—the blues lyric as a poem is only half of that dialogue. And all
the elements of technique in performance, the flattened and shaded
notes that produce their unnerving and mournful sound, the qualities of timbre in the voice typical of African singing, the growl and

rasp of the vocal techniques, the suspensions and asides get lost on the page.

Another thing that makes transcription and literary presentation of the blues lyric difficult and in some way falsifies it is that it was improvised, so that each recording—recording began in the 1920s—arrests a thing in motion. And the particular versions that got recorded may or may not have been attending to things like narrative shape that the aesthetic of the page highlights. For all of these reasons, the transcribed blues lyric is much less a poem than the poetry that's in it. But the poetry is often so powerful that it is worth having it in print nevertheless. A good source is Eric Sackheim's *The Blues Line*, published by Ecco Press. The best book about the culture of the blues is Amiri Baraka's *Blues People*. The invaluable anthology of the uses of the blues form is Kevin Young's *Blues Poems*.

Almost as soon as the blues began to be disseminated by small recording companies aimed at a black audience—race records, they were called—African American poets began to experiment with literary adaptation of the blues form. The most interesting, I think, is the work of Langston Hughes and Sterling Brown.

EXPERIMENTS WITH THE BLUES FORM

Langston Hughes: The first blues to be published was W. C. Handy's *St. Louis Blues*. The first recording, by Mamie Smith, appeared in 1920. Hughes began publishing his experiments with the blues form in 1925–1926. His poems are wildly expensive to reprint, so it's best to go to the collected poems. The early experiments with taking the oral, improvisatory blues lyric into the territory of the printed poem include "Midwinter Blues," "Gypsy Man," "Ma Man," "Listen Here Blues," "Lament over Love," "Fortune Teller Blues," "Wide River," and "Suicide."

By the 1930s Hughes's poems became more militant. Here is a

blues he wrote in collaboration with the novelist Richard Wright. It was published in *New Masses* in 1939 when "red" was a buzzword for revolution:

Red Clay Blues

I miss that red clay, Lawd, I
Need to feel it in my shoes.
Says miss that red clay, Lawd, I
Need to feel it in my shoes.
I want to get to Georgia cause I
Got them red clay blues.

Pavement's hard on my feet, I'm
Tired o' this concrete street.
Pavement's hard on my feet, I'm
Tired o' this city street.
Goin' back to Georgia where
That red clay can't be beat.

I want to tramp in the red mud, Lawd, and
Feel the red clay round my toes.
I want to wade in that red mud,
Feel that red clay suckin' at my toes.
I want my little farm back and I
Don't care where the landlord goes.

I want to be in Georgia, when the
Big storm starts to blow.
Yes, I want to be in Georgia when that
Big storm starts to blow.
I want to see the landlords runnin' cause I
Wonder where they gonna go!

I got them red clay blues.

In the 1940s Hughes experimented with shorter versions, the epigram buried in the blues, in "Curious," "Evil," which is too good not to quote—

> Looks like what drives me crazy
> Don't have no effect on you—
> But I'm gonna keep on at it
> Till it drives you crazy too.

—"Hope" and "Wake":

> Tell all my mourners
> To mourn in red
> Cause there ain't no sense
> In my bein' dead.

Sterling Brown: Sterling Brown published his remarkable *Southern Road* in 1936, after the Harlem Renaissance had lost its charm for white readers and the book disappeared with hardly a trace. His versions of blues are, I think, subtler and darker than those of Hughes.

Kentucky Blues

> I'm Kentucky born,
> Kentucky bred,
> Gonna brag about Kentucky
> Till I'm dead.
>
> Thoroughbred horses,
> Hansome, fas',
> I ain't got nothin'
> But a dam' jackass.

Women as purty
As Kingdom Come,
Ain't got no woman
'Cause I'm black and dumb.

Cornland good,
Tobacco land fine,
Can't raise nothin'
On dis hill o' mine.

Ain't got no woman,
Nor no Man O' War,
But dis nigger git
What he's hankerin' for—

De red licker's good,
An' it ain't too high,
Gonna brag about Kentucky
Till I die . . .

See also "Old King Cotton," "Tin Roof Blues," "New St. Louis
Blues," which makes a triptych of "Market Street Woman," "Tornado
Blues," and "Low Down." Here is a little of "Market Street Woman":

Market Street woman is known fuh to have dark days.
Market Street woman noted fuh to have dark days,
Life do her dirty a hundred ornery ways.

Let her hang out de window and watch de busy worl' go pas',
Hang her head out de window and watch de careless worl' go pas',
Maybe some good luck will come down Market Street at las'.

Put paint on her lips, purple powder on her choklit face,
Paint on her lips, purple powder on her choklit face,
Take mo' dan paint to change de luck of dis dam place.

Whatever is so haunting in the basic form—say it, say it again, give it a twist and secure it with a rhyme—has echoes in other forms. Something of the 4-4-3-3 of the sonnet. The say-it-and-turn-it is a bit like the haiku. Sterling Brown, who read Hardy and Yeats and Scottish ballads at Williams College and at Harvard, came to the South as an outsider. And, in "Memphis Blues," he makes a ballad, almost a nursery rhyme rhythm, out of the blues sensibility:

> Memphis go
> By flood or flame;
> Nigger won't worry
> All de same—
> Memphis go
> Memphis come back—
> Ain' no skin
> Off de nigger's back.

THE THREE-LINE POEM

8 . *In English:* There aren't many three-line poems in English poetry. They thought of the short poem as an epigram and used the couplet or the quatrain for that purpose with its neat and final-sounding rhymes. Occasionally in Ben Jonson, Richard Crashaw, and others the epigram got stretched to three lines, but with no memorable results. Robert Herrick wrote one lyrical triplet:

> See'st thou that cloud as silver cleare,
> Plump, soft & swelling every where?
> 'Tis Julia's bed and she sleeps there.

And Emily Dickinson wrote a few:

An Hour is a Sea
Between a few, and me—
With them would Harbor be—

Then there are the fragments in Coleridge's journals. Images that
gathered themselves as blank verse and never found their way into
poems. He did not call them poems, having no theory of poetry that
would allow it, but they suggest what he might have done if he had:

                    The swallows
Interweaving there, mid the pair'd sea-mews
At distance wildly wailing!
    *

The Brook runs over sea-weeds.
Sabbath day—from the Miller's merry wheel
The water-drops dripp'd leisurely.
    *

                              A long deep lane
So overshadowed, it might seem one bower—
The damp clay-banks were furr'd with mouldy moss.
    *

                    The subtle snow
In every breeze rose curling from the Grove
Like pillars of cottage smoke.

And Whitman, who experimented with everything using his
new line, experimented with the three-line form:

I am he that aches with amorous love;
Does the earth gravitate? does not all matter, aching, attract
    all matter?
So the body of me to all I meet or know.

A Farm Picture

Through the ample open door of the peaceful country barn,
A sunlit pasture field with cattle and horses feeding,
And haze and vista, and the far horizon fading away.

A Child's Amaze

Silent and amazed even when a little boy
I remember hearing the preacher every Sunday put God in
    his statements
As contending against some being or influence.

And there is, of course, Ezra Pound:

Coda

O my songs,
Why do you look so eagerly and so curiously into people's faces,
Will you find your lost dead among them?

Alba

As cool as the pale wet leaves
of lily-of-the-valley
She lay beside me in the dawn.

T'ai Chiu

The petals fall to the fountain,
        the orange-colored rose-leaves.
Their ochre clings to the stone.

Here are some more recent three-line poems.

Michael Palmer:

Purples of Barley

And all of the time you are seeing these things she
sings "not
loudly but with authority"

Carol Snow:

And another

"massacre of the innocents."

And that there is a form
even for that.

Brenda Hillman scatters brief remark poems in three lines in her
books; they seem to comment on her process:

—Nice going but you don't
have to decide anything that leaves
anything else out—

(And you thought
you had learned health
but had only met some of the characters)

(agonized
by the glazed multitude
of unusable lines—)

and the mistake wasn't that heavy
but it had ropes tying it to
all my other mistakes!

My friend called;
   she was telling
the pain "what to think"—

Unfinished Glimmer

   (Look, you. You're getting
most of them. If there are more
   we'll write them later—)

9. *Haiku and renga:* Haiku is of course the classic three-line un-rhymed form. As we've seen, it is sometimes thought of as a three-phrase one-line poem. And we have seen above how it deploys the possibilities of the three-part structure. Because its impulse is met-onymic, pictorial, direct, it had some influence on imagist poets. I don't think I need to give more examples here.

There are two things to understand about it formally. The first is the importance of the *kigo*, or seasonal reference, that each haiku contains. These phrases—autumn evening, spring rain, harvest moon, plum blossoms—are so packed with associations to classi-cal Japanese poetry and to Japanese social life that they anchor the poem and give it, almost always, a two-part structure within the three-phrase sequence. The poem is almost always a commentary on its kigo. It would be as if we had developed a popular form in which one line was a quotation from Shakespeare and the other two a subtle comment on it drawn from direct, spontaneous ob-servation:

   To be or not to be—
she's walking to the store
   in the raw spring wind

> Out, out, brief candle—
> he has a toothache,
> he's working on a poem—

So the basis of the form in a way is to rub two sticks together, one that floats into the mind and one that comes up from the world.

The second thing is that the haiku evolved from the *renga*, which evolved from the *tanka*. From the point of view of form, the *renga* may be the most interesting thing, at the moment, about haiku. In a *renga*, the first poet writes a haiku. I'm going to use a famous one, Matsuo Bashō's and his group's *Monkey's Raincoat*, as an example. A poet named Mukai Kyorai began the poem:

> The kite's feather
> cleaned up a bit
> by the first winter rain.

To which Bashō added a couplet, making the two verses a tanka:

> The withered leaves, stirred
> by a gust of wind, then still

A third poet, Nozawa Bonchō, writes another haiku, which, taken together with Bashō's lines, produces a completely new tanka, entirely independent of Kyorai's verse:

> Since morning
> his trouser drenched
> from fording streams

The next poet, Nakamura Fumikuni, writes a couplet to make a new poem with Boncho's haiku:

In the fields bamboo traps
to ward off badgers

Notice that the season has changed. In the first it is the very beginning of winter. In the second it's sometime in the fall. In the third it's sometime in the summer. And notice that each of the verses, after the first, both begins one poem and ends another. These combinations of things—the constantly shifting seasons, the beginnings that are ending—are formal expressions of a deeply Buddhist attitude toward time and change.

We have so far three five-line poems:

The kite's feathers
cleaned up a bit
by the first winter rain.

The withered leaves, stirred
by a gust of wind, then still.

Since morning
his trousers drenched
from fording streams—

in the fields bamboo traps
to ward off badgers

Here's a little more of it. Bashhō:

Through the lush ivy
crawling over the lattice door
an evening moon

Then Kyorai:

He won't share the pears
The place is famous for

Then Fumikuni:

He's playing at sketching
with ink and brush
at the end of autumn

Then Bonchō :

How pleasant it is, wearing
stylish & expensive knitted stockings

Then Kyorai:

Wordless all morning
and nothing happens
to break the inner quiet

Then Bashō :

Just as the village comes into view
they sound the noontime horn

And so on. One way to get the rapidity of this is to see it as a series
of prose sentences:

The kite's feathers cleaned up a bit by the first winter
rain. Withered leaves, stirred by a gust of wind, then
still. Since morning his trousers drenched from fording
streams. They've set bamboo traps in the fields to scare
off badgers. Through the lush ivy crawling over the

lattice door an evening moon. He won't share the pears
the place is famous for. He's playing at sketching with
ink and brush at the end of autumn. How pleasant to
be wearing stylish and expensive knitted stockings.
Wordless all morning and nothing happened to break
the inner quiet. Just as the village comes into view, they
sound the noon horn. Frayed at the edge, the straw
sleeping mat is getting moldy. The lotus petals falling
one by one. At Suizen temple very good soup. He
pleads off—he's got another eight miles to travel. This
spring too the servants, loyal as Lu T'ung's, stay on.
New growth on the tree's graft in the hazy moonlight.
Covered with moss, the old stone basin by the flowering
cherry. By midday his anger had subsided. In just one
sitting: bolts down two days' rations. North wind on the
island, and the feel of snow in it. Every day, dusk falling,
he climbs the temple hill to light the lamp. The wood
thrushes are finished with their summer songs. Weak,
bone-thin, he can't get out of bed. Her visitor finds the
place cramped and borrows carriage-space next door.
My faithless lover: let him crawl to me through the
quince hedge. At parting she helps him put on his sword.
Restless she combs her hair out carelessly. He musters
himself the night before the battle. What moon there
is dissolving in the dawn. Autumn to Biwa Lake and to
Mount Hira a first frost. Somebody stole his cache of
buckwheat, he goes on writing poems. Winter wind:
heavy jackets for awhile. Jostled by others, having slept
badly, he sets out again. Clouds from *tatara* still crimson
in the sky. A cottage: they're repairing harnesses, the
window onto cherry trees. Among old loquat leaves, new
buds.

The form is a *kasen*, thirty-six stanzas. Solo, the renga suggests a form—in verse or prose—for catching both the rapidity of the mind and the phantasmal solidity of the world.

Readers may want to consult Eliot Weinberger's essay on Octavio Paz and the renga, and his translation of a very rare instance in which a poet wrote a solitary rather than collaborative renga, a one-hundred-stanza verse by the medieval poet Sora.

FOUR

1. Old English, *feower;* Latin, *quattuor;* Greek, *tettares.* The four cardinal points of the compass, the four sides of a square. This number expresses and stands for evenness and completeness in several ways.

In most preliterate cultures, the world was organized into fours. Almost all Native American peoples, for example, not using anything like a Linnaean system to classify phenomena, put things in four categories based on the points of the compass. Plants, animals, clans, numbers, genders, weathers, colors were associated with the four directions.

THE FOUR-LINE STANZA IN METRICAL POETRY

2. There is no four-line form in English, but the four-line stanza, the *quatrain,* is basic to most English lyric forms, one of the earliest of which was the *ballad stanza,* which consists of four lines, a tetrameter line followed by a trimeter followed by a tetrameter followed by

a trimeter, with an abab or an abcb rhyme scheme. This form was adapted to the hymn and has been called the *common measure* or the *hymn stanza*. As soon as Middle English verse found its way to accentual syllabic meters, the lyric is given shape by the four-line stanza, as in this one (author unknown):

> Sumer is icumen in,
> Lhude sing cuccu;
> Groweth sed and bloweth med
> And spingeth the wode nu—

To which it added a playful refrain:

> Sing cuccu!

The abcb stanza was particularly attractive because it used rhyme to secure a conclusion and gave some freedom to the other two lines. Not surprising that the best-known four-line poem in the language is in that form (author also unknown):

> Western wind, when wilt thou blow?
> The small rain down can rain.
> Christ! that my love were in my arms
> And I in my bed again.

And one of the best-known eight-line poems:

> O Rose, thou art sick.
> The invisible worm
> That flies in the night
> In the howling storm
> Has found out thy bed
> Of crimson joy,

And his dark secret love
Does thy life destroy.

3 . Again the number of possible structures increases: $1 + 1 + 1 + 1$, $2 + 2, 3 + 1, 1 + 3, 1 + 2 + 1, 1 + 1 + 2, 2 + 1 + 1$, so that great variety is possible in a longer form. "Western Wind" is $2 + 2$.

Blake's "The Sick Rose" consists of two sentences, one of them compound. So it is at the first level $1 + 7$. Taking the compound into consideration, the rhythmic pattern is $1 + 5 + 2$, enjambed across the stanza break (to suggest the worm's terrifying ability to penetrate), and the poem also lays down one perception per line, $1 + 1 + 1 + 1 + 1 + 1 + 1 + 1$ in a fatal cadence. Unless you think of that "bed of crimson joy" as a single image, in which case, the movement lingers a little there, $1 + 1 + 1 + 1 + 2 + 1 + 1$. Enjambment, of course, multiplies and complicates all these possibilities. It can also be doled out this way, $1 + 3 + 2 + 2$:

One image, one line:

O Rose, thou art sick.

One image, three lines:

The invisible worm
That flies in the night
In the howling storm

One image, two lines:

Has found out thy bed
Of crimson joy

One image, two lines:

And his dark, secret love
Does thy life destroy.

4. In the late teens of the new century, when Pound and Eliot, talking, decided that the *vers libre* movement in America was descending into sloppiness, and they decided to put some starch back into modernism, to go back, as Pound said, to "the Bay State Hymnal," it was the quatrain they turned to. Pound in the pyrotechnic bravura of "Hugh Selwyn Mauberly":

> For three years, out of touch with his time,
> He strove to resuscitate the dead art
> Of poetry; to maintain 'the sublime'
> In the old sense. Wrong from the start—
>
> No, hardly, but seeing he had been born
> In a half savage country, out of date;
> Bent resolutely on wringing lilies from the acorn;
> Capaneus; trout for factitious bait;
>
> ἴδμεν γάρ τοι πάν πάνθ', ὅσ' ἐνι Τροίη
> Caught in the unstopped ear;
> Giving the rocks small lee-way
> The chopped seas held him, therefore, that year.

And Eliot in various poems, including this one in which he elects to have an Irishman stand for gross sensuality:

> Apeneck Sweeney spreads his knees
> Letting his arms hang down to laugh,
> The zebra stripes along his jaw
> Swelling to maculate giraffe.

The circles of the stormy moon
Slide westward toward the River Plate,
Death and the Raven drift above,
And Sweeney guards the horned gate.

It was the first neoformalist retrenching.

5 . The best way to get a sense of the four-line stanza in English is
to pick up an anthology and read through it. Probably, for this form,
metrical pattern is just as important as stanza patterning. Five basic meters, rhyme scheme aside, have been used regularly with the
four-line stanza: the pentameter quatrain, the tetrameter quatrain,
the headless tetrameter quatrain, the ballad stanza, and the trimeter
quatrain. Here's an example of each:

William Butler Yeats, pentameter quatrain:

When you are old and gray and full of sleep,
And nodding by the fire, take down this book,
And slowly read, and dream of the soft look
Your eyes had once, and of their shadows deep;

Robert Frost, tetrameter quatrain:

Whose woods these are, I think I know.
His house is in the village, though;
He will not see me stopping here
To watch his woods fill up with snow.

John Donne, headless tetrameter quatrain:

Go and catch a falling star,
Get with child a mandrake root,

> Tell me where all past years are,
> Or who cleft the Devil's foot,

William Wordsworth, the ballad stanza:

> A slumber did my spirit seal.
> I had no human fears.
> She seemed a thing who could feel
> The touch of earthly years.

Theodore Roethke, trimeter quatrain:

> The whiskey on your breath
> Could make a small boy dizzy;
> But I hung on like death:
> Such waltzing was not easy.

And there are, of course, endless variations, like the stanza of Elizabeth Bishop's "The Armadillo," a trimeter quatrain with a pentameter third line:

> This is the time of year
> when almost every night
> the frail, illegal fire balloons appear.
> Climbing the mountain height,

Or Hardy's trimeter with a tetrameter third line:

> But Time, to make me grieve,
> Part steals, lets part abide;
> And shakes this fragile frame at eve
> With throbbings of noontide.

And here is Emily Dickinson's dimeter quatrain:

> Wild Nights! Wild Nights!
> Were I with thee
> Wild Nights should be
> Our luxury!

6 . The form got used for different purposes in different periods. In the Renaissance, for example, it is a song form:

> When that I was and a little tiny boy,
> With hey, ho, the wind and the rain,
> A foolish thing was but a toy,
> For the rain it raineth every day.

> *(William Shakespeare)*

But the tetrameter quatrain also was associated with old-fashioned, non-Italian common sense, with English plainness:

> My friends, the things that do attain
> The happy life be these, I find:
> The riches left, not got with pain;
> The fruitful ground; the quiet mind;

> *(Walter Raleigh)*

And the more ambitious work was carried on in Italian and classical forms, pastorals, elegies, and sonnets.

In the seventeenth century, among the Royalist poets, it was almost always associated with song:

> Gather ye rosebuds while ye may,
> Old time is still a-flying;
> And this same flower that smiles today
> Tomorrow will be dying.
>
> (Robert Herrick)

When the devotional poets, and later the Puritan poets used it, they tended to complicate it. George Herbert, for example, gives the tetrameter a dying fall in "Virtue":

> Sweet day, so cool, so calm, so bright,
> The bridal of the earth and sky:
> The dews shall weep thy fall tonight;
> For thou must die.

And in his "Horation Ode," Andrew Marvell invents a curious-sounding quatrain of two tetrameter lines followed by two trimeters:

> 'Tis time to leave the books in dust,
> And oil the unused armor's rust,
> Removing from the wall
> The corslet in the hall.

The crucial development in the eighteenth century was the Protestant hymn. It begins with Isaac Watts:

> Our God, our help in ages past,
> Our hope for years to come,
> Our shelter from the stormy blast,
> And our eternal home.

It kept the English plainness, and the form's roots in song, and gave it Protestant inwardness. And it was this form that migrated to Protestant America in "Rock of Ages" and "Amazing Grace" (written by John Newton, the reformed captain of a slaving ship) and in carols like "It came upon a midnight clear." In the nineteenth century in America a New York minister named Robert Lowry wrote "Shall We Gather at the River" to commemorate parishioners killed in a virulent epidemic of influenza. Philadelphia minister Phillips Brooks wrote a Christmas carol two years after the Civil War that was also a prayer for peace:

> *O little town of Bethlehem*
> *How still we see thee lie!*
> *The hopes and fears of all the years*
> *Are gathered here tonight.*

In the literary tradition, the Protestant hymn gave a form to the only two poets in the language for whom the quatrain was central, Blake for the *Songs of Innocence and Experience* and Dickinson for the infinite variations she wrung on the common measure in a thousand poems. The other major poet for whom it was important was Thomas Hardy. For him it was a ballad form, a late flowering of the ballad revival that was the other important development in the eighteenth century. Thomas Percy's *Reliques,* a late-eighteenth-century collection of old ballads, seemed like fresh air to the young romantics like Wordsworth and Coleridge after a century of the heroic couplet, and the desire to return to roots in song, narrative, and plain English diction gave a title to their collaborative collection, *Lyrical Ballads.* And a form to Coleridge's "Rime of the Ancient Mariner":

> All in a hot and copper sky,
> The bloody Sun, at noon,

Right up above the mast did stand,
      No bigger than the moon.

The other eighteenth-century development had to do with the pentameter quatrain. In "Elegy in a Country Churchyard," Thomas Gray used it to write a lulling descriptive line that got imitated all through the next century:

The curfew tolls the knell of parting day,
The lowing herd winds slowly o'er the lea,
The plowman homeward plods his weary way,
And leaves the world to darkness and to me.

Victorians used all these forms—the descriptive-philosophical pentameter (it's the one Yeats used in 1893 for "When You Are Old and Grey"), the narrative quatrain, the song, the prayer or ballad. The two notable developments in the later nineteenth century are Alfred Lord Tennyson's quatrain for "In Memoriam," the only well-known long poem in English to use such a simple form. It's written as a series of short lyrics, four quatrains long (the form, minus meter and rhyme, John Ashbery used in *Shadow Train*).
      Here's Tennyson:

He is not here; but far away
The noise of life begins again,
And ghastly through the drizzling rain
On the bald street breaks the blank day.

The other Victorian excitement was Edward Fitzgerald's *Rubaiyat* quatrain, which we'll look at below. The century ends with Hardy's grim, exacting uses of the ballad:

That night your great guns, unawares,
Shook all our coffins as we lay,
And broke the chancel window-squares,
We thought it was the Judgement Day

And sat upright—

As we have seen, in another few years, Eliot and Pound would be reviving, with peculiar modernist twists, the plain-spoken tetrameter quatrain to beat it over the heads of Amy Lowell and Carl Sandburg and what they regarded as the slovenliness of the new American free verse movement.

7. *Russian acmeist verse:* Acmeism was the Russian equivalent of imagism in the early twentieth century. It wasn't a free verse movement, but a movement against symbolist obscurity and toward classical hardness. Its preferred mode was the Russian tetrameter couplet, which mixed monosyllabic and polysyllabic rhyme. Osip Mandelstam, Anna Akhmatova, Marina Tsvetaeva, and Boris Pasternak—not a member of the group—all did brilliant work in the short tetrameter form, and Mandelstam's *Stone* (1913) begins with a couple of four-line poems in the stanza. Here are some translations of each. Maybe some of you know Russian and can do better:

An apple drops to the ground,
toneless, precise
—and all around
the song of the trees, the forest silence . . .

(*Tr. Burton Raffael*)

The shy speechless sound
of a fruit falling from its tree,
and around it the silent music
of the forest, unbroken . . .

(Tr. W. S. Merwin and Clarence Brown)

The careful and hollow thud
of a fruit snapped from a tree
amidst the neverending song
of the deep forest silence . . .

(Tr. David McDuff)

A tentative hollow note
As a pod falls from a tree
In the constant melody
Of the wood's deep quiet . . .

(Tr. Robert Tracy)

Here is another one:

You appeared out of the half-
dark hall, suddenly, wearing a shawl—
we disturbed no one,
we woke no servants . . .

(Tr. Burton Raffael)

All the lamps were turned low.
You slipped out quickly in a thin shawl.

We disturbed no one.
The servants went on sleeping.

(Tr. W. S. Merwin and Clarence Brown)

Suddenly in a light shawl
you slipped out of the half-darkened hall—
we disturbed no one,
we did not wake the sleeping servants . . .

(Tr. David McDuff)

In a light shawl, you suddenly slipped
Out of the shadowed hall—
We disturbed no one at all
Nor woke the servants up . . .

(Tr. Robert Tracy)

THE FOUR-LINE STANZA
IN FREE VERSE

8 . So we've seen the expressive associations of the quatrain inherited by the poets who made a break from metrical poetry.

It's interesting, in this way, to see how Whitman uses it in "Song of Myself." Mostly, he avoids it—it's too balanced. But he seems to use it sometimes when he wants to say an important thing plainly and forcibly:

Creeds and school in abeyance,
Retiring back awhile sufficed at what they are, but never
    forgotten,

I harbor for good or bad, I permit to speak at every hazard,
Nature without check with original energy.

—

There was never any more inception than there is now,
Nor any more youth or age than there is now,
And will never be any more perfection than there is now,
Nor any more heaven or hell than there is now.

And occasionally for descriptive purposes as in the pentameter quatrain of Thomas Gray:

I mind how once we lay such a transparent summer morning,
How you settled your head athwart my hips and gently turn'd
    over upon me,
And parted the shirt from my bosom-bone, and plunged your
    tongue to my bare-stripped heart,
And reach'd till you felt my beard, and reach'd till you held
    my feet.

—

. . . The big doors of the country barn stand open and ready,
The dried grass of the harvest-time loads the slow-drawn wagon,
The clear light plays on the brown gray and green intertinged,
The armfuls are pack'd to the sagging mow.

And, in a memorable riff in "The Sleepers," Whitman makes a kind
of lullaby of its sense of completion:

The married couple sleep calmly in their bed, he with his
    palm on the hip of his wife, and she with her palm on the
    hip of her husband,
The sisters sleep lovingly side by side in their bed,
The men sleep lovingly side by side in theirs,

And the mother sleeps with her little child carefully wrapt.

The blind sleep, and the deaf and dumb sleep,
The prisoner sleeps well in the prison, the runaway son
    sleeps,
The murderer that is to be hung next day, how does he sleep?
And the murder'd person, how does he sleep?

The female that loves unrequited sleeps,
And the male that loves unrequited sleeps,
The head of the money-maker that plotted all day sleeps,
And the enraged and treacherous dispositions, all, all sleep.

9. Probably the most famous quatrain in modernist verse is Pound's translation of Li Bai in *Cathay* (1915), "The Jewel Stairs' Grievance":

The jewelled steps are already quite white with dew,
It is so late that the dew soaks my gauze stockings,
And I let down the crystal curtain
And watch the moon through the clear autumn.

This accomplishes several things. It contains the imagist ideal of clear presentation. It shows a way to write a four-line poem that's not an epigram. It shows a way, by following the presentation of the Chinese characters, to write free verse based on limpid English sentence rhythms. And it shows a way to use the effects of both Gray's pentameter quatrain and the full tetrameter quatrain without evoking the effects of meter.

The last two lines could in fact be scanned as tetrameter:

Ănd Í/ lĕt dówn/ thĕ crýs/ tăl cúr/ tain
Ănd wátch/ thĕ móon/ thrŏúgh thĕ cleár aút/umn

but the first two lines don't scan so easily:

> The jew/ elled steps/ are al/ ready /quite white/ with dew
> It is/ so late/ that the dew/ soaks my/ gauze stock/ ings

Easier to scan it accentually, six beats and six beats, then four and four tending to five:

> The jewelled steps already quite white with dew

> It is so late that the dew soaks my gauze stockings

> And I let down the crystal curtain

> And watch the moon through the clear autumn

The first line is six stresses parceled out between slight pauses like this: 2/3/1. The second line is also six stresses with a slightly different rhythmic character: 2/1/3. The third line is four stresses: 2/2, a contraction, and the fourth line is an expansion, but to five stresses not six. It relaxes the pattern. 2/1/2, as if it were the balance the first two lines were trying to find. (This depends, I know, on hearing "through" as a stressed syllable. Monosyllabic prepositions in ordinary speech don't receive stress, but the slight pause after "And watch the moon" and the article before "clear" does, to my ear, throw weight onto "through." If the line read "And watched the moon through clear autumn air," one wouldn't hear a stress on "through.") The effect Pound achieves seems from this distance wonderfully calculated, but, of course, he was feeling his way. And the combination of the apparent simplicity of Chinese sentence construction and the clear-mindedness of the Taoist sensibility had allowed something new to happen to the sound of English verse—but the effect is too quiescent to have interested Pound for long. In fact, he avoided the four-line stanza in general. I can only think of one in all of the *Cantos*:

> Nor can he who has passed a month in the death cells
> believe in capital punishment
> No man who has passed a month in the death cells
> believes in cages for beasts.

There are none to speak of in Eliot, and very few in Stevens, who much preferred twos and threes.

10. H.D., trying to work out a free verse song form, uses the stanza but almost always in poems that mix stanza lengths. Here is the first poem from her first book, *Sea Garden* (1916):

> Rose, harsh rose,
> marred and with stint of petals,
> meagre flower, thin,
> sparse of leaf,
>
> more precious
> than a wet rose
> single on a stem—
> you are caught in the drift.
>
> Stunted, with small leaf,
> you are flung on the sand,
> you are lifted
> in the crisp sand
> that drives the wind.
>
> Can the spice-rose
> drip such acrid fragrance
> hardened in a leaf?

So it was Williams who experimented with it most, hardly at all at first, and then in the '30s and '40s more and more. He seemed to like it, especially the rough four-beat line that approached the te-trameter, for its definiteness:

> Sometimes I envy others, fear them
> a little too, if they write well.
> For when I cannot write I'm a sick man
> and want to die. The cause is plain.
>
> But they have no access to my sources.
> Let them write then as they can and
> perfect it as they can they will never
> come to the secret of that form
>
> interknit with the unfathomable ground
> where we walk daily and from which
> among the rest you have sprung
> and opened flower-like to my hand.

For more recent instances, Ashbery's *Shadow Train* is particularly interesting to look at. And there is Frank O'Hara's "Poem" of 1952, which has an extremely complicated attitude toward the notion of order a stanza proposes.

> The eager note on my door said, "Call me,
> call when you get in!" so I quickly threw
> a few tangerines into my overnight bag
> straightened my eyelids and shoulders, and
>
> headed straight for the door. It was autumn
> by the time I got around the corner, oh all
> unwilling to be either pertinent or bemused, but
> the leaves were brighter than grass on the sidewalk!

Funny, I thought, that the lights are on this late
and the hall door open; still up at this hour, a
champion jai-alai player like himself? Oh fie!
For shame! What a host, so zealous! And he was

there in the hall, flat on a sheet of blood that
ran down the stairs. I did appreciate it. There are few
hosts who so thoroughly prepare to greet a guest
only casually invited, and that several months ago.

THE FOUR-LINE POEM: CHUEH-CHU AND RUBA'I

11. The Chinese quatrain was one of the great literary forms of the
Tang dynasty. It was called *chueh-chu,* or "curtailed verse." It was a
form of "regulated verse," or *chin-t'i-shih,* in which the pattern of
tones followed certain rules. The poem of Li Bai that Pound translated was a chueh-chu. But there were also four-line poems in the
"old" or unpatterned style—nearer to the rhythm of folk songs—
and Li Bai particularly favored that form. Arthur Cooper: ". . . the
fourfold structure has something at once like a little sonata-form and
like the composition of a painting. The sonata form of these poems is
reflected in the Chinese names of each of the lines: the first is called
'Raising,' that is, introduction of the theme; the second is called 'For-
warding,' that is, development; the third, 'Twisting,' or introduction
of a new theme,; and the fourth 'Concluding.'"

All of the great Tang masters, Du Fu, Li Bai, Bai Juyi, Wang Wei,
and the eccentric Han Shan, worked in the form. There is even a long
poem by Li He, often called the Chinese Rimbaud, which is about all
the ways the bureaucratic system and its examinations did in poets.
It consists of twenty-six quatrains and it's called "Twenty-six Ways of
Breaking Wild Horses." Impossible to represent these poets, whom

some think the greatest constellation of lyric poetry in any language ever, in a few lines.

Here's one poem by Du Fu:

> My rain-soaked herbs: some still sparse, some lush.
> They freshen the porch and pavilion with their color.
> These waste mountains are full of them. But what's what?
> I don't know the names and the root shapes are terrifying.

That's the seven-syllable form. Here's a five:

> *Through Censor Ts'ui I Send a Quatrain to Kao Shih*
>
> Half my hundred-year life gone—
> Another autumn, hunger and cold return.
> Ask the Prefect of P'eng-chou how long,
> In such distress, one must await rescue.

12 . *The ruba'i:* The term means "foursome."[1] This Persian couplet, divided into rhyming half lines, emerged sometime around 900, and became the traditional short form in the Islamic world. It got introduced into English, of course, by Edward Fitzgerald's translation of the ruba'i of the Persian mathematician and philosopher, Omar Khayyam. Their hedonism and skepticism went off like a bomb in late Victorian England. Our age has been more interested in Sufi mystical traditions, and, probably, Coleman Bark's translations of Rumi are now the best-known rendering of Middle Eastern verse. Fitzgerald holds up remarkably well. If you've never read him, or not read him lately, it is worth taking a look. In the 1960s Robert Graves retranslated the poems, arguing that Fitzgerald had misrepresented Omar. And there was another version in the 1970s by the scholar Pe-

ter Avery and the poet John Heath-Stubbs, which tried, they said, to convey the "hard directness of the Persian."

A recent scholarly translation by L. P. Elwell-Sutton may get nearer to the bone.

Omar Khayyam was a mathematician and astronomer. He wrote a treatise on algebra, helped devise the Islamic calendar, and made important contributions to astronomy. The poems were the by-blows, musings, of a very sophisticated intelligence living in a very rich civilization at a time when Europe was mostly a bunch of thuggish robber barons hacking out their territories. Here are some of the Elwell-Sutton versions:

> This circle in which we come and go
> Has neither origin nor final end.
> Will no one ever tell us truthfully
> Whence we have come and whither do we go?
>
> ⋆
>
> Even a drunk would never propose
> To smash to bits his neatly-fashioned cup.
> By whom then were so many comely bodies,
> fashioned in love, yet smashed in angry hate?
>
> ⋆
>
> Every particle of dust upon this earth
> Was once a moon-like face, a Venus brow.
> Wipe the dust gently from your lover's cheek.
> For that dust too was once a lover's cheek.
>
> ⋆
>
> The boundless universe was born of night.
> No man has ever pierced its secrets.
> They all have much to say for their own good,
> But they can't tell you who they are, or why.
>
> ⋆

The dawn is here; wake up, lovely.
Pour wine slowly, slowly; pluck the lute.
For those who are here aren't staying long,
And those who've gone aren't ever coming back.

What moved Fitzgerald about Omar, whose poems he was piec-
ing out of very old and hard-to-read Persian manuscripts with the
one available English-Persian dictionary, was what he called the "Ep-
icurean pathos." And it was this flavor that so took Algernon Charles
Swinburne, Christina Rossetti, and the other rebellious Victorians
when they came across the poem—the entire edition had been re-
maindered; they bought their copies for a penny apiece at a Thames-
side used book stall—ten years after its publication:

> There was a door to which I found no key;
> There was a veil through which I might not see:
> Some little talk awhile of ME and THEE
> There was—and then no more of THEE and ME.
>
>   *
>
> And lately, by the tavern door agape,
> Came shining through the dusk an Angel Shape
> Bearing a vessel on his shoulder; and
> He bid me taste of it; and 'twas—the Grape!

The late-nineteenth-century poets sort of combined Keats and
Fitzgerald to produce their poems of rebellion and sensuality. Here
is Swinburne in "Laus Veneris," using the Omar stanza. As far as I
know, it's the only Victorian poem about a hickey:

> Asleep or waking is it? for her neck,
> Kissed over close, wears yet a purple speck
> Wherein the pained blood falters and goes out,
> Soft, and stung softly—fairer for a fleck.

13 . Here are a couple quatrains by Yeats:

Spilt Milk

We that have done and thought,
That have thought and done,
Must ramble and thin out
Like milk spilt on a stone.

The Spur

You think it horrible that lust and rage
Should dance attendance upon my old age;
They were not such a plague when I was young;
What else have I to spur me into song.

14 . Jump ahead. Harryette Mullen's *Muse and Drudge* in 1995, a long
poem made out of more than three hundred four-line stanzas in a
punning bluesy diction. The first one begins with a nod to Sappho's
quatrain:

Sapphire's lyre styles
plucked eyebrows
bow legs and hips
whose lives are lonely too

my last nerve's lucid music
sure chewed up the juicy fruit
you must don't like my peaches
there's some left on the tree.

A NOTE ON NUMBERS

1. Almost all the likely formal propositions in both metrical and free verse poems can be derived from one-, two-, three-, and four-line stanzas.

2. There are stanza shapes hallowed by some particular use that students of English literature used to learn. Rime royal, the seven-line stanza of Chaucer's *Troilus and Criseyde* is one. Before the sonnet came to England, two stanzas of rime royal made a sort of sonnet, though for Chaucer it was a form used for narrative, and rhyme dependent if one is to hear its shape. Hard to imagine an unrhymed nine-line free verse stanza. One might measure out a narrative or expository or associative poem in nines, though. It seems possible, a sort of lumbering ordinariness if the lines tended to be roughly the same length. Or could be made of sets of three threes, with a pattern of lines of irregular length, for example, long, short, long, to make an intricate patterning.

And there is ottava rima, an eight-line stanza with a particularly thumping rhyme scheme that was supposed to have been originated by Giovanni Boccaccio and brought into English by Thomas Wyatt, which Lord George Gordon Byron used in *Don Juan* and Kenneth Koch revived in *Ko*, his epic poem about a Japanese baseball player. And the Spencerian stanza of *The Faerie Queen*. Nine lines with an intricately repetitive rhyme scheme and a slow alexandrine (twelve syllables) for a final line.

Rime royal and Edmund Spenser's stanza came from a culture full of craft ornamentation in its weaving and embroidery. Were one to use them today, in their full rhymed forms, it's not clear to me what in our culture their expressive force would be. Free verse seven- or nine-line stanzas will probably read as mechanical regularity or give a kind of architectural solidity (as in the editing of some Japanese films) to the progression of thought or narrative.

3. All of them, and others, are made out of ones, twos, threes, and fours. In the way that most sonnets are made from either a 4/4/3/3 pattern or a 4/4/4/2 pattern. And then within a line, we might hear one or two or three, even four phrases, which also make rhythmic units, as the line usually makes a rhythmic unit.

Two phrase units:

Th' expense of spirit in a waste of shame

Three phrase units:

Is lust in action, and till action, lust

Four phrase units:

is perjured, murderous, bloody, full of blame,

Five phrase units:

> savage, extreme, rude, cruel, not to trust,

And in this way the formal imagination is about numbers falling through numbers, as it is in music.

4. The idea of form contains some notion of measure. The things to be measured in poems might be syllables, words, stressed and unstressed syllables, lines, even syntactical structures. If three sentences have the same syntactical disposition:

> The Curfew tolls the knell of parting day,
> The lowing herd winds slowly o'er the lea,
> The plowman homeward plods his weary way—

. . . we notice; and the noticing is a form of counting; we are, probably for very good evolutionary reasons, counters and noticers of patterns and disruptions of patterns at the core of our being. Line itself, of course, is in poetry a primary measure. The stanza another one. Though they can be enjambed, that is, not syntactically a completed unit of the kind that a sentence is, the poet's choice to make a line invites us to see and usually to hear it as a unit. In the same way we are invited to sense the stanza—in its printed form, visually; in its aural form by way of some other marker, rhyme the most common—as a unit.

5. Rhythm, pattern, play. I think about this four-line poem by Blake we looked at before:

> What is it men in women do require?
> The lineaments of gratified desire.

What is it women do in men require?
The lineaments of gratified desire.

The parallelism gives pleasure; it is a syntactical parallelism. And so does the small variation in the structure—to avoid a variation in the meter. The moving around of the verb is a little celebration of difference. And the rhymes of course make an emphatic repetition. We count those, too. Long I, long I, long I, long I. And the doubling of it in *gratified, gratified*. Here is a little Irving Berlin lyric, two lines:

What'll I do, if you are far away
And I am blue, what'll I do?

Notice the sound play, first. The first phrase, *What'll I do,* has a particular rhythm, stressed syllable, unstressed syllable, unstressed syllable, stressed syllable. I've heard it called a cradle, because, marked, it looks like one: / _ _ /, and it's so common to the rhythm of English speech that it functions—counting paired stressed and unstressed syllables as "feet" the way prosodists do—as a two-foot rhythmic unit, the way the double iamb—unstressed, unstressed, stressed, stressed—does. *Chiasmus* is the Greek name for the crossing pattern—

A   B
B   A

—in the Berlin lyric. The winsomeness and humor of it has to do with the mix of the rhyme—*do, you, blue, do*—and the truncation in the pattern, the skipping lilt in the cradle—*what'll I do*—then three, slow, rising iambs—*If you, are far, away* and then the shorter two iambs, *And I, am blue,* and then the lilt of the cradle again. And the sense of distance created by the assonance and rhyme of *are far*—the human imagination making such expressive complexity in the simplest forms.

The double iamb is such a rhythmic signature in English because the sequence of preposition-article-adjective-noun is so common. A poem by Theodore Roethke, for example, begins like this: "In a dark wood the eye begins to see." *The eye begins to see* functions like *when you are far away*, establishing the rising rhythm of iambs after the initial figure. And hearing it one could imagine how Berlin's trick of crossing, rhyming, and shortening might work:

> In a dark wood the eye begins to see.
> Or could, in a dark wood.

6 . So the pulsing and shaping made by rhythmic play is going on all the time in poems. You can learn how to write a sonnet or a pantoum, but the kind of expressive force that makes interesting poems come alive occurs more or less intuitively and out of sight, out of sight even of the writer who creates those effects. Poets mostly do not make a blueprint and then build an airplane. Mostly they listen and record what they are just hearing or have just heard.

BLANK VERSE

1. Instances of formal invention can be absorbed, consciously or unconsciously learned—not so much as templates but as instinctive promptings from the memory of the movement of the mind in reading (or hearing) poems. For large movements of form, like the organization of whole poems, it's interesting to think about blank verse because it's not organized around two-, three-, or four-line stanzas. It didn't come in stanzas because it doesn't rhyme . . . and in English it's mostly been rhyme, until the twentieth century, that proposed stanza shape. So poets writing free verse had to have gotten their idea of what constitutes a stanza from somewhere, and my hunch is they got it from blank verse.

2. Because it doesn't rhyme, and doesn't propose a specified stanza length, I think blank verse became the implicit model, or an implicit model, for how to write free verse. In two ways: first, blank verse does dazzling things with the relation between the sentence and the line, and second, its practice served as a model for what to do with the stanza, if it does not have a fixed pattern, in the free verse poem.

3. Quick history of blank verse: Read a little of Henry Howard, Earl of Surrey's translation of the second and fourth books of Virgil's *Aeneid*. It introduced (as far as I know) blank verse into English. Supposedly it was modeled on an Italian blank verse translation of the poem. The earl was Anne Boleyn's first cousin, which wasn't lucky. He accomplished this work some time before 1547, when Henry VIII had him beheaded. Then read a little of Christopher Marlowe's *Tamburlaine* and a little of any Shakespeare play; read, maybe, the great soliloquies, then a book of *Paradise Lost,* then a little of James Thomson's *The Seasons* (1726), maybe the beginning of the "Winter" book, then—to see the high method of John Milton humanized, something from William Cowper's "The Task," maybe Book IV, "The Winter Evening." Here he is describing in what had been the grand idiom of Milton's epic theological drama the arrival of the postman:

> Hark! 'tis the twanging horn! O'er yonder bridge
> That with its wearisome but needful length
> Bestrides the wintry flood, in which the moon
> Sees her unwrinkled face reflected bright,
> He comes, the herald of a noisy world,
> With spattered boots, strapped waist, and frozen locks,
> News from all nations, lumbering at his back.

(Sweet that he calls the length of the bridge "needful." Reminds me of Stephen Dedalus's remark. "A pier? Oh yes, a disappointed bridge.") From Cowper, proceed to any of the great blank verse poems of Wordsworth and Coleridge, which are probably for readers of English poetry the crucial models for how blank verse is supposed to move. And then the Browning of "Fra Lippo Lippi" or a little of *The Ring and the Book;* he was probably a model for Pound's and Eliot's blank-verse-like free verse. Then the Frost of "Directive" and "Out, Out—" and "Two Look at Two." And Stevens, "Sunday Morning" and "The Idea of Order at Key West." This is—for glimpsing, not

absorbing—a couple of nights' reading. And you could conclude this
survey with a more contemporary poem not in blank verse but moving like blank verse except with more disconcerting enjambments,
like John Ashbery's "Clepsydra," which begins like this:

> Hasn't the sky? Returned from moving the other
> Authority recently dropped, wrested as much of
> That severe sunshine as you need now on the way
> You go. The reason why it happened only since
> You woke up is letting the steam disappear
> From those clouds when the landscape all around
> Is hilly sites that will have to be reckoned
> Into the total for there to be more air: that is,
> More fitness read into the undeduced result, than land.

4 . To study how the stanza is used, a quick way would be to look
closely at a couple of great poems, Wordsworth's "Tintern Abbey"
and Coleridge's "Frost at Midnight." At the simplest level the blank
verse stanza works like a paragraph does in prose. But it can also
mime the rivery movement of the mind in quietly spectacular ways,
as in "Tintern Abbey," or the pulses of thought as it does in "Frost at
Midnight." For the stanza not used, Frost, "Directive."

5 . Here are a couple of passages from Wordsworth's "The Prelude," a bit of Browning (channeling Shakespeare in "Fra Lippo
Lippi"), some of a descriptive poem, "In a London Drawing Room,"
by George Eliot (blank verse in the age of the novel), and then Frost
and Stevens. The thing to attend to here is the relation between the
line and the sentence, what the expressive uses of enjambment are,
how and when the identity of line and sentence is used and to what
effect.

(Wordsworth)

Nor less, when spring had warmed the cultured Vale,
Moved we as plunderers where the mother-bird
Had in high places built her lodge; though mean
Our object and inglorious, yet the end
Was not ignoble. Oh! When I have hung
Above the raven's nest, by knots of grass
And half-inch fissures in the slippery rock
But ill-sustained, and almost (so it seemed)
Suspended by the blast that blew amain,
Shouldering the naked crag, oh, at that time
While on the perilous ridge I hung alone
With what strange utterance did the loud dry wind
Blow through my ear! The sky seemed not a sky
Of earth—and with what motion moved the clouds.

*

. . . The sands of Westmoreland, the creeks and bays
Of Cumbria's rocky limits, they can tell
How, when the sea threw off his evening shade,
And to the shepherd's hut on distant hills
Sent welcome notice of the rising moon.
How I have stood, to fancies such as these
A stranger, linking with the spectacle
No conscious memory of a kindred sight,
And bringing with me no peculiar sense
Of quietness or peace; yet have I stood,
E'en while my eye hath moved o'er many a league
Of shining water, gathering as it seemed
Through every hair-breadth in that field of light,
New pleasure like a bee among the flowers.

*

(Browning)

Lord, I'm not angry! Bid your hang-dogs go

Drink out this quarter-florin to the health
Of the munificent house that harbors me
(And many more beside, lad, more beside)
And all's come square again! I'd like his face—
His, elbowing on his comrade in the door
With the staff and lantern—for the slave that holds
John Baptist's head a-dangle by the hair
With one hand ("Look you now," as who should say)
And his weapon in the other, still unwiped!

     *

(Eliot)
The sky is cloudy, yellowed by the smoke.
For view there are the houses opposite
Cutting the sky with one long line of wall
Like solid fog: far as the eye can stretch
Monotony of surface and of form
Without a break to hang a guess upon.
No bird can make a shadow as it flies
For all is shadow, as in ways o'erhung
By thickest canvass, where the golden rays
Are clothed in hemp. No figure lingering
Pauses to feed the hunger of the eye
Or rest a little on the lap of life.

     *

(Frost)
A doe from round a spruce stood looking at them
Across the wall, as near the wall as they.
She saw them in their field, they her in hers.
The difficulty of seeing what stood still,
Like some upended boulder split in two,
Was in her clouded eyes: they saw no fear there.
She seemed to think that, two thus, they were safe.
Then, as if they were something that, though strange,

She could not trouble her mind with too long,
She sighed and passed unscared along the wall.

    *

(Stevens)
Complacencies of the peignoir, and late
Coffee and oranges in a sunny chair,
And the green freedom of a cockatoo
Upon a rug mingle to dissipate
The holy hush of ancient sacrifice.
She dreams a little, and she feels the dark
Encroachment of that old catastrophe,
As a calm darkens among water lights.
The pungent oranges and bright, green wings
Seem things in some procession of the dead,
Winding across wide water, without sound.
The day is like wide water without sound,
Stilled for the passing of her dreaming feet
Over the seas, to silent Palestine,
Dominion of the blood and sepulcher.

The last is a single section of "Sunday Morning," but it also has the feel and shape of an (almost) unrhymed sonnet. Notice that of the preceding, Wordsworth's lines are the maziest, the closest to Milton's immensely flexible syntax (which probably came from studying Latin since he was a little kid).

SONNET

The sonnet is the one durable, widely used form in English poetry in the last five hundred years. It came into English in the early sixteenth century through the translation of Petrarch. Its content was psychological and erotic, it brought Italianate extended metaphor into English, and it had philosophical roots in the Neoplatonic tradition of courtly love. It exploded in the sonnet sequences of the 1590s—Shakespeare's is the most famous—and was transformed in the early seventeenth century by Donne's use of it for religious poems and in midcentury by Milton's grand and masterly summation in poems on literary, personal, and political subjects.

(The Italian sonnet is Sicilian in origin. It is said to have been invented at the court of Frederick II, the Holy Roman Emperor and King of Sicily who had his court at Palermo and patronized poets writing in Sicilian, Provencal, Arabic, and Greek. Among them was Giacomo da Lentini, a notary at the court, who wrote in Sicilian and supposedly hit upon the sonnet some time around 1222–1225 by adding to a pair of quatrains a pair of triplet stanzas from a Sicilian folk song form he had heard. This established the fourteen lines and 4-4-

3-3 pattern of the form to which he gave the name of *sonetta*, or small song. Lentini wrote in Sicilian, adapting the idiom and subject matter of Provencal poetry, and eighteen sonnets by him survive in Tuscan transliterations. Guittone d'Arezzo (1235–1294) took the form into Tuscany—he produced three hundred sonnets—and passed it to Guido Cavalcanti (1250–1300) and Dante Aligheri (1265–1321), who passed it to Francesco Petrarch (1304–1374) and Michaelangelo Buonarroti (1475–1564).)

That form, for me, was roughly—state it; dance it. Or—state it; dance the undoing of it. Without Italian, especially without medieval Italian, I found that the best way to study the relation of octet to sestet was a read through Dante Gabriel Rossetti's *Early Italian Poets*, one of the sweetest of all books of Victorian poetry.

In English the sonnet evolved into two forms. One was an Italianate sonnet that retained the 4-4-3-3 rhyme scheme and with it its rhetorical structure—an eight-line development, a turn at the ninth line that initiates the six-line conclusion; the other came to be called the English sonnet and employed a 4-4-4-2 rhyme scheme, borrowing from the native tradition the strong finish of a concluding couplet rhyme. This was, of course, the form that Shakespeare made famous, and, though it still tended to introduce a turn at the ninth line, it allowed for other rhetorical strategies—twelve lines of development, for example, and the resolution or turn or summation in the couplet.

Peter Sacks has remarked that some of the appeal of the sonnet may have to be because it has the same proportions as the human face. Hans Holbein, painting in the heyday of the sonnet, observed that the proportions of the human face were upper half, brow, eyes, nose 8, and lower half, mouth, jaw, chin 6, proportions that mimic those of the sonnet. And, Sacks writes, the sonnet originates as a kind of staring into the eyes of the beloved. So it suggests one formal energy of the sonnet: it can be thought of as an intense gaze at a subject. Though that doesn't quite capture the rhetorical flourish of the form. It's a very showy form in the sixteenth century, when skill at rhetoric and argument was part of a classical education. Some sonnets seem to sit comfortably in their basic formal proposition, but the best of them bring intensity or playfulness of imagination to the way energy moves in the form.

The English sonnet fell into disuse toward the end of the seventeenth century and was revived by poets at the very end of the eighteenth. See Wordsworth's "Scorn Not the Sonnet." The form got memorable use in the poems of Charlotte Smith, Wordsworth, Shelley, Clare, and Keats; and the Victorians revived the sonnet sequence in George Meredith's "Modern Love," Elizabeth Browning's "Sonnets from the Portuguese," the two volumes of Frederick Tuckerman's "Sonnets," as well as Dante Gabriel Rossetti's "House of Life" and his reinvestigation of the origin of the form in his great translation, *Early Italian Poets.* As Milton capped the first cycle of the sonnet, Gerard Manley Hopkins capped the second with his dark, explosive poems in the form. The sonnets of Edwin Arlington Robinson, narrative and naturalistic, are another powerful late transformation.

With the exception of Frost and Yeats and the early poems of Ezra Pound, the modernist project—partly because it radically de-emphasized rhyme—avoided or covertly adapted the sonnet, though it continued to be used. The best-known later sequences are Louis Zukofsky's ingenious deployment of it in "A-7"; John Berryman's *Berryman's Sonnets;* the late sequences of Robert Lowell, *History* and *The Dolphin;* and Ted Berrigan's *The Sonnets.* As a formal proposition the form has appealed also to neoformalist and language poets—Berrigan's Ashbery-and-O'Hara-inflected cutup sequence is an initiating instance, and so are the poems of Bernadette Mayer.

QUICK TAKE ON
THE HISTORY OF THE SONNET

There are lots of sources. One of the best is Phyllis Levin's *The Penguin Book of the Sonnet*. Another is Stephen Burt's *The Art of the Sonnet*.

So the form comes into English in the 1530s, begins with Thomas Wyatt's translations of Petrarch, and experiments with the sonnet form in original poems in English. Wyatt died, age thirty-eight or thirty-nine, in 1542. Poems were first printed in *Tottel's Miscellany* in 1557. Henry Howard, fifteen years younger than Wyatt, was translating Petrarch at the same time or just after. Howard died five years after Wyatt, aged twenty-nine or thirty.

TRANSLATIONS OF PETRARCH

* Thomas Wyatt: "The Long Love That in My Thought Doth Harbor"; "My Galley Charged with Forgetfulness"
* Henry Howard: "Love That Doth Reign and Live Within My Thought"

EARLIEST ENGLISH SONNETS

* Thomas Wyatt: "Whoso List to Hunt" (c. 1542)
* Henry Howard: "The Soote Season" (c. 1547)

THE NEXT GENERATION (1560–1580)

* George Turberville: "The Lover to the Thames of London to Favor His Lady Passing Thereon" (experiment with sixteen-line sonnet, 1567)
* George Gascoigne: "For That He Looked Not Upon Her" (1573)

THE GREAT DECADES (1580–1610)

* William Shakespeare: Sonnets—printed 1609, earliest written in the 1580s, WS in his twenties
* Edmund Spenser: *Amoretti*—printed in 1595
* Philip Sidney: *Astrophil and Stella*—1582, printed in 1591
* Samuel Daniel: *Delia*—printed in 1592
* Michael Drayton: printed in 1619, written in the 1580s and '90s
* Sir Walter Raleigh: "Three Things There Be"—1610, the pure English tone, plain, moralizing
* Fulke Greville: *Caelica*—printed 1633, written mostly in 1580s and '90s

THE NEXT GENERATION (1610–1630)

* Ben Jonson: classical models, took no interest in the sonnet
* John Donne: same age as Jonson, no sonnets in his "Songs & Sonnets" presumably because he felt it had been used up for purposes of eroticism and wit; came to the form relatively late, in the 1620s and 1630s, for the "Holy Sonnets," which would completely reframe the subject matter of the form. Possible that he took hints from Shakespeare, Greville, and Raleigh, as they moved away from the rhetoric of Platonic love toward a more spoken diction and graver, darker matter.
* Lady Mary Wroth: *Pamphilia to Amphilanthus*—published 1621, first sequence of sonnets by an Englishwoman, many with an ababcdcdceefggf rhyme scheme that is variant version of the Italian sonnet.

THE SONNET IN THE MID-SEVENTEENTH CENTURY (1630–1680)

* George Herbert: "Redemption"—probably imitating Donne (1633); "Prayer I" (1633): but Herbert mainly worked in his reli-

gious poems from the strenuous new stanza forms invented by Donne in his erotic and secular poems
* John Milton: "On Shakespeare" (1630); "How Soon Hath Time" (1631); "I Did But Prompt the Age" (1645); "When I Consider How My Light Is Spent" (1652); "On the Late Massacre in Piedmont" (1658)

Then, in the Restoration and the early eighteenth century, with the ascendancy of the heroic couplet, the sonnet falls into disuse. It's not interesting to the best poets. It doesn't show up again until after the Pope-Swift generation. The poets of midcentury and after, in the so-called age of sensibility, were attracted to the ode, the elegy, the epitaph, the hymn. But some of them began to write sonnets.

* Thomas Gray: "Sonnet on the Death of Mr. Richard West" (1742; see Wordsworth's dismantling of the diction of this poem in the preface to the *Lyrical Ballads*)

THE SONNET REVIVAL IN THE ROMANTIC PERIOD (1780–1828)
* William Blake: "To the Evening Star" (1783; so eccentric from the point of view of its time as not to be a sonnet but fourteen lines of blank verse; notice the wildly unusual enjambments, but also the conventional turn at line 10)
* Charlotte Smith: "Written in the Churchyard at Middleton in Sussex" (1789); "Written Near a Port on a Dark Evening" (1797); "Written in October" (1797); "Nepenthe" (1797)
* William Wordsworth: "It Is a Beauteous Evening; London" (1802); "Composed Upon Westminster Bridge, September 3, 1802" (the signature poetics of immediacy in the dating, borrowed perhaps from Smith, marks the romantic turn in the

form); "On the Extinction of the Venetian Republic" (resurrects Milton's use of the form on a political theme); "Nuns Fret Not; The World Is Too Much With Us" (classical allusion and contemporary theme, Wordsworth soaked in Milton)—all printed in 1807; "Surprised by Joy" (1815); "Mutability" (1822); "Scorn Not the Sonnet" (1827; interesting take on the status of the form and the sense of its pastness)

* Samuel Coleridge: "Work Without Hope, Lines Composed 21st February 1825" (imitates W's dating; uses stanza breaks to emphasize unusual 6/8 turn; unconventional rhyme scheme)
* Percy Bysshe Shelley: "To Wordsworth" (1816); "Ozymandias" (1818); "England in 1819" (1819)
* John Keats: "On First Looking into Chapman's Homer" (1816); "On the Sea" (1817); "On Sitting Down to Read King Lear Again, When I Have Fears, To Homer" (1818); "On the Sonnet, Bright Star" (1819)

SONNET IN THE 1830s

* Edgar Allan Poe: "Sonnet to Science" (1829)
* Ralph Waldo Emerson: "The Rhodora" (1834)
* John Clare: "Gypsies" (1837; see also "Badger," which is written in three stanzas, the first two of which are fourteen lines of couplets, almost sonnets, and "Farewell," with its 6/4/4 pattern) and all the Northborough Sonnets, 1832–1837, for the radical use of it as a purely descriptive form

THE VICTORIAN SONNET (1840–1880)

* Alfred Lord Tennyson: "The Kraken" (1830, very Shelleyan, written when he was twenty-one); "Now Sleeps the Crimson Petal" (1847, disguised sonnet from *The Princess*)
* Elizabeth Browning: *Sonnets from the Portuguese* (1845–1846)

* Matthew Arnold: "Shakespeare" (1849); "Dover Beach" (1867, notice that the first stanza is a loose, Wordsworthian sonnet)
* Dante Rossetti: *The House of Life* (1847–80); *Early Italian Poets* (1860–70; Rossetti translated all the early Italian sonnets in two volumes; after Fitzgerald's *Rubaiyat* they are probably the best literary translations of the nineteenth century)
* Christina Rossetti: "In an Artist's Studio" (1856)
* George Meredith: "Modern Love" (1862; a remarkable turn for the form, a kind of novel in sonnets); "Lucifer in Starlight" (1883); "Winter Heavens" (1888)
* Henry Wadsworth Longfellow: "Mezzo Cammin, Written at Boppard on the Rhine, August 25, 1842"; "Chaucer" (1873); "Milton" (1873; literary subjects having become naturalized to the form)
* Frederick Tuckerman: *Sonnets* (1854–60; maybe the intensest psychologically, after Meredith, of the Victorian sonnets)

TINKERERS, ENGLISH AND AMERICAN (1840–1924)

* Henry Thoreau: "Haze," "Smoke," "Low-Anchored Cloud" (1843; descriptive poems that hover around the sonnet form)
* Walt Whitman: "I Saw in Louisiana a Live-Oak Growing" (1860; a thirteen-line free verse poem, perhaps the first free verse sonnet)
* Herman Melville: "The Maldive Shark" (1888; sixteen lines sonnetish)
* Thomas Hardy: "Hap" (1866); "Jezreel, On Its Seizure by the English Under Allenby, September 1918" (1918; four long-lined quatrains with the tone and feel of a Miltonic sonnet)
* Gerard Manley Hopkins: "God's Grandeur," "The Windhover," "Duns Scotus' Oxford," "Pied Beauty" (truncated sonnet for which Hopkins invented the term "curtal sonnet"; all these poems 1877); "Felix Randal" (1880, astonishing long-lined son-

net); "Spring and Fall" (1880, 15 fifteen lines, couplet rhyme, trochaic meter); "As Kingfishers Catch Fire" (1882), the 'Terrible Sonnets' (1885); "That Nature Is a Heraclitean Fire" (1888, an exploded sonnet?); "Thou Art Indeed Just, Lord" (1889).

VICTORIAN TO MODERN: SURVIVAL OF THE SONNET (1880–1930)

* Edwin Arlington Robinson: "George Crabbe," "Reuben Bright" (1897); "How Annandale Went Out" (1910); "New England," "The Sheaves" (1925)
* W. B. Yeats: "In the Seven Woods" (1903); "Leda and the Swan" (1923); "Meru" (1934, the political-apocalyptic sonnet, Milton to Shelley to Yeats)
* Robert Frost: "The Oven Bird," "Range-Finding" (1916); "Acquainted With the Night" (sonnet with a terza terza rima rhyme scheme, 1928); "Design" (1936); "Never Again Would Birds' Song Be the Same" (1942); "The Gift Outright" (1942, read at John F. Kennedy's inauguration in 1960)
* D. H. Lawrence: "Baby Running Barefoot" (1916), "When I Read Shakespeare" (1929); "Trees in the Garden" (fifteen lines, 1932); "Andraitx—Pomegranate Flowers" (1932)
* Edna St. Vincent Millay: "Euclid Alone Has Looked on Beauty Bare" (1920); "I, Being Born a Woman and Distressed" (1923); "I Dreamed I Moved Among the Elysian Fields" (1930)
* Robinson Jeffers: "Shane O'Neill's Cairn" (1931); "Love the Wild Swan" (1935); "The Eye" (1941); "Carmel Point" (1954); "Vulture, Birds and Fishes" (1963, late work, sonnet based)
* e e Cummings: "the Cambridge ladies who live in furnished rooms" (1923), "next to of Course god America i" (1926)

MODERNISTS AND THE SONNET (1913–1933)

* Gertrude Stein: "Susie Asado" (1913; if you look for a more de-
  cisive break in the tradition than Hopkins, this would be it, a
  cubist sonnet)
* Wallace Stevens: "The Snow Man" (1923; a fifteen-line poem.
  Stevens showed no interest in the sonnet after 1910)
* William Carlos Williams: Avoided the sonnet after 1911
* Ezra Pound: Avoided the sonnet after 1914, but published his
  translation of Cavalcanti's sonnets in 1934 and embedded parts
  of them in the *Cantos* as tracers of a neo-Platonism that inter-
  ested him
* H.D.: Avoided the sonnet
* Marianne Moore: Seems to have avoided the sonnet
* T. S. Eliot: Didn't work in the sonnet form, but see the first
  fourteen-line stanza of "The Dry Salvages" and the first stanza
  of the third section of "Little Gidding"
* Hart Crane: "To Emily Dickinson" (1933)

People kept experimenting with the form though it is hard to
name a decisive instance after Yeats's "Leda and the Swan" in 1923
and Frost's "Design" in 1936. The most ambitious instances are Robert Lowell's sonnet sequences of the early 1970s and John Berryman's sonnet sequence, which is not his best work. The New York
School poets were drawn to the form—see the work of Berrigan and
Mayer—and Seamus Heaney did important work in "The Glanmore
Sonnets" (1979), "Clearances" (1987), and elsewhere.

THE SONNET 1939–1989

* W. H. Auden: "Sonnets from China" (1939)
* John Berryman: *Berryman's Sonnets* (1967)
* Robert Lowell: *Notebooks 1967–68* (1969), *Notebook* (1970), *The
  Dolphin* (1973), *For Lizzie and Harriet* (1973), *History* (1972)
* Adrienne Rich: *21 Love Poems* (1976)

* Seamus Heaney: "Glanmore Sonnets" (1979), "Clearances" (1987)
* Ted Berrigan: *The Sonnets* (1967)
* Bernadette Mayer: *Sonnets* (1989)

THE SONNET AFTER 1990

* A range of work in the form can be found in *The Penguin Book of the Sonnet*, ed. Phyllis Levin, 2006.

READING THE SONNET

And now a quick run-through of this history. As a craftsperson, you'd want to notice and absorb the way the rhyme schemes and the turns are used, the relation of thematic development to the possibilities in this structure. For example, noticing what happens when a poem begins—"When in disgrace with fortune and men's eyes," "When I consider how my light is spent"—with a subordinate clause, what unwinding that implies. As opposed to the assault on his subject in the first line of Donne's "Batter my heart, three-personed God," with its subordinate clause following: "For you as yet but knock, breathe, shine, and seek to mend . . ."

1. *The beginning:* two versions of Petrarch

Wyatt:

> The long love that in my thought doth harbor, a
> And in my heart doth keep his residence, b
> Into my face presseth with bold pretense b
> And there encampeth, spreading his banner. a

She that me learns to love and suffer c
And wills that my trust and lust's negligence d
Be reined by reason, shame, and reverence d
With his hardiness takes displeasure. c

Wherewithal unto the heart's forest he fleeth, e
Leaving his enterprise with pain and cry, f
And there him hideth and not appeareth. e
What may I do, when my master feareth, e
But in the field with him to live and die? f
For good is the life ending faithfully f

Surrey:

Love, that doth reign and live within my thought, a
And built his nest within my captive breast, b
Clad in the arms wherein with me he fought, a
Oft in my face he doth his banner rest. b

But she that taught me love and suffer pain, c
My doubtful hope and eke my hot desire d
With shamefast look to shadow and refrain, c
Her smiling grace converteth straight to ire. d

And coward Love, then, to the heart apace e
Taketh his flight, where he doth lurk and plain, c
His purpose lost, and dare not show his face. e

For my lord's guilt thus faultless bide I pain, c
Yet from my lord shall not my foot remove: f
Sweet is the death that taketh end by love. f

Note: The basic feudal/military metaphor was standard already
in the Italian sonnet. The Renaissance was a sort of classicizing of
a thug culture (vide Dante). So the new "knights," formerly sol-

diers of ducal gangs, are lovers on whom the platonizing restraint of the Lady works a transformation. Both Wyatt and Surrey follow the quatrain-quatrain-tercet-tercet pattern of Petrarch but vary the rhyme scheme. And Surrey uses the English couplet finish.

2. *First English sonnets:*

Wyatt:

> Whoso list to hunt, I know where is an hind, a
> But as for me, alas, I may no more; b
> The vain travail hath wearied me so sore, b
> I am of them that furthest come behind. a
>
> Yet may I by no means my wearied mind a
> Draw from the deer, but as she fleeth afore b
> Fainting I follow; I leave off therefore, b
> Since in a net I seek to hold the wind. a
>
> Whoso list her hunt, I put him out of doubt, c
> As well as I, may spend his time in vain. d
> And graven with diamonds in letters plain, d
> There is written her fair neck round about, c
> *"Noli me tangere,* for Caesar's I am, e
> And wild for to hold, though I seem tame." e

Note: A Petrarchan sonnet. Hunting was another of the basic aristocratic-erotic metaphors. One poached the King's deer under penalty of death. The new thing—typical of Wyatt's more English song lyrics—is the absolute credibility of the speaking voice, compared to his Italian translations. And the writing: the sensational second quatrain with its enjambments followed by trochaic substitutions—"draw from," "fainting." Also interesting is the way that the sense is not completed at the end of the first tercet, but leaps across to the next. And the way the repetition of the first quatrain rhymes in the second stanza helps get the dream-exhaustion and obsession. The phrase *noli me tangere*—do not touch me—often appears in Renaissance portraits of young women. In Neoplatonist thought, the dance of desire—restraint—beauty was a trinity carried in the emblem of the three graces—the one near you, the one turned away, and the one coming back. But Wyatt is not typically a platonizing idealist, and this feels like something else. It was thought to have been written about Henry VIII's wife, Anne Boleyn.

Surrey:

The soote season, that bud and bloom forth brings, a
With green hath clad the hill and eke the vale; b
The nightingale with feathers new she sings; a
The turtle to her make hath told her tale. b

Summer is come, for every spray now springs; a
The hart hath hung his old head on the pale; b
The buck in brake his winter coat he flings, a
The fishes float with new repaired scale; b

The adder all her slough away she slings, a
The swift swallow pursueth the flies small; b
The busy bee her honey now she mings. a
Winter is worn, that was the flowers' bale. b

And thus I see among these pleasant things, a
Each care decays, and yet my sorrow springs. a

Note: Looked at in one way, this is the first English-style sonnet: quatrain-quatrain-quatrain-couplet. But the repetition of the singing "ing" rhyme and the basic list structure and the syntactic parallelism belong to an English style older than the couplet; they de-emphasize the quatrains. The reversal at the couplet is the one Shakespeare will use so often. It means that the poem needs a punch line. The pretty descriptive writing is like Chaucer's and anticipates Spenser's, but the reversal, the psychological moment, seems a rhetorical cuteness. Which is a problem with the couplet reversal generally.

Note: *Tottel's Miscellany, or Book of Songs and Sonnettes* was published in 1557 and went through seven editions by 1584.

3 . *The next generation:*

Gascoigne:

> You must not wonder, though you think it strange, a
> To see me hold my louring head so low, b
> And that mine eyes take no delight to range a
> About the gleams which on your face do grow. b
>
> The mouse which once hath broken out the trap c
> Is seldom 'ticed with the trustless bait, d
> But lies aloof for fear of more mishap, c
> And feedeth still in doubt of deep deceit. d
>
> The scorched fly, which once hath 'scaped the flame, e
> Will hardly come to play again with fire, f
> Whereby I learn that grievous is the game e
> Which follows fancy dazzled by desire: f
>
> So that I wink or else hold down my head g
> Because your blazing eyes my bale have bred. g

Note: This is the English sonnet. And the native tone: the speaking voice, the homely rather than grand metaphors, and this early Tudor love of alliteration. The alliteration is associated with desire, the Italianate or fancy style: "gleams which on your face do grow,"

"grievous is the game," "dazzled by desire," "blazing eyes my bale."
The poem doesn't end with a reversal but a restatement in line 13
and an intensification in line 14. Coming back and nailing down as
a form of closure. Sure rhythms, sure enjambments: Gascoigne is a
wonderful writer.

Turberville:

> Thou stately stream that with the swelling tide a
> 'Gainst London walls incessantly dost beat, b
> Thou Thames, I say, where barge and boat doth ride, a
> And snow-white swans do fish for needful meat: b
> When so my love, of force or pleasure, shall c
> Flit on thy flood as custom is to do, d
> Seek not with dread her courage to appall, c
> But calm the tide, and smoothly let it go, d
> As she may joy, arrived to siker shore, e
> To pass the pleasant stream she did before. e
>
> To welter up and surge in wrathful wise, f
> As did the flood when Helle drenched was, g
> Would but procure defame of thee to rise; f
> Wherefore let all such ruthless rigor pass. g
> So wish I that thou mayest with bending side a
> Have power for aye in wonted gulf to glide. a

Note: Experiment with a 4-6-6 structure, or a quatrain-quatrain-
couplet-quatrain-couplet structure, which never took. I think Swinburne was the first person to point out that, in the tenth line of this
supremely silly poem, the poet gives the impression that he is asking
the Thames to let his love live to pee another day. "And snow-white
swans do fish for needful meat" is also a famously ridiculous line.
The Italianate idealizing mode in an English setting.

4 . *The 1580s:*

Thomas Watson, *Passionate Century of Love* (1581):

Note: 18-line sonnets, all translations and imitations, later a work of his own in 14-line poems, *The Tears of Fancie.*

> I saw the object of my pining thought a
> Within a garden of sweet nature's placing: b
> Where is an arbor artificial wrought a
> By workman's wondrous skill the garden gracing b
>
> Did boast his glory, glory far renowned, c
> For on his shady boughs my mistress slept, d
> And with a garland of his branches crowned, c
> Her dainty forhead from the sun ykept. d
>
> Imperious love upon her eyelids tending, e
> Playing his wanton sports at every beck, f
> And into every finest limb descending, e
> From eyes to lips, from lips to ivory neck: f
>
> And every limb supplied and 't every part, g
> Had free access, but durst not touch her heart. g

Note: The preceding is the English sonnet in form but tries to get the equivalent of Italian rhymes with the "-ing" endings. This interweaving of one-syllable and two-syllable rhymes is much easier to do in an inflected language; it's very strong in Slavic languages and is the basis for the prosody of Pushkin and of the great Russian modernists like Pasternak, Mandelstam, and Akhmatova. Here, notice that the turn doesn't come until the second half of the last line.

5 . *1590–1610:*

Phillip Sidney, *Astrophil and Stella* (1590):

69.

Dear, why make you more of a dog than me?
If he do love, I burn. I burn for love.
If he wait well, I never thence would move.
If he be fair, yet but a dog can be;
Little he is, so little worth is he;
He barks, my songs thine own voice yet doth prove:
Bidden, perhaps, he fetched thee a glove,
But I unbid, fetch even my soul to thee.
Yet while I languish, him thy bosom clips,
That lap doth lap, nay lets, in spite of spite,
This sour-breath'd mute taste of those sugar'd lips.
Alas, if you grant only such delight
To witless things, then Love, I hope—since wit
Becomes a clog—will soon ease me of it.

On Her Toothache

The scourge of life, and death's extreme disgrace,
The smoke of hell, the monster called Pain;
Long shamed to be accurst in every place,
By them who of his rude resort complain;
Like crafty wretch, by time and travail taught,
His ugly evil in other's good to hide
Late harbours in her face, whom Nature wrought
As treasure house where her best gifts do bide.
And so by privilege of sacred seat—
A seat where beauty shines and virtue reigns—

He hopes for some small praise, since she has great;
Within her beams wrapping his cruel stains.
Ah, saucy Pain! Let not thy error last;
More loving eyes she draws, more hate thou hast.

Samuel Daniel, *Delia* (1591)
Barnabe Barnes, *Parthenophil and Partnenope* (1593):
Note: see also Thomas Lodge, *Phillis Honored with Pastoral Son-nets,* and Giles Fletcher, *Licia, or Poems of Love in Honor of the Admirable and Singular Virtues of His Lady.*

Jove for Europa's love took shape of Bull,
And for Calisto played Diana's part
And in a golden shower, he filled full
The lap of Danae with celestial art,
Would I were chang'd but to my mistress's gloves,
That those white, lovely fingers I might hide,
That I might kiss those hands, which mine heart loves
Or else the chain of pearls, her neck's vain pride,
Made proud with her neck's veins, that I might fold
About that lovely neck, and her paps tickle,
Or her to compass like a belt of gold,
Or that sweet wine, which down her thoat doth trickle,
To kiss her lips, and lie next at her heart,
Run through her veins, and pass by pleasure's part.

Note: Barnes's editor, Victor Doyno, observes that this poem "has brought a good deal of adverse criticism upon" the poet, and notes that the tradition of the lover's transformation has a long and honorable history. It is even picked up by Shakespeare's Romeo:

O that I were a glove upon that hand,
That I might touch that cheek.

(*II, ii, 24–25*)

The play may have been written in the summer of 1593, so it's possible that Shakespeare was reading Barnes. And Philip Marston refers to the poem in 1598:

Parthenophell, thy wish I will omit,
So beastly tis I may not utter it

And as late as 1875 the Victorian editor, the Reverend Alexander Grosart, is still fuming: "Certes 'pleasure's part' is unpardonable." Barnes was the fourth son of the Bishop of Nottingham. He was baptized in York in March 1570. So this is a youthful poem. He went to Oxford.

Henry Constable, *Diana* (1594):

To live in hell, and heaven to behold, a
To welcome life, and die a living death, b
To sweat with heat, and yet be freezing cold, a
To grasp at stars, and lie the earth beneath, b
To tread a maze that never shall have end, c
To burn in sighs, and starve in daily tears, d
To clime a hill and never to descend, c
Giants to kill, and quake at childish fears, d
To pine for food, and watch th' Hesperian tree, e
To thirst for drink, and nectar still to draw, f
To live accurst, whom men hold blest to be, e
And weep those wrongs, which never creature saw; f

If this be love, if love in these be founded, g
My heart is love, for these in it are grounded. g

Note: The courtly love clichés in the list-of-paradoxes style that
was popular in English verse a hundred years before.

William Percy, "Sonnets to the Fairest Celia" (1594):

Receive these writs, my sweet and dearest friend,
The lively pattern of my lifeless body;
Where thou shalt find in ebon picture penn'd,
How I was meek, but thou extremely bloody.

I'll walk forlorn along the willow shades,
Alone, complaining of a ruthless dame;
Where'er I pass, the rocks, the hills, the glades,
In piteous yells shall sound her cruel name.

There I will wail the lot which fortune sent me,
And make my moans unto the savage ears;
The remnant of the days which Nature lent me,
I'll spend them all, conceal'd, in ceaseless tears.

Since unkind fates permit me not t'enjoy her,
No more (burst eyes!) I mean for to annoy her.

Note: The mediocre poems have a way of making the basic sil-
liness of the emotional convention starker. The lesson is, I guess,
that young poets, writing in the going style, are very likely to be
saying things they don't really mean, rendering emotions they
don't really feel.

Barnfield, *Cynthia, With Certain Sonnets* (1595):

Note: see also Spenser, *Amoretti,* and Barnes, *Divine Centurie of Spiritual Sonnets.*

Note: My Victorian source says that Richard Barnfield "wrote several really fine pieces which, however, are not suitable for quotation." He offers this:

> It is reported of fair Thetis' son
> Achilles, famous for his chivalry,
> His noble mind and magnanimity,
> That when the Trojan wars were new begun,
> Whos'ever was deep-wounded with his spear,
> Could never be re-cured of his maim,
> Nor ever after be made whole again,
> Except with that spear's rust he holpen were:
> Even so it fareth with my fortune now,
> Who being wounded with his piercing eye,
> Must either thereby find a remedy,
> Or else to be relieved I know not how.
> Then if thou hast a mind still to annoy me,
> Kill me with kisses, if thou wilt destroy me.

Barnfield's *Cynthia, With Certain Sonnets* was published when he was twenty-two years old. The chief interest of his work is that he wrote the one explicitly homoerotic sonnet sequence to come out of the Tudor sonnet boom, a sequence of twenty poems in which the author is, in the pastoral convention, Daphnis and the object of his desire the beautiful Ganymede. Except for the gender of the beloved, the sonnets are quite conventional. They are more ardent than witty, and gracefully written; Barnfield uses the abba-cddc-effe-gg rhyme scheme throughout.

William Smith, *Chloris* (1596):

My love, I cannot thy rare beauties place
Under those forms which many writers use.
Some like to stones compare their mistress' face
Some in the name of flowers do love abuse;
Some make their love a goldsmith's shop to be,
Where orient pearls and precious stones abound:
In my conceit these far do disagree,
The perfect praise of beauty forth to sound.
O Cloris! thou dost imitate thyself!
Self-imitating passeth precious stones;
For all the Eastern-India golden pelf,
Thy red and white with purest fair attones.
Matchless for beauty Nature hath thee fram'd
Only unkind and cruel thou art nam'd.

R. L. Gentleman, *Diella* (1596):

When Love had first beseig'd my heart's strong wall,
Rampir'd and countermur'd with chastity,
And had with ordnance made his tops to fall,
Stooping their glory to his surquedry;
I called a parley and withal did crave
Some composition, or some friendly peace:
To this request he his consent soon gave,
As seeming glad such cruel wars should cease.
I, nought mistrusting, open'd all the gates,
Yea, lodg'd him in the palace of my heart;
When lo! in dead of night he seeks his mates,
And shows each traitor how to play his part;
With that they fir'd my heart, and thence 'gan fly,
Their names, sweet smiles, fair face, and piercing eye.

Shakespeare, *Sonnets* (1609):

The early Shakespeare of the sweet and noble style:

> Shall I compare thee to a summer's day?
> Thou art more lovely and more temperate:
> Rough winds do shake the darling buds of May,
> And summer's lease hath all too short a date;
> Sometimes too hot the eye of heaven shines,
> And often is his gold complexion dimmed;
> And every fair from fair sometimes declines,
> By chance or nature's changing course untrimmed;
> But thy eternal beauty shall not fade,
> Nor lose possesion of that fair thou ow'st;
> Nor shall death brag thou wander'st in his shade,
> When in eternal lines to time thou grow'st:
> So long as men can breathe or eyes can see,
> So long lives this, and this gives life to thee.

The idealist Shakespeare the Victorians loved:

> Let not to the marriage of true minds
> Admit impediments. Love is not love
> Which alters when it alteration finds,
> Or bends with the remover to remove:
> Oh, no! It is an ever-fixed mark
> That looks on tempests and is never shaken;
> It is the star to every wander'ng bark,
> Whose worth's unknown, although his height be taken.
> Love's not time's fool, though rosy lips and cheeks
> Within his bending sickle's compass come;
> Love alters not with his brief hours and weeks,
> But bears it out even to the edge of doom.

If this be error and upon me proved,
I never writ, nor no man ever loved.

The melancholy-confessional Shakespeare:

When, in disgrace with fortune and men's eyes,
I all alone beweep my outcast state,
And trouble deaf heaven with my bootless cries,
And look upon myself, and curse my fate,
Wishing me like to one more rich in hope,
Featured like him, like him with friends possessed,
Desiring this man's art and that man's scope,
With what I most enjoy contented least;
Yet in these thoughts myself almost despising,
Haply I think on thee—and then my state,
Like to the lark at break of day arising
From sullen earth, sings hymns at heaven's gate;
For thy sweet love remembered such wealth brings
That then I scorn to change my state with kings.

The poet of the grand style:

Not mine own fears, nor the prophetic soul
Of the whole world dreaming on things to come,
Can yet the lease of my true love control,
Supposes as forfeit to a confined doom.
The mortal moon hath her eclipse endured,
And the sad augurs mock their own presage;
Incertainties now crown themselves assured,
And peace proclaims olives of endless age.
Now with the drops of this most balmy time
My love looks fresh, and death to me subscribes,

Since, spite of him, I'll live in this poor rhyme,
While he insults o'er dull and speechless tribes:
And thou in this shall find thy monument,
When tyrants' crests and tombs of brass are spent.

The furious style:

Th' expense of spirit in a waste of shame
Is lust in action; and till action, lust
Is perjured, murderous, bloody, full of blame,
Savage, extreme, rude, cruel, not to trust,
Enjoy'd no sooner but despised straight:
Past reason hunted, and no sooner had,
Past reason hated, as a swallowed bait
On purpose laid to make the taker mad:
Mad in pursuit, and in possession so;
Had, having, and in quest to have extreme;
A bliss in proof, and proved, a very woe;
Before, a joy proposed, behind, a dream.
All this the world well knows; yet none knows well
To shun the heaven that leads men to this hell.

The sardonic, truth-telling Shakespeare:

When my love swears that she is made of truth,
I do believe her though I know she lies,
That she might think me some untutored youth,
Unlearned in the world's false subtleties.
Thus vainly thinking that she thinks me young,
Although she knows my days are past the best,
Simply I credit her false-speaking tongue:
On both sides thus is simple truth suppressed.
But wherefore says she not she is unjust?

And wherefore say not I that I am old?
Oh, love's best habit is in seeming trust,
And age in love loves not to have years told.
Therefore I lie with her and she with me,
And in our faults by lies we flattered be.

The poet who sends up the whole erotic-idealist style of the love sonnet:

My mistress' eyes are nothing like the sun;
Coral is far more red than her lips' red;
If snow be white, why then her breasts are dun;
If hair be wires, black wires grow on her head.
I have seen roses damask'd, red and white,
But no such roses see I in her cheeks;
And in some perfumes is there more delight
Than in the breath that from my mistress reeks.
I love to hear her speak, yet well I know
That music hath a far more pleasing sound;
I grant I never saw a goddess go;
My mistress, when she walks, walks on the ground.
And yet, by heaven, I think my love as rare
As any she belied with false compare.

The moralist of the last sonnets:

Poor soul, the center of my sinful earth,
Lord of these rebel powers that thee array,
Why dost thou pine within and suffer dearth,
Painting thy outward walls so falsely gay?
Why so large cost, having so short a lease,
Dost thou upon thy fading mansion spend?
Shall worms, inheritors of this excess,

Eat up thy charge? Is this the body's end?
Then, soul, live thou upon thy servant's loss,
And let that pine to aggravate thy store;
Buy terms divine in selling hours of dross,
Within be fed, without be rich no more.
So shalt thou feed on death, that leads on men,
And death once dead, there's no more dying then.

Joshua Sylvester, *Sonnets* (1610):

They say that shadows of deceased ghosts
Do haunt the houses and the graves about,
Of such whose lives-lamp went untimely out,
Delighting still in their forsaken hostes:
So, in a place where cruell love doth shoote
The fatal shaft that slew my loves delight,
I stalke and walke and wander day and night,
Even like a ghost with unperceived foote.
But those light ghosts are happier far than I,
For, at their pleasure, they can come and goe
Unto the place that hides their treasure, so,
And see the same with their fantastick eye.
Where I (alas) dare not approach the cruell
Proud Monument, that doth inclose my Jewell.

Sylvester died in 1618. His *Sonnets* were printed in 1641.

Michael Drayton, *Idea* (1619):

Three sorts of serpents do resemble thee;
That dangerous eye-killing cocatrice,
Th' enchanting syren, which doth so entice
The weeping crocodile; these vile pernicious three.

The basilisk his nature takes from thee,
Who for my life in secret wait doth lie,
And to my heart sends't poison from thine eye:
Thus do I feel the pain, the cause ye cannot see.
Fair-maid no more, but mer-maid be thy name,
Who with thy sweet alluring harmony
Hast played the thief, and stol'n my heart from me,
And, like a tyrant, mak'st my grief thy game.
The crocodile, who, when thou hast me slaine,
Lament'st my death with tears of thy disdaine.

His Remedie for Love

Since to obtain thee, nothing me will stead,
I have a med'cine that shall cure my Love,
The powder of her heart dry'd, when she is dead,
That gold nor honor ne'er had power to move;
Mix'd with her tears that ne'er her true-love crost,
Nor at fifteen ne'er long'd to be a bride;
Boil'd with her sighs, on giving up the ghost,
That for her late-deceased husband died;
Into the same then let a woman breathe,
That being chid, did never word reply,
With one thrice-married's prayers, that did bequeath
A legacy to stale virginity.
If this receit hath not the pow'r to win me,
Little I'll say, but think the Devil in me.

As Love and I, late harbour'd in one inn,
With proverbs thus each other entertain,
In love there is not lack, thus I begin;
Fair words make fools, replieth he again;
That spares to speak, doth spare to speed, quoth I.

As well, saith he, too forward as too slow.
Fortune assists the boldest, I reply.
A hasty man, quoth he, ne'er wanted woe.
Labour is light, where love, quoth I, doth pay;
Saith he, light burthen's heavy, if far borne;
Quoth I, the main lost, cast the by away:
You have spun a fair thread, he replies in scorn.
And having thus a while each other thwarted,
Fools as we met, so fools again we parted.

Note: These are dates of publication. Many of the sequences were written earlier, *Astrophil and Stella* in 1582, and were widely known in manuscript before they were published in books. Drayton died in 1631.

6 . *The sonnet in the seventeenth century:*

Fulke Greville:
Note: Greville died in 1628. His sonnets were published in 1633 in *Caelica;* it included many poems, which he called sonnets that were not sonnets in form. The turn from erotic to moral themes—which often appears at the end of sonnet sequences—is reflected in his poems from the beginning, and they thus mark the beginning of the shift from the Petrarchan themes of the sixteenth century to the religious themes of the seventeenth.

John Donne:

I

Thou hast made me, and shall Thy work decay?
Repair me now, for now mine end doth haste,
I run to death, and death meets me as fast,

And all my pleasures are like yesterday;
I dare not move my dim eyes any way,
Despair behind and death before doth cast
Such terror, and my feebled flesh doth waste
By sin in it, which it towards hell doth weight;
Only Thou art above, and when towards Thee
By Thy leave I can look, I rise again;
But our old subtle foe so tempteth me
That not one hour myself I can sustain;
Thy grace may wing me to prevent his art,
And thou like adamant draw mine iron heart.

V

I am a little world made cunningly
Of elements and an angelic sprite,
But black sin hath betrayed to endless night
My world's both parts, and oh, both parts must die.
You which beyond that heaven which was most high
Have found new spheres, and of new lands can write,
Pour new seas in mine eyes, that so I might
Drown my world with my weeping earnestly,
Or wash it if it must be drowned no more.
But oh it must be burnt! Alas, the fire
Of lust and envy have burnt it heretofore,
And made it fouler; let their flames retire,
And burn me, O Lord, with a fiery zeal
Of Thee and Thy house, which doth in eating heal.

VII

At the round earth's imagined corners, blow
Your trumpets, angels, and arise, arise
From death, your numberless infinities

Of souls, and to your scattered bodies go,
All whom the flood did, and fire shall o'erthrow,
Despair, law, chance, hath slain, and you whose eyes
Shall behold God and never taste death's woe.
But let them sleep, Lord, and me mourn a space,
For if above all these my sins abound,
'Tis late to ask abundance of thy grace
When we are there; here on this lowly ground,
Teach me how to repent; for that's as good
As if Thou hadst sealed my pardon with Thy blood.

IX

If poisonous minerals, and if that tree
Whose fruit threw death on else immortal us,
If lecherous goats, if serpents envious
Cannot be damned, alas, why should I be?
Why should intent or reason, born in me,
Make sins, else equal, in me more heinous?
And mercy being easy, and glorious
To God, in His stern wrath why threatens He?
But who am I that dare dispute with Thee?
O God, oh! of thine only worthy blood
And my tears, make a heavenly Lethean flood
And drown in it my sin's black memory.
That Thou remember them, some claim as debt,
I think it mercy, if Thou wilt forget.

X

Death be not proud, though some have called thee
Mighty and dreadful, for thou art not so;
For those whom thou think'st thou dost overthrow
Die not, poor death, nor yet canst thou kill me.

From rest and sleep, which but thy pictures be,
Much pleasure; then from thee much more must flow,
And soonest our best men with thee do go,
Rest of their bones, and soul's delivery.
Thou art slave to fate, chance, kings, and desperate men,
And dost with poison, war, and sickness dwell;
And poppy or charms can make us sleep as well,
And better than thy stroke; why swell'st thou then?
One short sleep past, we wake eternally,
And death shall be no more; death, thou shalt die.

XIV

Batter my heart, three-person'd God, for you
As yet but knock, breathe, shine, and seek to mend;
That I may rise and stand, o'erthrow me, and bend
Your force to break, blow, burn, and make me new.
I, like an usurp'd town to another due,
Labor to admit you, but oh, to no end;
Reason, your viceroy in me, me should defend,
But is captiv'd, and proves weak or untrue.
Yet dearly I love you, and would be lov'd fain,
But am betroth'd unto your enemy;
Divorce me, untie or break that knot again,
Take me to you, imprison me, for I,
Except you enthrall me, never shall be free,
Nor ever chaste, except you ravish me.

Note: Donne died in 1631. The "Holy Sonnets" published in his *Divine Poems* in 1633 are a radical reorientation of the sonnet form. This was the work in which the possibility of the sonnet got profoundly reordered. Notice the rhyme pattern: abba, abba, and then the turn and cdcd, ee. A slightly more Italianate version of the Shakespearean pattern. Hard to imagine these poems without the example of Shakespeare, or for that matter without the soliloquies in Elizabethan plays. "Batter my heart" seems especially to belong to the same invention of psychological interiority that critics have described as the achievement of the sonnets and the plays of Shakespeare. What Harold Bloom called—going too far, no doubt—"the invention of the human."

George Herbert:

Redemption

Having been tenant long to a rich lord,
   Not thriving, I resolvèd to be bold,
   And make a suit unto him, to afford
A new small-rented lease, and cancel th' old.
In heaven at his manor I him sought;
   They told me there that he was lately gone
   About some land, which he had dearly bought
Long since on earth, to take possession.
I straight returned, and knowing his great birth,
   Sought him accordingly in great resorts;
   In cities, theaters, gardens, parks, and courts;
At length I heard a ragged noise and mirth
   Of thieves and murderers; there I him espied,
   Who straight, *Your suit is granted,* said, and died.

Prayer (I)

Prayer the Churchs banquet, Angels age,
   Gods breath in man returning to his birth,
   The soul in paraphrase, heart in pilgrimage,
The Christian plummet sounding heav'n and earth;
Engine against th' Almightie, sinners towre,
   Reversed thunder, Christ-side-piercing spear,

The six-daies world transposing in an houre,
A kinde of tune, which all things heare and fear;
Softness, and peace, and joy, and love, and blisse,
    Exalted Manna, gladnesse of the best,
    Heaven in ordinarie, man well drest,
The milkie way, the bird of Paradise,
    Church-bels beyond the starres heard, the souls
        bloud,
    The land of spices; something understood.

Note: Herbert seems to have moved away from the sonnet and was one of the crucial inventors, after Donne, of new forms.

7. *Milton:*

Note: Milton wrote twenty-three sonnets, five of them in Italian, for which he provided English translations. His first sonnet was probably written in 1628 when he was twenty years old, the last in 1655 when he was forty-seven. The serious work starts about 1642. Interest is in the sheer variety of subjects. In this, especially in the political poems, he seems to have used the form in an entirely new way.

Sonnet XI: To Mr. Henry Lawes on His Airs

Harry whose tuneful and well-measured song
First taught our English music how to span
Words with just note and accent, not to scan
With Midas' ears, committing short and long,
Thy worth and skill exempts thee from the throng,
With praise enough for Envy to look wan;
To after age thou shalt be writ the man
That with smooth air could humor best our tongue.
Thou honor'st verse, and verse must lend her wing

To honor thee, the priest of Phoebus' choir,
That tun'st their happy lines in hymn or story.
Dante shall give Fame leave to set thee higher
Than his Casella, whom he wooed to sing,
Met in the milder shades of Purgatory.

Henry Lawes composed the music for Milton's masque *Comus*. Midas preferred the music of Pan to the music of Apollo. Dante met Casella in Purgatorio II, 76–117. Casella sings one of Dante's own canzone so sweetly that the spirits around him pause to listen. The rhyme scheme is abba-cddc-efg-feg.

Sonnet XVIII: On the Late Massacres in Piedmont

Avenge O Lord thy slaughtered saints, whose bones
        Lie scattered on the Alpine mountains cold,
        Ev'n them who kept thy truth so pure of old
        When all our fathers worshipped stocks and stones,
Forget not: in thy book record their groans
        Who were thy sheep and in their ancient fold
        Slain by the bloody Piemontese that rolled
        Mother with infant down the rocks. Their moans
The vales redoubled to the hills, and they
        To Heav'n. Their martyred blood and ashes sow
        O'er all th' Italian fields where still doth sway
The triple tyrant; that from these may grow
        A hundred-fold, who having learnt thy way
        Early may fly the Babylonian woe.

As far as I know, this is the first sonnet on a political theme. It must have felt like an unexpected departure for the form. Generations thought of Milton, the poet and Puritan thinker, as embodying a kind of nobility that gave authority to his work, and this formal extension of the private psychology of the sonnet to the public realm must have been a part of that feeling. It shows up in the sonnets of Wordsworth and Shelley and Hart Crane and Robert Lowell.

Sonnet XIX

When I consider how my light is spent,
> Ere half my days, in this dark world and wide,
> And that one talent which is death to hide,
> Lodged with me useless, though my souls more bent

To serve therewith my Maker, and present
> My true account, lest He returning chide,
> "Doth God exact day-labor, light denied,"
> I fondly ask; But patience to prevent

That murmur, soon replies, "God doth not need
> Either man's work, or his own gifts; who best
> Bear his mild yoke, they serve him best, his state
> Is kingly. Thousands at his bidding speed
> And post o'er land and ocean without rest:
> They also serve who only stand and wait.

Sonnet XXIII

Methought I saw my late espouséd saint
> Brought to me like Alcestis from the grave,
> Whom Jove's great son to her glad husband gave,
> Rescued from death by force, though pale and faint.

Mine, as whom washed from spot of child-bed taint,
> Purification in the Old Law did save,
> And such as yet once more I trust to have
> Full sight of her in Heaven without restraint,

Came vested all in white, pure as her mind:
> Her face was veiled, yet to my fancied sight,
> Love, sweetness, goodness in her person shined

So clear as in no face with more delight.
> But O as to embrace me she inclined
> I waked, she fled, and day brought back my night.

These sonnets belong to the powerful strain of interior mono-logue begun in the lover's psychology in the Italian sonnet and deep-ened and intensified in the work of Shakespeare and Donne. Hard to account for their quiet radiance. Milton's second wife, Katherine Woodcock, died in February 1658, after giving birth to a son three months before.

Alcestis offered herself as a victim to Death in place of her hus-band and was brought back from the other world by Hercules.

Leviticus, 12. After a certain period following childbirth, women were expected to bring offerings to the temple and the priest to make atonement on her behalf.

These poems seem to mark the end of the use of the sonnet form by English poets for about a hundred years. Excepting, perhaps, one curiosity, a poem published by Philip Ayres (1638–1712) in *Lyric Poems in Imitation of the Italians* in 1687.

On a Fair Beggar

Barefoot and ragged, with neglected Hair,
She whom the heavens at once made poor and fair,
With humble voice and moving words did stay,
To beg an Alms of all who passed that way.

But thousands viewing her became her Prize,
Willingly yielding to her conquering eyes,
And caught by her bright Hairs, whilst careless she
Makes them pay homage to her Poverty.

So mean a boon, said I, what can extort
From that fair mouth, where wanton Love to sport

> Amidst the Pearls and Rubies we behold?
> Nature on thee has all her Treasures spread,
> Do but incline thy rich and precious Head,
> And those fair locks shall pour down showers of Gold

A different form: five couplets and an abab quatrain. Ayres was a contemporary of John Dryden. He published *Lyric Poems in Imitation of the Italians* in 1687. This may be the nearest thing to a Caravaggio in English poetry.

8 . *The revival in the late eighteenth century:*

Thomas Gray (1742, published 1775):

Sonnet on the Death of Mr. Richard West

> In vain to me the smiling mornings shine,
> And reddening Phoebus lifts his golden fire;
> The birds in vain their amorous descant join,
> Or cheerful fields resume their green attire;
> These ears, alas! for other notes repine,
> A different object do these eyes require;
> My lonely anguish melts no heart but mine,
> And in my breast the imperfect joys expire.
> Yet morning smiles the busy race to cheer,
> And new-born pleasure brings to happier men;
> The fields to all their wonted tribute bear;
> To warm their little loves the birds complain:
> I fruitless morn to him that cannot hear,
> And weep the more, because I weep in vain.

This poem marks the revival of the sonnet by a poet-scholar in the mid-eighteenth century after its more or less complete disappearance from English literature in the middle of the seventeenth century: it returns in the form of a kind of antiquarian melancholy. It was written in 1742, published, after his death, in 1775. abab-cdcd-efe-fef.

Thomas Warton the Younger (1777):

Sonnet VIII: On King Arthur's Round Table at Winchester

Where Venta's Norman castle still uprears
Its raftered hall, that o'er the grassy foss,
And scattered flinty fragments clad in moss,
On yonder steep in naked state appears;
High hung remains, the pride of war-like years,
Old Arthur's Board: on the capacious round
Some British pen has sketched the names renowned,
In marks obscure, of his immortal peers.
Though joined by magic skill, with many a rhyme,
The Druid frame, unhonoured, falls a prey
To the slow vengeance of the wizard Time,
And fade the British characters away;
Yet Spenser's page, that chants in verse sublime
Those Chiefs, shall live unconscious of decay.

Note: The diagram of King Arthur's Round Table that hangs from the Great Hall in Winchester has been dated to the thirteenth century.

9 . *The romantic sonnet:*

William Blake (1783):

To the Evening Star

Thou fair-haired angel of the evening,
Now, while the sun rests on the mountain, light

Thy bright torch of love; thy radiant crown
Put on, and smile upon our evening bed!
Smile on our loves, and while thou drawest the
Blue curtains of the sky, scatter thy silver dew
On every flower that shuts its sweet eyes
In timely sleep. Let thy west wind sleep on
The lake, speak silence with thy glimmering eyes,
And wash the dusk with silver. Soon, full soon,
Dost thou withdraw; then the wolf rages wide,
And the lion glares through the dun forest:
The fleeces of our flocks are covered with
Thy sacred dew: protect them with thine influence.

Blake (1757–1827) apparently wrote this somewhat astonishing poem between the ages of twelve and twenty. It was published in *Poetical Sketches* when he was twenty-six. Three things surprise me about it: it is, as far as I know, the first unrhymed sonnet in the English language (not therefore—some would argue—a sonnet); it has, six years after Thomas Warton's sonnet, for the most part thrown off the hackneyed diction of eighteenth-century poetry; and the line endings in line 5—"drawest the" and line 13—"covered with"—are unlike anything in English until the advent of twentieth-century free verse.

Charlotte Smith, "Written in the Churchyard at Middleton" (1789):

Pressed by the moon, mute arbitress of tides,
While the loud equinox its power combines,
The sea no more its swelling surge confines,
But o'er the shrinking land sublimely rides.
The wild blast, rising from the western cave,
Drives the huge billows from their heaving bed,
Tears from their grassy tombs the village dead,
And breaks the silent sabbath of the grave!

With shells and sea-weed mingled, on the shore
Lo! their bones whiten in the frequent wave;
But vain to them the winds and waters rave;
They hear the warring elements no more:
While I am doomed—by life's long storm oppressed,
To gaze with envy of their gloomy rest.

Charlotte Smith, "Written Near a Port on a Dark Evening" (1797):

Huge vapors brood above the clifted shire,
Night on the Ocean settles, dark and mute,
Save where is heard the repercussive roar
Of drowsy billows, on the rugged foot
Of rocks remote; or still more distant tone
Of seamen in the anchored bark that tell
The watch relieved; or one deep voice alone
Singing the hour and bidding "Strike the bell."
All is black shadow, but the lucid line
Marked by the light surf on the level sand,
Or where afar the ship-lights faintly shine
Like wandering fairy fires, that oft on land
Mislead the Pilgrim—Such the dubious ray
That wavering reason lends, in life's long darkling way.

Charlotte Smith, "Written in October (1797):

The blasts of Autumn as they scatter round
The faded foliage of another year,
And muttering many a sad and solemn sound,
Drive the pale fragments o'er the stubble sere,
Are well attuned to my dejected mood;
(Ah! better far than airs that breathe of Spring!)
While the high rooks, that hoarsely clamoring

Seek in black phalanx the half leafless-wood,
I rather hear than that enraptured lay
Harmonious, of Love and Pleasure born,
Which from the golden furze, or flowering thorn
Awakes the Shepherd in the ides of May;
Nature delights *me* most when most she mourns,
For never more in me the Spring of Hope returns!

Smith (1749–1806) married a West Indies merchant, who fled England to avoid imprisonment for debt and left her with twelve children to raise, which she set about doing by earning a living as a writer. Her first book of poems, *Elegiac Sonnets,* was published in 1774. The sonnets are striking in several ways: the freshness and accuracy of description—she might have invented the descriptive sonnet; the relative freedom from poeticisms—a few years ahead of Wordsworth's and Coleridge's efforts to reform the diction of poetry; and their intense melancholy.

Wordsworth:

It Is a Beauteous Evening, Calm and Free

It is a beauteous evening, calm and free,
The holy time is quiet as a Nun
Breathless with adoration; the broad sun
Is sinking down in its tranquility;
The gentleness of heaven broods o'er the Sea;
Listen! the mighty Being is awake,
And doth with his eternal motion make
A sound like thunder—everlastingly.
Dear child! dear Girl! that walkest with me here,
If thou appear untouched by solemn thought,
Thy nature is not therefore less divine:

Thou liest in Abraham's bosom all the year;
And worshipp'st at the Temple's inner shrine,
God being with thee when we know it not.

Composed on Westminster Bridge, September 3, 1802

Earth has not anything to show more fair:
Dull would he be of soul who could pass by
A sight so touching in its majesty:
This City now doth, like a garment, wear
The beauty of the morning; silent, bare,
Ships, towers, domes, theatres, and temples lie
Open unto the fields, and to the sky;
All bright and glittering in the smokeless air.
Never did sun more beautifully steep
In his first splendour, valley, rock, or hill;
Ne'er saw I, never felt, a calm so deep!
The river glideth at his own sweet will:
Dear God! the very houses seem asleep;
And all that mighty heart is lying still!

London, 1802

Milton! thou shouldst be living at this hour:
England hath need of thee: she is a fen
Of stagnant waters: altar, sword, and pen,
Fireside, the heroic wealth of hall and bower,
Have forfeited their ancient English dower
Of inward happiness. We are selfish men;
Oh! raise us up, return to us again;
And give us manners, virtue, freedom, power.
Thy soul was like a Star, and dwelt apart:
Thou hadst a voice whose sound was like the sea:
Pure as the naked heavens, majestic, free,

So didst thou travel on life's common way,
In cheerful godliness; and yet thy heart
The lowliest duties on herself did lay.

The World Is Too Much With Us

The world is too much with us; late and soon,
Getting and spending, we lay waste our powers;
Little we see in Nature that is ours;
We have given our hearts away, a sordid boon!
This Sea that bares her bosom to the moon;
The winds that will be howling at all hours,
And are up-gathered now like sleeping flowers,
For this, for everything, we are out of tune;
It moves us not.—Great God! I'd rather be
A pagan suckled in a creed outworn;
So might I, standing on this pleasant lea,
Have glimpses that would make me less forlorn;
Have sight of Proteus rising from the sea;
Or hear old Triton blow his wreathèd horn.

Percy Bysshe Shelley:

Ozymandias

I met a traveller from an antique land,
Who said—"Two vast and trunkless legs of stone
Stand in the desert. . . . Near them, on the sand,
Half sunk a shattered visage lies, whose frown,
And wrinkled lip, and sneer of cold command,
Tell that its sculptor well those passions read
Which yet survive, stamped on these lifeless things,
The hand that mocked them, and the heart that fed;
And on the pedestal, these words appear:

My name is Ozymandias, King of Kings;
Look on my Works, ye Mighty, and despair!
Nothing beside remains. Round the decay
Of that colossal Wreck, boundless and bare
The lone and level sands stretch far away."

To Wordsworth

Poet of Nature, thou hast wept to know
That things depart which never may return:
Childhood and youth, friendship and love's first glow,
Have fled like sweet dreams, leaving thee to mourn.
These common woes I feel. One loss is mine
Which thou too feel'st, yet I alone deplore.
Thou wert as a lone star, whose light did shine
On some frail bark in winter's midnight roar:
Thou hast like to a rock-built refuge stood
Above the blind and battling multitude:
In honoured poverty thy voice did weave
Songs consecrate to truth and liberty,—
Deserting these, thou leavest me to grieve,
Thus having been, that thou shouldst cease to be.

England in 1819

An old, mad, blind, despised, and dying King;
Princes, the dregs of their dull race, who flow
Through public scorn,—mud from a muddy spring;
Rulers who neither see nor feel nor know,
But leechlike to their fainting country cling
Till they drop, blind in blood, without a blow.
A people starved and stabbed in th' untilled field;
An army, whom liberticide and prey
Makes as a two-edged sword to all who wield;

Golden and sanguine laws which tempt and slay;
Religion Christless, Godless—a book sealed;
A senate, Time's worst statute, unrepealed—
Are graves from which a glorious Phantom may
Burst, to illumine our tempestuous day.

Keats:

On First Looking into Chapman's Homer

Much have I travelled in the realms of gold,
And many goodly states and kingdoms seen;
Round many western islands have I been
Which bards in fealty to Apollo hold.
Oft of one wide expanse had I been told
That deep-browed Homer ruled as his demesne;
Yet did I never breathe its pure serene
Till I heard Chapman speak out loud and bold:
Then felt I like some watcher of the skies
When a new planet swims into his ken;
Or like stout Cortez, when with eagle eyes
He stared at the Pacific—and all his men
Looked at each other with a wild surmise—
Silent, upon a peak in Darien.

On the Elgin Marbles

My spirit is too weak; mortality
Weighs heavily on me like unwilling sleep,
And each imagined pinnacle and steep
Of Godlike hardship tells me I must die
Like a sick eagle looking at the sky.
Yet 'tis a gentle luxury to weep,
That I have not the cloudy winds to keep

Fresh for the opening of the morning's eye.
Such dim-conceived glories of the brain
Bring round the heart an indescribable feud;
So do these wonders a most dizzy pain,
That mingles Grecian grandeur with the rude
Wastings of old Time—with a billowy main
A sun, a shadow of a magnitude.

Bright Star

Bright Star! would I were steadfast as thou art—
Not in lone splendor hung aloft the night,
And watching, with eternal lids apart,
Like Nature's patient, sleepless Eremite,
The moving waters at their priest-like task
Of pure ablution round earth's human shores,
Or gazing on the new soft fallen mask
Of snow upon the mountains and the moors—
No—yet still steadfast, still unchangeable,
Pillowed upon my fair love's ripening breast
To feel for ever its soft fall and swell,
Awake forever in a sweet unrest,
Still, still to hear her tender-taken breath,
And so live ever—or else swoon to death.

10 . *The Victorian sonnet:*

Tuckerman:

from Sonnets, Third Series: IV

Thin little leaves of wood fern, ribbed and toothed,
Long curved sail needles of the green pitch pine,

With common sandgrass, skirt the horizon line,
And over these the incorruptible blue!
Here let me gently lie and softly view
All world asperities, lightly touched and smoothed
As by his gracious hand, the great Bestower.
What though the year be late? some colors run
Yet through the dry, some links of melody.
Still let me be, by such, assuaged and soothed
And happier made, as when, our schoolday done,
We hunted on from flower to frosty flower,
Tattered and dim, the last red butterfly,
Or the old grasshopper molasses-mouthed.

Tuckerman's fine detail, and a really odd rhyme scheme. I assume
he meant "toothed" and "smoothed" and "soothed" to rhyme with
"blue" and "view" and for them to sort of rhyme with "-mouthed."
And "melody" with "butterfly" and "Bestower" with "flower." Tuckerman said that he worshipped Tennyson's ear. You can see why.

Elizabeth Barrett Browning:

from Sonnets from the Portuguese

XXIII

Is it indeed so? If I lay here dead,
Wouldst thou miss any life in losing mine?
And would the sun for thee more coldly shine
Because of grave-damps falling round my head?
I marvelled, my Belovèd, when I read
Thy thought so in the letter. I am thine—
But . . . so much to thee? Can I pour thy wine
While my hands tremble? Then my soul, instead

Of dreams of death, resumes life's lower range.
Then, love me, Love! look on me—breathe on me!
As brighter ladies do not count it strange,
For love, to give up acres and degree,
I yield the grave for thy sake, and exchange
My near sweet view of heaven, for earth with thee!

XXIX

I think of thee!—my thoughts do twine and bud
About thee, as wild vines, about a tree,
Put out broad leaves, and soon there's nought to see
Except the straggling green which hides the wood.
Yet, O my palm-tree, be it understood
I will not have my thoughts instead of thee
Who art dearer, better! Rather, instantly
Renew thy presence; as a strong tree should,
Rustle thy boughs and set thy trunk all bare,
And let these bands of greenery which insphere thee,
Drop heavily down,—burst, shattered everywhere!
Because, in this deep joy to see and hear thee
And breathe within thy shadow a new air,
I do not think of thee—I am too near thee.

The rhyme scheme in the first: abba, abba, cdcdcd. In the second: abba, abba, cbcbcb. To get the "thee, thee, thee!" effect of the love poem. And, though the rhymes make for the 8-6 rhythm, the turn in each of these poems comes earlier than the ninth line, which mutes the feeling of rhetorical display so common in the Elizabethan sonnet.

Meredith:

Modern Love XXX

What are we first? First, animals; and next
Intelligences at a leap; on whom
Pale lies the distant shadow of the tomb,
And all that draweth on the tomb for text.
Into which state comes Love, the crowning sun:
Beneath whose light the shadow loses form.
We are the lords of life, and life is warm.
Intelligence and instinct now are one.
But nature says: "My children most they seem
When they least know me: therefore I decree
That they shall suffer." Swift doth young Love flee,
And we stand wakened, shivering from our dream.
Then if we study Nature we are wise.
Thus do the few who live but with the day:
The scientific animals are they—
Lady, this is my sonnet to your eyes.

Sixteen lines!

11. *Modernism:*

Walt Whitman:

I Saw in Louisiana a Live-Oak Growing

I saw in Louisiana a live-oak growing,
All alone stood it and the moss hung down from the
    branches,
Without any companion it grew there uttering joyous leaves
    of dark green,

And its look, rude, unbending, lusty, made me think of
     myself,
But I wonder'd how it could utter joyous leaves standing
     alone there without its friend near, for I knew I could not,
And I broke off a twig with a certain number of leaves upon
     it, and twined around it a little moss,
And brought it away, and I have placed it in sight in my room,
It is not needed to remind me as of my own dear friends,
(For I believe lately I think of little else than of them,)
Yet it remains to me a curious token, it makes me think of
     manly love;
For all that, and though the live-oak glistens there in
     Louisiana solitary in a wide flat space,
Uttering joyous leaves all its life without a friend a lover near,
I know very well I could not.

A thirteen-line poem, with a turn at the tenth line. Must be Whitman's first experiment with a sonnetish version of the free verse poem he was inventing.

Gerard Manley Hopkins:

God's Grandeur

The world is charged with the grandeur of God.
     It will flame out, like shining from shook foil;
     It gathers to a greatness, like the ooze of oil
Crushed. Why do men then now not reck his rod?
Generations have trod, have trod, have trod;
     And all is seared with trade; bleared, smeared with toil;
     And wears man's smudge and shares man's smell: the soil
Is bare now, nor can foot feel, being shod.

And for all this, nature is never spent;
   There lives the dearest freshness deep down things;
And though the last lights off the black West went
   Oh, morning, at the brown brink eastward, springs—
Because the Holy Ghost over the bent
   World broods with warm breast and with ah! bright wings.

Pied Beauty

Glory be to God for dappled things—
   For skies of couple-colour as a brinded cow;
     For rose-moles all in stipple upon trout that swim;
Fresh-firecoal chestnut-falls; finches' wings;
   Landscape plotted and pieced—fold, fallow, and plough;
     And áll trádes, their gear and tackle and trim.

All things counter, original, spare, strange;
   Whatever is fickle, freckled (who knows how?)
     With swift, slow; sweet, sour; adazzle, dim;
He fathers-forth whose beauty is past change:
          Praise him.

Felix Randal

Felix Randal the farrier, O is he dead then? my duty all ended,
Who have watched his mould of man, big-boned and hardy-
   handsome
Pining, pining, till time when reason rambled in it, and some
Fatal four disorders, fleshed there, all contended?

Sickness broke him. Impatient, he cursed at first, but mended
Being anointed and all; though a heavenlier heart began some
Months earlier, since I had our sweet reprieve and ransom
Tendered to him. Ah well, God rest him all road ever he offended!

This seeing the sick endears them to us, us too it endears.
My tongue had taught thee comfort, touch had quenched
    thy tears,
Thy tears that touched my heart, child, Felix, poor Felix Randal;

How far from then forethought of, all thy more boisterous years,
When thou at the random grim forge, powerful amidst peers,
Didst fettle for the great grey drayhorse his bright and
    battering sandal!

I think the meter of this poem is intended to be the classical elegiac meter—Felix RANdal the FARrier O is he DEAD then my DUty
all ENDED.

Carrion Comfort

Not, I'll not, carrion comfort, Despair, not feast on thee;
Not untwist—slack they may be—these last strands of man
In me ór, most weary, cry I can no more. I can;
Can something, hope, wish day come, not choose not to be.
But ah, but O thou terrible, why wouldst thou rude on me
Thy wring-world right foot rock? lay a lionlimb against me?
    scan
With darksome devouring eyes my bruisèd bones? and fan,
O in turns of tempest, me heaped there; me frantic to avoid
    thee and flee?

    Why? That my chaff might fly; my grain lie, sheer and clear.
Nay in all that toil, that coil, since (seems) I kissed the rod,
Hand rather, my heart lo! lapped strength, stole joy, would
    laugh, chéer.
Cheer whom though? the hero whose heaven-handling flung
    me, fóot tród

Me? or me that fought him? O which one? is it each one? That
   night, that year
Of now done darkness I wretch lay wrestling with (my God!)
   my God.

I wake and feel the fell of dark, not day

I wake and feel the fell of dark, not day.
What hours, O what black hours we have spent
This night! what sights you, heart, saw; ways you went!
And more must, in yet longer light's delay.
   With witness I speak this. But where I say
Hours I mean years, mean life. And my lament
Is cries countless, cries like dead letters sent
To dearest him that lives alas! away.

   I am gall, I am heartburn. God's most deep decree
Bitter would have me taste: my taste was me;
Bones built in me, flesh filled, blood brimmed the curse.
   Selfyeast of spirit a dull dough sours. I see
The lost are like this, and their scourge to be
As I am mine, their sweating selves; but worse.

No worst, there is none. Pitched past pitch of grief.

No worst, there is none. Pitched past pitch of grief,
More pangs will, schooled at forepangs, wilder wring.
Comforter, where, where is your comforting?
Mary, mother of us, where is your relief?
My cries heave, herds-long; huddle in a main, a chief
Woe, wórld-sorrow; on an áge-old anvil wince and sing—
Then lull, then leave off. Fury had shrieked 'No ling-
ering! Let me be fell: force I must be brief."'

O the mind, mind has mountains; cliffs of fall
Frightful, sheer, no-man-fathomed. Hold them cheap
May who ne'er hung there. Nor does long our small
Durance deal with that steep or deep. Here! creep,
Wretch, under a comfort serves in a whirlwind: all
Life death does end and each day dies with sleep.

Edward Arlington Robinson:

George Crabbe

Give him the darkest inch your shelf allows,
Hide him in lonely garrets, if you will,
But his hard, human pulse is throbbing still
With the sure strength that fearless truth endows.
In spite of all fine science disavows,
Of his plain excellence and stubborn skill
There yet remains what fashion cannot kill,
Though years have thinned the laurel from his brows.

Whether or not we read him, we can feel
From time to time the vigor of his name
Against us like a finger for the shame
And emptiness of what our souls reveal
In books that are as altars where we kneel
To consecrate the flicker, not the flame.

How Annandale Went Out

"They called it Annandale—and I was there
To flourish, to find words, and to attend:
Liar, physician, hypocrite, and friend,
I watched him, and the sight was not so fair
As one or two that I have seen elsewhere:

An apparatus not for me to mend—
A wreck, with hell between him and the end,
Remained of Annandale; and I was there.

"I knew the ruin as I knew the man;
So put the two together if you can,
Remembering the worst you know of me.
Now view yourself as I was, on the spot—
With a slight kind of engine. Do you see?
Like this . . . You wouldn't hang me? I thought not."

This is the sonnet as a narrative poem and as a dramatic mono-
logue. The "slight kind of engine" is presumably a hypodermic needle.

William Butler Yeats:

Leda and the Swan

A sudden blow: the great wings beating still
Above the staggering girl, her thighs caressed
By the dark webs, her nape caught in his bill,
He holds her helpless breast upon his breast.

How can those terrified vague fingers push
The feathered glory from her loosening thighs?
And how can body, laid in that white rush,
But feel the strange heart beating where it lies?

A shudder in the loins engenders there
The broken wall, the burning roof and tower
And Agamemnon dead.
                              Being so caught up,
So mastered by the brute blood of the air,
Did she put on his knowledge with his power
Before the indifferent beak could let her drop?

Robert Frost:

Acquainted with the Night

I have been one acquainted with the night.
I have walked out in rain—and back in rain.
I have outwalked the furthest city light.

I have looked down the saddest city lane.
I have passed by the watchman on his beat
And dropped my eyes, unwilling to explain.

I have stood still and stopped the sound of feet
When far away an interrupted cry
Came over houses from another street,

But not to call me back or say good-bye;
And further still at an unearthly height,
One luminary clock against the sky

Proclaimed the time was neither wrong nor right.
I have been one acquainted with the night.

A terza rima sonnet.

D. H. Lawrence:

Baby Running Barefoot

When the white feet of the baby beat across the grass
The little white feet nod like white flowers in a wind,
They poise and run like puffs of wind that pass
Over water where the weeds are thinned.

And the sight of their white playing in the grass
Is winsome as a robin's song, so fluttering;

Or like two butterflies that settle on a glass
Cup for a moment, soft little wing-beats uttering.

And I wish that the baby would tack across here to me
Like a wind-shadow running on a pond, so she could stand
With two little bare white feet upon my knee
And I could feel her feet in either hand

Cool as syringa buds in morning hours,
Or firm and silken as young peony flowers.

12 . *Modernist sonnet and after:*

Louis Zukofsky:

from A

Horses: who will do it? out of manes? Words
Will do it, out of manes, out of airs, but
They have no manes, so there are no airs, birds
Of words, from me to them no singing gut.
For they have no eyes, for their legs are wood,
For their stomachs are logs with print on them;
Blood red, red lamps hang from necks or where could
Be necks, two legs stand A, four together M.
"Street Closed" is what print says on their stomachs;
That cuts out everybody but the diggers;
You're cut out and she's cut out, and the jiggers
Are cut out. No! we can't have such nor bucks
As won't, tho they're not here, pass thru a hoop
Stayed on a manhole—me? Am on a stoop.

Note: From "A-7," which consists of seven sonnets. Written in the
early '30s. The horses are sawhorses, probably, also the Zukofskian

horse, a recurrent symbol of "the perfection and opulence of living organisms." The manes are also manes, Roman ancestral spirits. Singing gut: his son was a violinist. A+M=am, as in being or perhaps the "I am who am" of Yahweh. Zukofsky on sonnets: "Williams said it was impossible to write sonnets. I don't know if anyone has been careful about it."

Robert Lowell:

from The Quaker Graveyard at Nantucket

> Whenever winds are moving and their breath a
> Heaves at the roped-in bulwarks of this pier, b
> The terns and sea-gulls tremble at your death a
> In these home waters. Sailor, can you hear b
> The Pequod's sea wings, beating landward, fall c
> Headlong and break on our Atlantic wall c
> Off 'Sconset, where the yawing S-boats splash d
> The bellbuoy, with ballooning spinnakers, e
> As the entangled, screeching mainsheet clears e
> The blocks: off Madeket, where lubbers lash d
> The heavy surf and throw their long lead squids f
> For blue-fish? Sea-gulls blink their heavy lids f
> Seaward. The wind's wings beat upon the stones, g
> Cousin, and scream for you, and the claws rush h
> At the sea's throat and wring it in the slush h
> Of this old Quaker graveyard where the bones g
> Cry out in the long night for the hurt beast i
> Bobbing by Ahab's whaleboats in the east. i

Note: Second section of the poem, eighteen lines—quatrain-couplet-quatrain-couplet-quatrain-couplet, enjambed at the end of each of the first two couplets to diminish any sense of stanza patterning. This is an example of the way the sonnet often informs the stanza shape and the work of binding and concentration in other kinds of poems.

After the Convention

Life, hope, they conquer death, generally, always;
and if the steamroller goes over the flower, the flower dies.
Some are more solid earth, they stood in lines,
blouse and helmet, a creamy de luxe sky-blue—
their music, savage, ephemeral.
After five nights of Chicago: police and mob,
I am so tired and had, cliches are wisdom,
the cliches of paranoia. On this shore,
the fall of the high tide waves is a straggling, joshing
march of soldiers . . . on the march for me.
How slender and graceful, the double line of trees,
how slender, graceful, irregular, and underweight,
the young in black folk-fire circles below the trees—
under their bodies, the green grass turns to hay.

Note: After the Democratic National Convention, Chicago 1968, where demonstrators, conducting a "festival of life" were dispersed by riot police, Lowell studied Milton. See his "After the Late Riots in Piedmont."

Ted Berrigan:

Sonnet #2

Dear Margie, hello. It is 5:15 a.m.
dear Berrigan. He died
Back to books. I read
It's 8:30 p.m. in New York and I've been running around all day

old come-all-ye's streel into the streets. yes, it is now.
How Much Longer Shall I Be Able To Inhabit The Divine
and the day is bright grey turning green
feminine marvelous and tough
watching the sun come up over the Navy Yard
to write scotch-tape body in a notebook
had 17 1/2 milligrams
Dear Margie, hello. It is 5:15 a.m.
fucked til 7 now she's late to work and I'm
18 so why are my hands shaking I should know better

Note: Berrigan's *Sonnets*, because of the cut-up method, is really a long poem and one needs to read the whole thing to see what he's up to, pouring relaxed daily notations through the sonnet form and then spraying lines in parts through the sequence in a sort of spatter technique that tries to get something of Jackson Pollock's method and something of the streets on Manhattan coming at you.

Bernadette Mayer:

Birthday Sonnet for Grace

I've always loved (your) Grace in 14 lines, sometimes
I have to fit my love for Grace into either
An unwieldy utopia or a smaller space,
Just a poem, not a big project for changing the world
    which I believe
It was the color of your hair that inspired me to try
    to do in words
Since such perfection doesn't exist in isolation
Like the Hyacinth, Royal, or Persian blues
That go so well with you.

Now older than we were before we were forty
And working so much in an owned world for rent money
Where there seems little time for the ancient hilarity
We digressed with once on the hypnopompic verges of the
    sublime
Now more engrossed in hypnagogic literal mysteries of
our age and ages I propose
To reiterate how I love you any time

Amazing the range of work in the form. There really isn't, as far
as I know, a good study of whatever it is, formal or psychological,
that has made the form—in all the European languages—so persis-
tent and compelling. It might, as Peter Sacks has suggested, be the
single gaze and the proportions of the face. But that doesn't account
for the importance of the turn. 8/6: say it long, say it a little shorter.
In the Italian sonnet with the more musical and twining rhymes in
the sestet: say it, then sing it. Or say it and sing the opposite, or the
qualification. And the Shakespearean sonnet, which usually has the
strong turn, doesn't have the formal change in the rhyme scheme, so
if it has an 8/6 structure, it also has a 4/4/4/2 structure: say it, say it,
contradict or qualify it, nail it. Though the form was, from the beginning, involved with representing states of mind, with the psychology of the Platonic lover, it was in Shakespeare's sonnets, it seems,
that the English sonnet got its striking interiority that plays through
Shakespeare, into Donne and the Milton of "When I Consider How
My Light Is Spent" and Keats and the Hopkins of the "terrible sonnets." It may be something in the turn that echoes the process that
we experience as constituting our subjectivity, though that doesn't
account for its occasional power and special dignity in the political
poem. And there are the descriptive sonnets, beginning with Charlotte Smith and Wordsworth, that fix the gaze on what sensibility or
imagination make of the world. And there are the descriptive poems

of John Clare that have no turn at all. And his experiments with the tetrameter, or curtailed, sonnet: seven couplets. Worth looking at his "Evening Primrose'" for what it does with sexual rhyming:

> When once the sun sinks in the west
> And dew-drops pearl the evening's breast
> Almost as pale as moonbeams are
> Or its companionable star
> The evening primrose opes anew
> Its delicate blossoms to the dew
> And hermit-like shunning the light
> Wastes its fair bloom upon the night
> Who blindfold to the fond caresses
> Knows not the beauty he possesses
> Thus it blooms on when night is by
> When day looks out with open eye
> Bashed at the gaze it cannot shun
> It faints and withers and is gone

VICTORIAN MEDIEVALISM: SESTINA AND VILLANELLE

1. Form, in the sense of a completely predetermined poetic pattern, one that tells you how long the poem will be, in lines of how many syllables, with what kind of rhyme scheme: the news is that the sonnet is the only one widely used in English.

2. There are a few others borrowed from medieval French and Provencal poetry by the French Pleiaide poets and used later by the romantics. They came into English in late Victorian times. They usually involve mesmeric repetition and suited the purposes of the English symbolist and symbolist-influenced poets; that is, for a poetry in which the music was tuned up in a way that turned down the sense and had the expressive effect either of obsessiveness or formal hauntedness. They include the ballade, rondeau, sestina, triolet, and villanelle. The two that came into some use among modernist poets and contemporaries are the sestina—obsessive repetition—and the villanelle—formal hauntedness.

3 . *Sestina:* Thought to have been invented around 1190 by the Provencal poet Arnaut Daniel whom Ezra Pound has translated. The form consists of six stanzas of six lines each, with a concluding three-line envoy. The sestina is usually unrhymed, but the six end-words in the first stanza are repeated in the following stanzas in a special order. The pattern is as follows:

> Stanza 1: abcdef
> 2: faebdc
> 3: cfdabe
> 4: ecbfad
> 5: deacfb
> 6: bdfeca
> Envoi: eca or ace

(with the other end-words bdf recurring within the lines)

Here is Anthony Bonner's translation, literal, clunky, of an Arnaut Daniel sestina. If you know anyone who knows Provencal, you should get them to read it to you, if you really want the idea of what this is about, formally. (Actually, now, wonder of wonders, you can hear it sung in Provencal on Youtube, accompanied by a lute or cittern:

> *Lo ferm voler qu'el cor m'intra*
>
> The firm desire which enters
> my heart cannot be taken from me by beak or nail
> of that talebearer whose evil words cost him his soul,
> and since I dare not beat him with a branch or rod,
> I shall at least, in secret, free from any spying uncle,
> rejoice in love's joy, in an orchard or in a chamber.

But when I think of that chamber
which, to my misfortune, no man enters
and is guarded as if by brother or by uncle,
my entire body, even to my fingernail,
trembles like a child before a rod,
such fear I have of not being hers with all my soul.

Would that I were hers, if not in soul
at least in body, hidden within her chamber;
for it wounds my heart more than blows of a rod
that I, her serf, can never therein enter.
No, I shall be with her as flesh and nail
and heed no warnings of friend or uncle.

Even the sister of my uncle
I never loved like this with all my soul!
As near as is the finger to the nail,
if it please her, would I be to her chamber.
It can bend me to its will, that love which enters
my heart, better than a strong man with a sharp rod.

Since flowered the dry rod,
or from Adam came forth nephew and uncle,
there never was a love so true as that which enters
my heart, neither in body nor in soul,
And wherever she may be, outside or in her chamber,
I shall be no further than the length of my nail.

As if with tooth or nail
my heart grips her, or as the bark the rod;
for to me she is a tower, palace and chamber
of joy, and neither brother, parent or uncle
I love so much; and in paradise my soul
will find redoubled joy, if lovers therein enter.

Arnaut sends his song of nail and uncle
(by leave of her who has, of his rod, the soul)
to his Desirat whose fame all chambers enters.

S. E. Hickman, "Forbidden Desires: Arnuat Daniel, Mathematician
and Troubadour"

Daniel is mainly known to us now because Dante Aligheri greeted
him as *"il miglio fabbro"*—the better craftsman—in the Purgatorio,
the phrase T. S. Eliot used when he dedicated "The Wasteland" to
Ezra Pound, and in textbooks, which describe him as the inventor of
the sestina. Pound and Eliot knew about him because in their youth
there was a kind of romance of the troubadour poets in popular culture. There was a bestselling book about them and theater pieces,
and there was Browning's poem "Sordello." It was a way—toward the
end of the century—of popularizing the art-for-art's-sake movement.
The troubadours stood for art; they were gay and footloose fellows
to be admired in opposition to what was perceived as the grimness of
practical and Protestant industrial culture. Hence the young Pound's
capes and his pointed beard. His early poems like "Cino"—"Bah! I
have sung of women in three cities, / But is all the same, / And I will
sing of the sun"—were a sort of calling card for a modern idea (an
anachronistically modern idea) of the poet as troubadour. Asked what
he thought of the early Pound when he was an undergraduate, Eliot
said, "I thought it was all cloak-and-dagger stuff."

What this view of the origins of the sestina leaves out is craftsmanship, the thing that made Daniel *"il miglio fabbor."* He was said
to be a mathematician and a composer as well as a poet and in his
day he was known for the musically complex end-rhyme and internal rhyming of his verse, a complexity of sound that gave him the
reputation of being difficult to understand, which would have been
another plus for Pound, who tried in some early translations to convey Daniel's sound:

Aye, life's a high thing,
where joy's his maintenance,
Who cries 'tis a wry thing,
hath danced never my dance,
I can advance
no blame against fate's tithing,
For lot and chance
Have deemed the best thing my thing.

The poems are convoluted enough that a modern scholar, Charles Jernigan, has interpreted a Daniel sestina as "mocking those formulaic troubadour sentiments by grinding them against the most disconcerting sexual reality and, by twisting them into the newly invented sestina form, he was also making fun of the difficult and complex types of verse, including his own" (*Studies in Philology* 71 [1974]). This proposes that the sestina was invented as a kind of parody of its own method. At the least there is a tension in the idea of it, from the beginning, between what was supposed to be the fine carelessness of the troubadour life and the meticulous craftsmanship the form required.

A few Renaissance poets had a hand at the sestina—the notable example is a double sestina by Sir Philip Sidney—and then it disappeared in English until it was revived by the Victorians, notably Swinburne. His sestina called "Sestina" can be found online. It was probably an instigation for Pound's famous one—with a medieval subject—"Sestina: Altaforte," about which Hugh Kenner tells a funny story. Pound was still trying to write like Browning when he was taken by Wyndam Lewis to visit the sculptor Henri Gaudier-Brzeska in London in his studio. Pound read him "Sestina: Altaforte," a poem implicitly praising the war-hungry restlessness of the mercenary Provencal princeling Bertran de Born, who made his living selling his army of peasants to the highest bidder. It was the age of Teddy Roosevelt. Pound's poem begins with De Born addressing his jongleur:

Damn it all! All this our South stinks peace.
You whoreson dog, Papiols, come! Let's to music!

After Pound had left, Gaudier-Brzeska remarked to Lewis in his French-accented English, "A bold man, using the word 'piss' in a poem." It was after that that he did the great cubist bust of Pound. The not-funny part of the story is that Gaudier-Brzeska enlisted in the French army when the war broke out and died in the trenches. After the war Pound would have a very different feeling—for a while at least—about the manly, martial spirit "Sestina: Altaforte" seems to celebrate:

There died a myriad . . .

Charm, smiling at the good mouth,
Quick eyes gone under earth's lid . . .

"Sestina: Altaforte" initiates the twentieth-century sestina, and it is haunted for me by that story. The repetitions of the sestina get something of the character of De Born—the poem is a dramatic monologue as well as a sestina—and it is written with terrific vigor, but I find I can't not see it as an early instance of Pound's terrible judgment. So it doesn't, except for its ingenuity, tell us much about the future uses of the form.

Elizabeth Bishop's "Sestina" is another story. She uses her repeated words—*house, grandmother, child, stove, almanac, tears*—to get something about a profound stuckness in a child's sense of the repetitions of daily life. One has to bring one's sense of Bishop's life to the poem, I think, to get the deep, suppressed melancholy of it, and of the way it is about orphaning and art:

With crayons the child draws a rigid house
and a winding pathway. Then the child

> puts in a man with buttons like tears
> and shows it proudly to her grandmother.

Bishop's plain, almost flat language. She lost her father in infancy, her mother to madness by the time she was five.

It was probably John Ashbery in "The Painter" and "Farm Implements with Rutabagas in a Landscape" who launched the sestina as a postmodern idiom. In those poems the repetitions also seem to be about the repetitiveness of the world and seem also, like the account of Arnaut's invention of the sestina, to be mocking poetry, or at least to be a kind of absurdist play, philosophical comedy about what language can deliver to us.

There's been a recent explosion of sestinas, noted and analyzed by Stephen Burt in a 2012 essay, "Sestina! Or, The Fate of the Idea of Form." He reads the phenomenon as a product of the teaching of creative writing and as a symptom of "diminished hope for the art," a way "to emphasize technique, and to disavow at once tradition, organicism, and social or spiritual efficacy."

For a form to which books on form give so much attention, there are remarkably few memorable poems in the English and American canon. Burt's essay provides a long list of contemporary sestinas from which readers can find out what's been going on with the form and decide for themselves about his assessment of them.

4 . *Villanelle:* The villanelle came into French from an Italian folk song form. Five tercets rhyming aba, followed by a quatrain rhyming abaa; first line of the first tercet recurring as the last line of the second and fourth tercets, and third line of the initial tercet recurring as the last line of the third and fifth tercets, these two refrain-lines again repeated as last lines of the poem. It was usually written in English in iambic pentameter. If a(1) stands for the first line and a(2) for the second, the pattern looks like this:

a(1) b a(2)
a b a(1)
a b a(2)
a b a(1)
a b a(2)
quatrain: a b a(1) a(2)

See Austin Dobson, "Essays in Old French Forms," *Old World Idylls* (1883).

It is a form that has produced at least these four quite powerful poems:

E. A. Robinson: "House on the Hill"
Dylan Thomas: "Do Not Go Gentle into That Good Night"
Theodore Roethke: "The Waking"
Elizabeth Bishop: "One Art"

All four of them are metrical poems. There are experiments with free verse and the villanelle form. But there is some right marriage between the insistence of meter and the relentlessness of the rhyming that seems to give the form its power.

5. *A note on the pantoum:* The pantoum was originally a Malaysian song form. It was brought into French by an orientalist scholar and was picked up by the French symbolist poets and brought into English, along with the sestina and villanelle, by Austin Dobson. It is composed of quatrains in which the second and fourth lines of each stanza serve as the first and third lines of the next. It can be any length, but the last line of the last stanza is usually the first line of the poem, and the third line of the first stanza appears as the second line of the last stanza.

Originally the idea was that the first two lines of each stanza and the second two developed different themes concurrently, the two parts of the stanza being linked by sound (rhyme and meter or some kind of grammatical parallelism). It became attractive to post-modernists in the 1970s and 1980s because it expressed even more forcefully than the sestina or the villanelle relentlessly boring or mysterious repetition.

The most memorable pantoum I know of is Donald Justice's "Pantoum of the Great Depression." And in Paul Hoover's anthology, *Postmodern American Poetry*, there are several recent poems:

David Trinidad: "Movin' with Nancy"
Elaine Equi: "A Date with Robbe-Grillet"

6. And for another use of hypnotic repetition altogether, borrowed from the surrealists, I think, see Kenneth Koch's "Sleeping With Women." It has no specified form, just drowns you in anaphora and unpredictable, predictable return of the repeated phrase. A little of it goes like this:

Sleeping with women: as in the poems of Pascoli.
Sleeping with women: as in the rain, as in the snow.
Sleeping with women: by starlight, as if we were angels,
    sleeping on the train,
On the starry foam, asleep and sleeping with them—sleeping
    with women.
Mediterranean: a voice.
Mediterranean: a sea. Asleep and sleeping.

This must come out of Gertrude Stein's "Lifting Belly," that great hymn to sexuality, domesticity, and dailiness.

A NOTE ON GENRE

1. So that's it for poetic forms. Four hundred and fifty years of the sonnet, occasional sestinas and villanelles, the rarer occasional pantoum. One could add the ballad—short narrative poems, traditionally in four-line stanzas. And a couple more recent English language adaptation—the ghazal (see Chapter 2) from Persian and Arabic, the blues from the American vernacular.

2. Much richer in the literary tradition is the idea of kinds of poems, poems with particular subject matter and/or particular angles of approach that don't, however, specify their length or a particular metrical pattern or rhyme scheme.

3. The *OED* is uncharacteristically unhelpful with the notion of genre. It means "kind" and got applied to people as well as stories in the nineteenth century, and it came to be used in art to describe paintings of ordinary life. In poetry it means types of poems, usually

with particular historical conventions attached to them. Lyric itself
is a genre.

4 . So it's interesting to think about the history of the lyric as we
glimpse it coming into view with the invention of writing.

EGYPT

The following song was said to be composed circa 1350 BC, possibly
by King Akhenaton himself (who is the speaker in the poem.)

> When in splendor you first took your throne,
> O living Aton,
> High in the precinct of heaven,
> O living God,
> Life truly began!
> Now from eastern horizon risen and streaming,
> You have flooded the world
> With your beauty.
> You are majestic, awesome, bedazzling, exalted,
> Yet your rays, they touch lightly, compass the lands
> To the limits of all your creation.
> There in the sun, you reach to the farthest
> Of those you would gather in
> For your son whom you love.
> Though you are far your light is wide upon the earth
> And you shine in the faces of all
> Who turn to follow your journeying
>
> (Ancient Egyptian Literature, translated by John L. Foster,
>   University of Texas Press, 2001)

ISRAEL

On the psalms: "We know little about how the anthology was made or when most of the pieces were composed . . . The biblical collection consists of poems written over a period of at least five centuries. Some psalms may well go back to the earliest centuries of the Davidic dynasty, that is, the 10th and 9th centuries BCE."

> The Lord is my shepherd;
> I shall not want.
> He makes me to lie down in green pastures;
> He leads me beside the still waters. He restores my soul;
> He leads me in the paths of righteousness
> For His name's sake;
> Yea, though I walk through the valley of the shadow of death.
> I will fear no evil.
> For You are with me;
> Your rod and your staff, they comfort me.
>
> You prepare a table before me in the presence of my enemies;
> You anoint my head with oil.
> My cup runs over.
> Surely goodness and mercy shall follow me
> All the days of my life;
> And I will dwell in the house of the Lord forever.

GREECE

This is one of the earliest fragments of a poem by Sappho. It comes from a poorly spelled inscription in a piece of pottery from the third century BC. It was probably composed in the late seventh/early sixth century BC. Nobody knows for sure whether the technology of writing had reached Lesbos in her lifetime.

Come to me from Crete to this holy place
Where your apple grove is,
And the sweet smoke of libanum rises
From your altar

Where cold water rushes through apple blossoms,
The whole place overshadowed by roses,
And from the shimmering apple leaves
   Sleep descends

Here where horses graze the meadow
And the spring flowers are blooming
And the winds are sweet and cooling
[a line or two missing here]

In this place, Kupris, goddess,
Pour nectar into the golden cups,
And bless our festivities
   With your good wine.

Kupris is a name for Aphrodite. (Should you ever go into the White Mountains on Crete to hike down the trail in Samaria Gorge to the Libyan Sea, someone is apt to point out to you on the way up the hillside cave where Aphrodite is said to have dwelt. It's surrounded by wild oleander and bearded goats grazing in the summer heat.) There are many translations of this poem.

CHINA

The *Shih Ching*, the oldest collection of Chinese poetry, is a collection of folk songs dating from 1,000 to 600 BC. They are traditionally believed to have been assembled by Confucius. They are full of the sense of daily living and ceremonial occasions. There are many translations. Ezra Pound translated the entire book. Mao Tse Tung edited an edition, establishing their modern order. This is the first of them in all editions, and it's learned by heart today by all Chinese schoolchildren.

Gwak! Gwak! cries the osprey
On sandbars in the river.
A good girl, mild-mannered,
Fine match for the gentleman.

Thick grows the watercress,
Left and right it grows.
A good girl, mild-mannered,
Sleeping and waking, he searches for her.

Searches and cannot find her.
Sleeping and waking, thinking of her.
Endlessly, endlessly
Tossing and turning.

Thick grows the watercress,
Left and right we pick it.
A good girl, mild-mannered,
The harp and the lute are her friends.

Thick grows the watercress.
Left and right we sort it.
A good girl, mild-mannered.
The bell and the drum delight her.

This is said (by whom?) to be a wedding song for a royal family. There are also many translations of this poem. See Burton Watson, *The Columbia Book of Chinese Poetry*, Columbia University Press, 1984.

A thing to notice about these poems is that three of the four are prayers. That is to say, the impulse of prayer seems to be very near the origin of the lyric.

5 . I learned the structure of prayer very early in a Catholic childhood. Others with other childhoods will have learned other prayers, or none, but we memorized ours and often rushed through them in the recitation, if there was recess or the end of Mass in the offing. For the "Hail Mary," for example, we could say the first part in one breath:

> Hail Mary, full of grace, the Lord is with thee, blessed art
> thou among women and blessed in the fruit of thy womb,
> Jesus.

And another breath for the second part:

> Holy Mary, mother of God, pray for us sinners now and at
> The hour of our death. Amen.

A transparent structure. Praise, then ask. The "Our Father" was the same. "Our Father who art in Heaven, hallowed be thy name" and then more of the same, and then the ask: "Give us this day our daily bread." It may be a clue to the deep, formal structure of various lyric forms. The function of prayer is to get into right relationship to a power or a desired good, or to ward off an evil. Even the Chinese folk song, after it has conjured fertility—the osprey, which is said to be a tradition symbol of conjugal accord (perhaps because those birds are so attentive to their nests) and the watercress—is about getting the man and the desirable sort of bride together.

6 . The praise part of the formula led to the litany. The corresponding part to do with warding off death or misfortune or other evils

would be not the list of great attributes of the desired person or condition, but a bill of complaints, as in this other poem from the *Shih
Ching*, a song of soldiers guarding the frontier:

> We pick ferns, we pick ferns,
> For the ferns are sprouting now.
> Oh to go home, to go home
> Before the year is over!
> No rooms, no houses for us,
> All because of the northern tribes,
> No time to kneel or sit down,
> All because of the northern tribes.
>
> We pick ferns, we pick ferns,
> The ferns now are tender;
> Oh to go home, to go home!
> Our hearts are saddened,
> Our sad hearts, smoulder and burn.
> We are hungry, we are thirsty,
> No limit to our border duty,
> No way to send home for news.

And so on through six stanzas. The poem ends:

> Slow, slow our march.
> We are thirsty, we are hungry,
> Our hearts worn with sorrow,
> No one knows our woe.

An example from another tradition comes from Tudor England, said
to have been composed by twenty-year-old Chidiock Tichborne on
the eve of his execution for treason:

My prime of youth is but a frost of cares,
My feast of joy is but a dish of pain,
My crop of corn is but a field of tares,
And all my good is but vain hope of gain.
The day is gone and yet I saw no sun,
And now I live, and now my life is done.

And so on—through three stanzas.

That is—as the litany is formally a list, so is the complaint, or dirge, or *planh*, as it came to be called in medieval Provencal. And lists in theory have no end. If they become prayers, they end with a wish, one way the formal imagination works at closure. If they get complicated, if they enact change, they evolve into the ode and the elegy, a place to begin to speak about genre.

7. Litany and surrealism. Maybe it has to do with Catholic countries.

André Breton, "Free Union":

My love whose hair is woodfire
Her thoughts heat lightning
Her waist an hourglass
My love an otter in the tiger's jaws
Her mouth a rosette bouquet of stars of the highest magnitude

Pablo Neruda: "Heights of Macchu Picchu," part 9:

Interstellar eagle, vine-in-a-mist.
Forsaken bastion, blind scimitar.
Orion belt, ceremonial bread.
Torrential stairway, immeasureable eyelids.

But see also Christopher Smart, "For I consider my cat Geoffrey";
Walt Whitman, "Song of Myself," various sections; Gertrude Stein,
"Lifting Belly"; Lyn Hejinian, "Happily."

8. Poem as prayer. It implies a psychic distance from the desired
object. In one way of thinking, then, lyric is the site of an absence.

> Western wind, when wilt thou blow?
> The small rain down doth rain.
> Christ! That my love were in my arms,
> And I in my bed again.

> *

> Wild nights! Wild nights!
> Were I with thee,
> Wild nights would be
> Our luxury!

And is incurably subjunctive—has a way of seeming to give us sym-
bolically what is absent physically. Martin Heidegger can speak of
the poem calling the world into being through the word. The work
of thinkers associated with deconstruction—Jacques Derrida, Paul
de Man—was to insist that the word is not the thing—that poetry
cannot, by definition, possess what it desires and seems to claim to
possess.

   Thinking about lyric, about the formal imagination working its
way from the beginning of a poem to the end, one can turn to the
work of genre, to the shapes of thought and arcs of feeling in the
traditional kinds.

9. So the rhythms of formal shaping in a poem are always working at at least a couple of levels—that of prosody, numbers falling

through numbers to create the expressive effect of a piece, and that of—don't know what to call it—thematic development, the way the poem makes its trajectory, creates its sense of movement (or doesn't) from beginning to end, some of which is apt to get prompts from generic expectations, conscious or not. Back to Emily Dickinson's "I cannot live with you—." The poem develops systematically every possible reason why the lovers couldn't live together and why neither could watch the other die and why they couldn't be in heaven either. It's about the faithfulness, the generative intensity of that impossibility. The movement has an inextinguishable finality and it ends with the killer lines that name the condition exactly. That's one way her formal imagination was working. Another was that she was, as she usually did, ringing another set of variations on the hymn stanza:

> I cannot live with you
> That would be life
> And life is over there
> Behind the shelf

This is the six syllables and three stresses followed by four syllables and two stresses version of the eight syllable, four stress followed by six syllable, three stress movement of the classic hymn meter. What the form expresses, especially in the curtailed version, is restraint, which is what the poem is about. And it matters that "life" and "shelf" don't quite rhyme. And the poem in a way explains why she had such a great ear for slant rhyme and off rhyme. Full rhyme expresses perfect union. Her theme was, to borrow Richard Wilbur's phrase, "sumptuous destitution."

This is why Robert Creeley's well-known formulation—"form is never more than an extension of content"—isn't quite adequate. The idea of "extension" doesn't quite capture the mysterious way in which prosodic form and the formal shape of the development of content interact.

Quite often the song can be there first, showing the conscious content the way, or resisting it. The main thing is that, in the great poems, we experience the relation between them as indissoluble. And that way in which they can't be teased apart is ultimately what we mean by form.

ODE

1. The word in ancient Greek meant "song," from *aeidein*, to sing or chant. In English the term is used very loosely and has come to mean, roughly, either a poem of praise—Neruda's *Odes*—or an emotional outburst—Ginsberg's "Plutonium Ode." "Plutonium Ode" in the 1950s felt like an oxymoron, marrying the world's newest poison to the quaint old poetic term. One idea of the ode was that it was a formal poem. And there is the other that it is a casual and spontaneous poem. There are reasons for this split history.

2. The form matters to us partly because, as it developed in the English tradition, it came to mean a poem that broke out of the other forms. By the nineteenth century it was a longish lyric poem, often with an elaborate stanza structure written in lines of varying and irregular length and often with different formal patterns in different parts. That meant that it came to seem an appropriate form for tracking a complicated emotion or series of emotions or thoughts and that, because of its irregularity, it was one of the natural—conscious or unconscious—models for the longish free verse poem.

3. And also because, begun as a formal and public, or informal and private poem of praise, it came to be the model for expressing or enacting a relationship to the values on which poetry seemed to depend. So it is particularly useful and interesting to study its history.

4. It evolved in Greece out of the choral songs sung at religious festivals that acted out the adventures and sufferings of gods, goddesses, and heroes. The Greek model of the form that came down to the European Renaissance was that of Pindar whose poems are said by critics to have, typically, three movements: strophe, antistrophe, and epode, to which Ben Jonson gave the English names of turn, counterturn, and stand. The strophe and antistrophe had the same stanza pattern, and the epode a different one. The movement was thought of on the analogy of dance.

Pindar's poems celebrated victories in sporting events, a genre that seems more or less incomprehensible to us now, and his were the only ones to survive, until a manuscript turned up in 1896. It contained remnants of fourteen victory odes by a poet named Bacchylides. Their form reinforced scholars' understanding of the way the genre worked.

In translation the three-part metrical pattern isn't evident, but the basic formal pattern is. In translation the odes read like very clever after-dinner speeches at a sports banquet. The poem begins by mentioning the victory and the winner, or if a horse or chariot race is involved, the winner and the owner, and then launches into the heart of the poem, which was intended to flatter the victor's place of origin, or the horse's, or the mythic origins of the particular festival. In a mix of geography, genealogy, and myth typical of the oral tradition, the poem tells stories, teases the audience with digressions, and returns at the end to compliments for the victor, or to a patron, or to useful platitudes. Bacchylides's poems seem fairly straightforward; one of his ends, in English translation:

To the wise my words have meaning: the sky
Is undefiled, the sea's water
Does not decay, and gold is joy,
But a man may not cast off

Gray age and recover the bloom
Of youth. Virtue's sheen
Never fades away like the body's;
The Muses preserve it, Hiero

Hiero was the owner of the chariot that won an Olympic race in 468 BC. Pindar's poems are more complex, but they follow the same pattern. The clue to the formal structure—what gets echoed in the history of the ode—is the way they begin in a place, and then take their audience on a journey—the entertaining stories in the middle part of the after-dinner speech—and then come to their graceful conclusion.

(Early Greek Lyric Poetry, *ed. David Mulroy, University of Michigan Press, 1992*)

5. Two thousand years later critics would notice this pattern in the romantic ode—in poems that announced themselves as odes and in the less formal poems that followed the same pattern. Wordsworth begins with the scene from a hillside above an old abbey, Coleridge with the midnight quiet in his cottage on a winter night, Keats with a moment of awe before a Greek vase in a museum. Then the poem takes you on what one critic, M. H. Abrams, describes as "an inward journey" where some work of transformation is done, and then returns you to the place where you began, with that place altered by the process. Perhaps this is a little neat. John Ashbery parodies it in "The Instruction Manual." In the beginning of that poem, the speaker is working in an office and bored. So in his imagination he

visits Mexico in a stretch of writing that reads like a 1940s movie travelogue with sunshine and sombreros and serapes and smiling señoritas, and then returns you to the office, where, a little nearer five o'clock and slightly refreshed, you have survived the day.

6 . The nineteenth-century poems were probably not modeled on Pindar or the eighteenth-century ode. They more nearly resemble the seventeenth-century meditative poem, which (see Louis Martz, *The Meditative Poem*) followed the pattern laid down for meditative prayer. Begin with a scene from the story of the man-god and his suffering. Take the story in, focusing on its details and their meaning, and then return yourself to the scene fully in possession of it. As we've seen, the ode begins in the praise poem and the prayer. The formal ode seems to be a way of conjuring and taking possession of the desired object or person or value. That's why it has been so easy to use the form of an erotic poem to write religious poetry or of a religious poem to write an erotic one. The ode impulse can take you to that place or conjure an anguished distance from it, or simply name it: "So much depends upon / a red wheelbarrow / glazed with rain water / beside the white chickens."

7. A tradition of English Pindarics developed; it seems to have started or at least been popularized by a seventeenth-century poet named Abraham Cowley (pronounced Cooley). There aren't any Pindaric odes in most anthologies of English or American poetry. As a strict form, it has not had legs. The best way to get a sense of it is to get a hold of a modern translation of Pindar and a volume of Cowley that includes his own odes and his Pindar translations.

8 . The other idea of the form comes from the odes of Horace.

9. Things change: I bought a hardback copy of his odes in Latin sometime in the 1970s for fifty cents in a used bookstore in Berkeley. It was published in 1898 and the editor begins this way: "What to say of these poems, every line of which is already well known to all students of literature?"

10. Horace wrote the four books of his odes between 23 and 13 BCE during the reign of Augustus. According to scholars, he called his poems *carmina,* or "songs." I'm not clear on when or how they came to be called odes. The Greek word *ode* means "song." For our purposes, the poems might just as well have been called "lyrics." His odes—probably the best known, most widely studied Roman poems in Europe from the Renaissance to the twentieth century—were mostly modeled on early Greek song forms. Horace was conscious of, in fact boasted of, having brought the Greek meters into the Latin language. His main models were Sappho and Alcaeus and he wrote in the stanza forms, various kinds of quatrains, in which they had composed. The idea of lyric—of written poems intended for reading, public or private, based on forms intended to be sung—may begin here, or a generation earlier with Catullus.

Of the 104 odes Horace wrote, all but twenty-five are written in quatrains, and the other twenty-five—a nineteenth-century German scholar reports—have a number of lines divisible by four. Like Emily Dickinson, Horace thought in fours, and he wrote about everything. "The situations of many of his poems," his translator David Ferry writes, "was pointedly ordinary: inviting a friend for a drink, pro- posing a party for a friend's return from abroad, advising somebody not to drink too much, praising a friend for his virtue, or his skill in poetry or public affairs, or his sexual success." There are also more public poems of occasion nearer to Pindar in spirit. But the idea of the ode that comes down to us from him is mostly informal: casual, unbuttoned, and elegant.

11. The other, the idea of his public poems, involved viewing the public world from a distance, with a certain detached irony. To track the influence of that sort of Horatian ode, much of which was tonal, once could look at I, 37, his ode about Cleopatra and compare it to Marvell's "Horatian Ode" to Cromwell, which is modeled on Horace, and then look at Robert Lowell's "Waking Early Sunday Morning," which is based on Marvell.

12. Among prosodists, Pindarics are often called "greater odes," Horatian "lesser odes," though these terms are almost meaningless now. Except in the sense that the smaller ode is a briefer lyric of praise like Neruda's and the longer ode takes its tradition from the romantic ode—a longer poem, often characterized by devices like apostrophe that enacts a crisis or celebration of the poet's relation to the sources of poetry.

13. This is pretty much the notion of the ode that has come down to us, the ode from the romantic poets, specifically from Wordsworth, Coleridge, Keats, and Shelley. And, I would add, the long Whitman poems modeled on the English odes, "Out of the Cradle Endlessly Rocking" and "Crossing Brooklyn Ferry." Some of their poems—Wordsworth's "Intimations" ode and Coleridge's "Dejection: An Ode"—are based on the formal idea that an ode is a poem in parts with varying metrical and rhyming schemes. Some of them, the blank verse poems like "Tintern Abbey" and "Frost at Midnight," seem formally nearer in their movement and prosody to seventeenth-century meditative poems. A helpful way to what's happening in these poems is in an essay by M. H. Abrams, "Style and Structure in the Greater Romantic Lyric." It's Abrams who observes the formal movement characteristic of many of these poems—that they begin in a place, that they take the reader (and the speaker of the

poem) on an inward journey, that they return by way of ending to a transformed place. If the ode evolved from a simple praise poem into a longish poem dramatizing an attempt to get into right relation to some power or good, then it gives us a way to track the work being done by the inward journey at the center of these poems.

14. The term *romantic* is a convenience for observing a shift in the notion of the poem from the idea that the work of the imagination was to make vivid and attractive the ideas that are available to us through reason or an empirical common sense to the idea that imagination was not illustrative, but creative, that the imagination embodied its own kind of knowledge, deeper, phenomenologically fuller, than the kinds of thing the other labors of knowing afford us. This was an idea being worked out—sometimes in startling form. Whitman could begin a poem "I celebrate myself." And it's a way to think about the formal movement of these poems. The power they are addressing, in one way or another, is the source of their own creative power.

15. The modernist generation steered clear of the word *ode*. For them, I think, it stood for an emotional effusiveness they aimed to avoid. They wanted to insist on the power of the artist as maker and not on inspiration as a breeze out of nature filling their sails. (Out the window a hawk just flew past as I wrote that sentence, riding the wind.) But it seems increasingly that their work doesn't represent a break with the romantic impulse but a reframing of the issue. Byzantium for Yeats is a symbol of the source of the power of art. "Among Schoolchildren" is the interior journey of an old man stunned into a memory by the beauty of a child in a classroom he is visiting. Several of Wallace Stevens's poems seem modeled fairly directly on Keats and Whitman. Many of Pound's early Cantos almost imitate Pindar by being shaped around a mythic journey. Each of the *Four Quartets* is a poem in parts

modeled on the formal ode. Langston Hughes's "Dream Deferred" is
a journey and a quest with an evolving formal shape.

16 . One of the great projects in the ode form in the second half of
the twentieth century was Pablo Neruda's. He wrote odes early on.
Some of them appear in the *Residencia en Tierra* volumes, but later
in life he contracted with a Venezuelan newspaper to write an ode a
week for a period on the condition that they appear in the news section, not the arts section, of the paper. And like Horace, only more
so, he wrote about everything, his socks, watermelons, tomatoes,
a woman's scent, Walt Whitman, movie theaters. They are mostly
written in very short lines—as a way of naturalizing and modern-
izing the formal ode. And they are mostly litanies, characteristic of
a Catholic culture. Here he is, for example, on elephants, a bit of the
poem laid out by me as if it were a litany in a prayer book, one item
of praise per line:

> Thick, pristine beast, Saint Elephant,
> sacred animal of perennial forests,
> sheer strength,
> fine and balanced leather of global saddle-makers,
> compact, satin-finished ivory,
> serene as the moon's flesh,
> with miniscule eyes—to see and not be seen—
> and a singing trunk, a blowing horn,
> hose of a creature rejoicing in its own freshness,
> earth-shaking machine, forest telephone

In his lineation it looks like this:

> Thick, pristine beast,
> St. Elephant,

sacred animal
of perennial forests,
sheer strength,
fine
and balanced
leather
of
global saddle-makers

Neruda knew elephants from his time in the diplomatic service in India, Ceylon, and Burma and the poem may well be an elegy, may be an instance of how close to elegy the ode often is. And a place to think about what work metaphor does in the ode tradition.

17. *Europe:* The German ode got called an elegy because it was written, by Friedrich Hölderlin principally, in an imitation of the Greek elegiac meter (alternating hexameter and pentameter lines). Rainer Maria Rilke's *Duino Elegies*—he was a reader of Keats—is a set of odes.

18. *Postwar Poland, the still life as ode:* Theodor Adorno said, famously, that to write poetry after Auschwitz was barbarism. After Auschwitz and in its neighborhood, Zbigniew Herbert wrote poems about objects that are a sort of dark, opposing mirror to Neruda's exuberance. They might be thought of as a turn taken by the ode form. What is a cup, after Auschwitz? What is the human hand for which the cup was designed, after Auschwitz? This is ode at the edge of satire: the world stripped bare. "Violins" is an instance:

Violins are naked. They have thin arms, with which, clumsily they try to protect themselves. They cry from shame and cold.

That's why. Not, as the music critics maintain, for beauty.
That isn't true.

(Selected Poems, tr. John and Bogdana Carpenter, Oxford, 1977)

See his "Object," "Drawer," "Study of the Object," "Pebble" in the
Selected Poems translated by Czesław Miłosz and Peter Dale Scott. See
also Czesław Miłosz's "Song on Porcelain" and Wisława Szymbor-
ska's "Still Life with a Balloon" and "Starvation Camp Near Jaslo."
And in the next generation Adam Zagajewski's "Ode to Plurality."

19 . *Postwar American poetry:* So much of it might be said to belong
to the manner of the lesser ode. Frank O'Hara especially. James
Schuyler seems a Horatian poet. Sylvia Plath's ferocious descriptive
poems like "Blackberrying" might belong with Herbert's poems to
the anti-ode. Charles Wright. Yusef Komunyakaa.

Some readings:

THE RENAISSANCE ODE

John Donne: "Good Friday, Riding Westward"
Ben Jonson: "An Ode to Himself"
Robert Herrick: "An Ode for Him"
John Milton: "On the Morning of Christ's Nativity"
Richard Crashaw: "A Hymn to the Name and Honor of the
Admirable Saint Theresa"
Andrew Marvell: "An Horation Ode"

RESTORATION AND EIGHTEENTH CENTURY

John Dryden: "A Song for St. Cecilia's Day"
Anne Finch: "On Melancholy"
John Dyer: "Grongar Hill"

Note: The mid-eighteenth-century ode. Dyer published his first in irregular stanzas and then modernized it into its present form by recasting it in headless tetrameter couplets. Compare the two and you can watch the classical ode get transformed into an early example of the landscape poem, which some critics have also described as a georgic.

Thomas Gray: "Ode on a Distant Prospect of Eton College"
    "Ode on the Death of a Favorite Cat, Drowned in a Tub of Goldfishes"
William Collins: "Ode Written in the Beginning of the Year 1746"
    "Ode on the Poetical Character"
    "Ode to Evening"
Christopher Smart: "For I Will Consider My Cat Jeoffry" [from *Jubilate Agno*]

ROMANTIC ODE

William Wordsworth: "Ode: Intimations of Immortality"
    "Lines Written Above Tintern Abbey"
    "Ode to Duty"
Samuel Coleridge: "Dejection: An Ode"
    "Frost at Midnight"
    "This Lime Tree Bower My Prison"
Percy Bysshe Shelley: "Ode to the West Wind"
    "To a Skylark"
    "To Night"
John Keats: "Ode to Psyche"
    "Ode to a Nightingale"
    "Ode to Melancholy"
    "Ode on a Grecian Urn"
    "To Autumn"

Walt Whitman: "Crossing Brooklyn Ferry"
             "Out of the Cradle Endlessly Rocking"

Note: Because it had come to seem the quintessential romantic form, the modernists avoided the term "ode." But many of their orienting poems have what seems very much an odelike structure. Later the form's open-endedness and shifts dissolve into the long free verse poem.

MODERNISM AND THE ODE

W. B. Yeats: "Among Schoolchildren"
Wallace Stevens: "The Idea of Order at Key West"
Ezra Pound: "Canto II"
T. S. Eliot: "Burnt Norton"
"The Dry Salvages"

Note: Interesting to compare the prayer in the fourth section to the prayer in the fourth section of Coleridge's "Dejection"

Hart Crane: "Voyages"
           "To Brooklyn Bridge"
Allen Tate: "Ode to the Confederate Dead"

MIDCENTURY AND AFTER

Lorine Niedecker: "Paean to Place"
Robert Lowell: "Waking Early Sunday Morning"
Allen Ginsberg: "Sunflower Sutra"
               "Wales Visitation"
               "America (MP)"
               "In the Baggage Room of the Greyhound"
A. R. Ammons: "Corson's Inlet"

John Ashbery: "The Instruction Manual"
       "Syringa (MP)"
       "Melodic Trains"
Adrienne Rich: "Toward the Solstice"
Yusef Komunyakaa: "Ode to the Chameleon"
       "Ode to the Guitar"
And see the odes of Pablo Neruda and of Adam Zagajewski.

Further reading: C. D. Wright, "The New American Ode"

READING THE ODE

1. So the ode, as a praise poem, probably emerged from the twinned forms of prayer and litany. Odes—here is a way to think about them—are about trying to get into right relation to an imagined good or power. Or, to say it the other way, they are about not being in possession of some desired good or power. If you were in possession of it, you wouldn't need to address it.

2. In this sense every love poem, every prayer, most descriptive poems, most poems that think through ideas (because the completed thought is the desired good) belong to the gesture of the ode. In this sense, "Western Wind" is a very short ode:

> O Western wind, when wilt thou blow?
> The small rain down doth rain.
> Christ! That my love were in my arms
> And I in my bed again!

And even this small, astonishing poem by Bashō, about not being in possession of what you are in possession of, is an ode:

> Even in Kyoto,
> Hearing the cuckoo's cry
> I long for Kyoto.

3. The ode is a request form, so it is a quest form, a motion-toward form, and it is therefore also inescapably a distance-from form, so that the membrane between ode and elegy, between desire and mourning, is in the best poems very permeable. That's why Coleridge could call his poem "Dejection: An Ode." Keats seems to have understood this very clearly in "Ode on a Grecian Urn" and "Ode to a Nightingale," and it is what gives those poems—and the great "To Autumn"—their aching beauty. Probably the clearest statement of the case is Emily Dickinson's "I Cannot Live with You," a poem made of a litany of reasons why the lovers want each other too much to ever get together. It's the poem that ends:

> So we must meet apart—
> You there—I—here
> With just the Door ajar
> That Oceans are—and Prayer—
> And that White Sustenance—
> Despair—

Which seems to say that in the end it is not the beloved object that is the good, it is desire, and therefore the very distance that the poem wants to traverse, that is the good.

Probably worth saying here that it is not always desire that initiates the ode. I remember being on a panel on poetics once with Seamus Heaney. I had quoted some of Robert Duncan's great poem,

"Often I am permitted to return to a meadow" in which Duncan writes about the source of his creativity being a place of "first permission" as an "everlasting omen of what is." It's not exactly automatic entry that he's speaking of, but the provocation toward a place of speech. Seamus, listening, squinted and demurred, and remarked that a poem for him almost always began in dissent, by saying no. Which, I think, makes immediate sense. If we agreed with the world in all its particulars, we would be identical with it and have nothing to say. Thought begins in disagreement, the terms of which demand to be articulated. The heart or mind opened to something by longing, by a felt absence is surely one movement of the ode. Thinking one's way out of an untenable place is another.

4. And there are also goods, and virtues implicit in them, that are relatively attainable so that our distance from them is, mostly, habit. "The function of art," Viktor Shklovsky, "is to make the stone stone and the grass grass by freeing us from the automatism of perception." So Pablo Neruda on tomatoes and sox, and this poem by Bashō:

> A fall night,
> Getting dinner, we peeled
> Eggplants, cucumbers.

BACCYLIADES, POUND, AND THE GREEK ODE

5. To begin to track this complex history, a place to start is the Greek ode. These poems were sung or recited, often in choral form, so they probably have some relation to the origins of drama, were perhaps danced, and thus have in their shape some ritual elements— some physical idea of how you dance toward or before the gods.

Scholars describe them as having three movements—strophe, in which the chorus moved from left to right; antistrophe, in which they moved from right to left; and epode, in which the chorus stood still. Typically, the poets varied the meter in the three parts. From our point of view the thing to notice is the obvious thing—their aim is praise, they have a beginning, a middle, and an end.

Here's an example from Baccylides, who was born on Ceos in the Cyclades about twenty-five hundred years ago. He was a younger contemporary of Pindar and was much admired in the ancient world. His poems disappeared altogether from the historical record—he survived as a name and a few scraps quoted by grammarians until fourteen of his odes were discovered in a papyrus in Egypt in 1896. Here is one of them—a victory ode to honor the winner of a chariot race in the Olympic games of 468. David Mulroy, the author of this translation, describes the poem as "containing all the standard ingredients: brief mention of the victory being commemorated, a mythical narrative indirectly related to the victory, and maxims that more or less tie the whole thing together."

This poem celebrates the owner of the horses, Hiero, the tyrant of Syracuse, who was a patron of poets. Why read this old oddity of another culture—a half-sung, half-danced version of an after-dinner speech at a sporting event? Well, we are looking at an old movement of the mind and of the formal imagination. The poem begins with praise and prayer. It moves to myth, that middle of the poem in which we can begin to ask what idea of development or transformation of a theme is at work. The myths and legends narrated in the middle of these odes were the common lore of their audience, the stories that bound them together. Scholars say they reach back in their motion to the Homeric hymns, the oldest extant Greek poems—called Homeric because they were written—and were recited before there was writing in which to record them—in Homer's meter, dactylic hexameter. The origins of drama were probably in the ritual enacting of these stories, all ways of soliciting and accommodating the powers that they understood to rule their universe, or, in the case of this story by Baccyliades, of a legendary king's relation to the gods.

Croesus, the hero of the poem's narrative middle, was king of Lydia, famous for his fabulous wealth. Lydia—western Turkey—functioned as a buffer state between the Greek world and the power of the Persian empire. When Lydia fell to Persia a hundred years before this poem was written, the Persian king Cyrus placed Croesus and his family on a funeral pyre to be burned alive. This is the story as Herodotus tells it. In Baccyliades's version, Croesus builds his own pyre to escape the humiliation of defeat, and his piety saves him.

The poem begins by addressing Clio, the muse associated with history and thus with memory and fame, and asks her to help him praise Demeter, the goddess of the fertility of nature whose cult was associated with Sicily (you can go online and find news of the discovery or her ancient temple there by archaeologists in 2012). Notice that, in the same breath, the poet celebrates the horses of Hiero, mentions his father, and lavishes praise on his prosperity. In this way it is very much a feudal poem, not so different in spirit and intent from the "great house" poems of the English Renaissance, celebrating the properties of the powerful landowners who were also the patrons of poets. And this beginning ends—we are on Olympus, not in Sicily—at the temple to Apollo and the sacred spring where visitors purified and refreshed themselves before presenting their petitions to the god.

> Sing, O generous Clio, the praise
> of fertile Sicily's queen,
> Demeter, her violet-wreathed girl, and Hiero's
> swift Olympian horses;

driven by Triumph and excellent Victory,
they flashed by the turbulent Alpheus
and placed the winner's garlands in the hands
of Deinomenes' fortunate son.

The people shouted, "Thrice
happy man!
who obtained from Zeus
the Greeks' widest rule
and knows better than to cloak his towering
wealth in darkness."

Precincts teem with sacrificial processions,
streets with hospitable feasts.
Gold glimmers amid rays
from graven tripods standing

in front of the temple, where Delphians care for
Phoebus' greatest shrine
by the Castalian foundation. Glorify God!
That is the crown of prosperity.

The transition to the story of Croesus depends on this, this and the
association of Lydia with the taming of wild horses. Hiero's victory is
imagined to inspire processions to the temple of Apollo and "the man
who led horse-taming / Lydia's hosts / when Zeus brought / the destined crisis to pass / and Sardis fell to the Persian army, Croesus was
saved by Apollo." It is a poet's transition—on the thinnest of pretexts,
but it allows Baccyliades to tell the edifying and entertaining story of
how Apollo snatched the king and his family from the flames:

For the man who led horse-taming
Lydia's hosts,
when Zeus brought

the destined crisis to pass
and Sardis fell to the Persian army—
Croesus was saved by Apollo,

god of the golden sword. That unexpected
day of grief, deciding
not to abide slavery, he built
a pyre facing the bronze

wall of his courtyard. With his virtuous wife
and daughters, who sobbed and tore
their elegant braids, he mounted, raised
his hands to the distant sky

and cried: "Overpowering deity,
where is the gods'
gratitude? Where
is Leto's lordly son?
Alyattes' palace has fallen. . . .
[Two lines are missing.]
The gold-bearing Pactolus is red
with blood, women are led away
from stately chambers to humiliation.

The hated is loved; death is sweetest."
He spoke and ordered his fastidious
servant to light the wood. The maidens
screamed and threw their hands

on their mother. Death foreseen
is bitterest for mortals,
but the fire no sooner
started to blaze than Zeus
positioned a cloud overhead and quenched
the golden flame.

Believe the will of the gods incapable
of nothing! Apollo transported
the elderly man to the Hyperboreans and settled him
there with his slim-ankled daughters

in return for sending mankind's greatest
gifts to holy Pytho.

End of the story. A story about right relation to the gods—a traditional piety, it would seem. Here is where Baccyliades takes his audience at the end of the poem:

Not one of Hellas' lords, O most
praiseworthy Hiero, would dare

to claim he has sent more
gold to Loxias.
[*Loxias* is one of Apollo's names.]

For one not fat
with envy it is easy to praise
a horse-loving martial man.
[Six lines are missing.]

... The lord Apollo
said to the son of Pheres: "A mortal,
you must be firm in two

convictions: that tomorrow's sun
is the last you will see
and that you will live
in luxury for fifty years."
Take pleasure in holy works,
the highest profit.

 To the wise my words have meaning: the sky

is undefiled; the sea's water
does not decay and gold is joy,
but a man may not cast off

   gray age and recover the bloom
of youth. Virtue's sheen
never fades away like the body's;
the Muse preserves it, Hiero,

   and yours are the finest flowers
of wealth. Silence
is not success'
ornament. By truth will live
the tale of your glories and the gift of the sweet-tongued
nightingale of Ceos.

(David Mulroy, Early Greek Lyric Poetry, *University of Michigan
   Press, 1992)*

At this distance a string of platitudes. But a very interesting turn in
the platitudes. From the idea that Croesus was saved by his piety to the
idea that only poetry can immortalize virtue. Gold is not power, then,
poetry is power. You can see now why the poem begins with Clio, the
muse who presides over fame. Funniest and oddest is that Baccyliades
ends by praising himself to Hiero. It's a description associated with
him in antiquity. He was "the sweet-tongued nightingale of Ceos."
And in this way it turns out to be—like "Ode to a Nightingale"—a
poem about mortality and imagination.

6 . If you are inclined to think of this use of the narrative middle
as antique, consider Ezra Pound's "Canto II." It's another poem that
falls fairly easily into three parts. I am not going to try to explicate the
poem, but look, briefly, at how it begins. Pound doesn't address Clio,

the muse of history, but he does address a mentor figure, Browning, and speaks of his envy and dismay at Browning's narrative poem, "Sordello." There's the poem, there's Browning interpretation of the old poet, there's Pound's interpretation, there's an extant scrap of a biography. The question of how you get at the real is transformed into an image of an old Chinese philosopher churning in the sea of the changeable world—which takes Pound to what he was great at, a flow of marine imagery, that calls up the story of Helen of Troy, that calls up many stories glimpsed in the waves, myth-stories that have been a human way of taking meaning from the changeable world, from the "blue-gray glass of the wave":

> HANG it all, Robert Browning,
> there can be but the one "Sordello."
> But Sordello, and my Sordello?
> Lo Sordels si fo di Mantovana.
> So-shu churned in the sea.
> Seal sports in the spray-whited circles of cliff-wash,
> Sleek head, daughter of Lir,
>   eyes of Picasso
> Under black fur-hood, lithe daughter of Ocean;
> And the wave runs in the beach-groove:
> "Eleanor, ἑλέναυς and ἑλέπτολις!"
>   And poor old Homer blind, blind, as a bat,
> Ear, ear for the sea-surge, murmur of old men's voices:
> "Let her go back to the ships,
> Back among Grecian faces, lest evil come on our own,
> Evil and further evil, and a curse cursed on our children,
> Moves, yes she moves like a goddess
> And has the face of a god
>   and the voice of Schoeney's daughters,
> And doom goes with her in walking,
> Let her go back to the ships,

back among Grecian voices."
And by the beach-run, Tyro,
Twisted arms of the sea-god,
Lithe sinews of water, gripping her, cross-hold,
And the blue-gray glass of the wave tents them,
Glare azure of water, cold-welter, close cover.
Quiet sun-tawny sand-stretch,
The gulls broad out their wings,
    nipping between the splay feathers;
Snipe come for their bath,
    bend out their wing-joints,
Spread wet wings to the sun-film,
And by Scios,
    to left of the Naxos passage,
Naviform rock overgrown,
    algæ cling to its edge,
There is a wine-red glow in the shallows,
    a tin flash in the sun-dazzle.

And here Pound comes to the myth-narrative. This is a story from Ovid (the Roman descendant of the myth tradition that passed through the Homeric hymns to Pindar and Baccyliades to the Greek tragic poets). It's one of those stories that must have derived from the physical look of a place, in this case "naviform rock / overgrown with algae." A small island that looked like a ship, from which grew the story of the kidnapping of Dionysus. Pirates stopping for water found the boy-god and seized him, thinking to sell him into slavery. And the god appeared in the boy, accompanied by his panthers, and covered the ships with his vines through "god-sleight," as the narrator of the story, an old sailor named Acoetes tells it, and turned the sailors into fish. It is a cautionary tale about messing with the god or pirating the fertility of the earth, told by the old sailor as a sort of inset Browningesque dramatic monologue:

The ship landed in Scios,
　　men wanting spring-water,
And by the rock-pool a young boy loggy with vine-must,
　　"To Naxos? Yes, we'll take you to Naxos,
Cum' along lad." "Not that way!"
"Aye, that way is Naxos."
　　And I said: "It's a straight ship."
And an ex-convict out of Italy
　　knocked me into the fore-stays,
(He was wanted for manslaughter in Tuscany)
　　And the whole twenty against me,
Mad for a little slave money.
　　And they took her out of Scios
And off her course . . .
　　And the boy came to, again, with the racket,
And looked out over the bows,
　　and to eastward, and to the Naxos passage.
God-sleight then, god-sleight:
　　Ship stock fast in sea-swirl,
Ivy upon the oars, King Pentheus,
　　grapes with no seed but sea-foam,
Ivy in scupper-hole.
Aye, I, Acœtes, stood there,
　　and the god stood by me,
Water cutting under the keel,
Sea-break from stern forrards,
　　wake running off from the bow,
And where was gunwale, there now was vine-trunk,
And tenthril where cordage had been,
　　grape-leaves on the rowlocks,
Heavy vine on the oarshafts,
And, out of nothing, a breathing,
　　hot breath on my ankles,

Beasts like shadows in glass,
    a furred tail upon nothingness.
Lynx-purr, and heathery smell of beasts,
    where tar smell had been,
Sniff and pad-foot of beasts,
    eye-glitter out of black air.
The sky overshot, dry, with no tempest,
Sniff and pad-foot of beasts,
    fur brushing my knee-skin,
Rustle of airy sheaths,
    dry forms in the æther.
And the ship like a keel in ship-yard,
    slung like an ox in smith's sling,
Ribs stuck fast in the ways,
    grape-cluster over pin-rack,
    void air taking pelt.
Lifeless air become sinewed,
    feline leisure of panthers,
Leopards sniffing the grape shoots by scupper-hole,
Crouched panthers by fore-hatch,
And the sea blue-deep about us,
    green-ruddy in shadows,
And Lyæus: "From now, Acœtes, my altars,
Fearing no bondage,
    fearing no cat of the wood,
Safe with my lynxes,
    feeding grapes to my leopards,
Olibanum is my incense,
    the vines grow in my homage."

The back-swell now smooth in the rudder-chains,
Black snout of a porpoise
    where Lycabs had been,

Fish-scales on the oarsmen.
    And I worship.
I have seen what I have seen.
    When they brought the boy I said:
"He has a god in him,
    though I do not know which god."
And they kicked me into the fore-stays.
I have seen what I have seen:
    Medon's face like the face of a dory,
Arms shrunk into fins. And you, Pentheus,
Had as well listen to Tiresias, and to Cadmus,
or your luck will go out of you.
Fish-scales over groin muscles,
lynx-purr amid sea . . .

That's one story coming up out of the flux, the metamorphoses
that Ovid described, and gazing into the sea, he conjures another:

And of a later year,
    pale in the wine-red algæ,
If you will lean over the rock,
    the coral face under wave-tinge,
Rose-paleness under water-shift,
    Ileuthyeria, fair Dafne of sea-bords,
The swimmer's arms turned to branches,
Who will say in what year,
    fleeing what band of tritons,
The smooth brows, seen, and half seen,
    now ivory stillness.

And this finishes the middle of the poem and returns us at the end
to the opening theme:

And So-shu churned in the sea, So-shu also,
　　　using the long moon for a churn-stick . . .
Lithe turning of water,
　　　sinews of Poseidon,
Black azure and hyaline,
　　　glass wave over Tyro,
Close cover, unstillness,
　　　bright welter of wave-cords,
Then quiet water,
　　　quiet in the buff sands,
Sea-fowl stretching wing-joints,
　　　splashing in rock-hollows and sand-hollows
In the wave-runs by the half-dune;
Glass-glint of wave in the tide-rips against sunlight,
　　　pallor of Hesperus,
Grey peak of the wave,
　　　wave, colour of grape's pulp,

Olive grey in the near,
　　　far, smoke grey of the rock-slide,
Salmon-pink wings of the fish-hawk
　　　cast grey shadows in water,
The tower like a one-eyed great goose
　　　cranes up out of the olive-grove,

And we have heard the fauns chiding Proteus
　　　in the smell of hay under the olive-trees,
And the frogs singing against the fauns
　　　in the half-light.
And . . .

In this case right relation to nature is, it would seem, an eye to beauty and an imagination open to the myth-world.

HORACE

7. Horace published—I am a little hazy about what constituted publication during the reign of Caesar Augustus—four books of poems that have come down to us as odes. Horace himself called his poems *carmina*, "songs" in Latin. Later editors—probably in the Alexandrian period—called them *odes*, "songs" in Greek, but the poems were completely unrelated to the kind of formal, celebratory odes that Pindar and Baccyliades wrote. So later poets and historians tended to distinguish between the formal, or Pindaric, ode, and the informal and Horation ode. John Milton's "On the Morning of Christ's Nativity" is a formal ode. Pablo Neruda's "To a Watermelon" is an informal ode. The odes of Keats, the middle- and late-eighteenth-century odes by poets you may or may not have read or heard of—Mark Akenside, William Collins, Thomas Gray, William Cowper, Charlotte Smith—are probably mixed cases. And Horace himself complicates the issue, because his books of songs include all sorts of poems, basically lyric poems on a wide range of subjects, that adapted the meters of early Greek poetry—of Sappho and Alcaeus—which got passed to the world through the schoolroom as odes.

Thus an Oxford University Press book on the ode by John Heath-Stubbs begins, "The term 'ode,' as applied to English poems, is, I suspect, a not infrequent source of puzzlement to the student." One English critic of the nineteenth century tried to settle the matter by saying that Horace's poems were not so much a genre as a flavor. Simplest to look at a couple of poems and at the way they passed into English. Early on in Horace's experiments with Greek meters, Rome received the news of the defeat of Mark Antony and the death of Cleopatra, a moment of Roman triumph, Horace wrote a poem, as if ripped from the headlines, that came to be called the Cleopatra ode:

At last the day has come for celebration,
For dancing and for drinking, bringing out
The couches with their images of gods
Adorned in preparation for the feast.

Before today it would have been wrong to call
For the festive Caecuban wine from the vintage bins,
It would have been wrong while that besotted queen,
With her vile gang of sick polluted creatures,

Crazed with hope and drunk with her past successes,
Was planning the death and destruction of the empire.
But, comrades, she came to and sobered up
When not one ship, almost, of all her fleet

Escaped unburned, and Caesar saw to it
That she was restored from the madness to a state
Of realistic terror. The way a hawk
Chases a frightened dove or as a hunter

Chases a hare across the snowy steppes,
His galleys chased this fleeing queen, intending
To put the monster prodigy into chains
And bring her back to Rome. But she desired

A nobler fate than that; she did not seek
To hide her remnant fleet in a secret harbor;
Nor did she, like a woman, quail with fear
At the thought of what the dagger does.

She grew more fierce as she beheld her death.
Bravely, as if unmoved, she looked upon
The ruins of her palace; bravely reached out,
And touched the poison snakes, and picked them up,

And handled them, and held them to her so
Her heart might drink its fill of their black venom.
In truth—no abject woman she—she scorned
In triumph to be brought in galleys unqueened

Across the seas to Rome to be a show.

The striking thing about the poem, of course, is that it begins in what seems like patriotic gloating and ends in something like a celebration not of Roman victory but of the grandeur of the Egyptian queen's pride and defiance. So it is indeed a praise poem, but it celebrates the vanquished, not the victor. The first two stanzas do the Pindaric celebrating, the middle of the poem tells the story of Octavian's success, and then veers, at the end of the fifth stanza in David Ferry's translation, to Cleopatra's point of view. A three-part structure of almost sonnetlike proportions, with the turn about two-thirds of the way through. Commentators have attended to the meter: this is an epic subject, but it doesn't get the treatment Horace's contemporary Varus would have given it—a full-fledged Homeric hexameter. He writes it in the meter of a love song by Sappho.

8 . You would not think this poem, so rooted in its circumstances, would have suggested a way forward for the ode, but it did, for at least one poet. Andrew Marvell, a poet of Puritan sympathies politically, mimicked Horace's method—and the poised irony of his means—in a poem about Oliver Cromwell, the Puritan military leader in the English civil wars of the mid-seventeenth century that led to the arrest and beheading of the king, Charles I, and the establishment of the Commonwealth with Cromwell as its Lord Protector. After disposing of Charles, Cromwell set about subjugating the Roman Catholic Irish with his Puritan troops. Marvell entitled his poem "An Horatian Ode Upon Cromwell's Return from Ireland."

Horace had suggested an ironic treatment of the praise poem and
Marvell jumped on it. I won't reproduce the whole poem here. You
can find it easily. But it begins like this:

> The forward youth that would appear
> Must now forsake his Muses dear,
>> Nor in the shadows sing
>> His numbers languishing.
>
> 'Tis time to leave the books in dust,
> And oil th' unused armour's rust,
>> Removing from the wall
>> The corslet of the hall.
>
> So restless Cromwell could not cease
> In the inglorious arts of peace,
>> But thorough advent'rous war
>> Urged his active star.

Looks like a straightforward call to heroic arms, if you do not read
too closely. But very shortly one notices the way the active man
is "forward" and wants to "appear," and the slightly comic Don
Quixote–ish idea of dusting off and oiling up the armor, and that
phrase "the inglorious arts of peace." And one would notice also the
way the meter of the poem gives a slightly mocking edge to its hero-
ics. Two lines of tetrameter, followed by two lines of trimeter, four
beats and then three, expand contract, and lock the lines together
with a jangling couplet rhyme. It ends like this:

> But thou, the war's and fortune's son,
> March indefatigably on;
>> And for the last effect
>> Still keep thy sword erect;

Besides the force it has to fright
The spirits of the shady night,
    The same arts that did gain
    A pow'r, must it maintain.

This echoes the truism about living by the sword and might remind some readers of the moral world of *Macbeth*. You can feel the way "the spirits of the shady night" might lead a man who has hazarded his fortune on power and so made enemies to tighten his grip on his sword.

I see the structure of the poem as having five parts—the introductory stanzas, the portrait of Cromwell and the question of the morality and legality of the war (which assumes blandly that power is right), the portrait of Charles's execution in the middle of the poem—an extraordinary bit of writing, and then the account of the bloody Irish campaign, and then the conclusion. Orderly, deft, judicious, skeptical. And suggests what might have been an unexpected direction for the prayer and the praise poem, that it could evolve into an instrument of assessment.

9. Here is another kind of poem by Horace that came to be associated with the ode. The translation is mine:

You talk very well about Inachus
And how Codrus died for the city,
And the offspring of old Aeacus
And the fighting at sacred Ilium under the walls.

But on the price of Chian wine,
And the question of who's going to warm it,
Under whose roof it will be drunk,
And when my bones will come unfrozen, you are mute.

Boy, let's drink to the new moon's silver
And drink to the middle of the night, and drink
To good Murena with three glasses
Or with nine. Nine, says the madman poet

Whom the muses love, Three
Should do nicely for a party,
Says the even-tempered grace who holds
Her naked sisters by the hands

And disapproves altogether of brawling.
But what I want's to rave. Why is the flute
From Phrygia silent? Why are the lyre
And the reed pipe hanging on the wall?

Oh, how I hate a pinching hand.
Scatter the roses! Let jealous old Lycus
Listen to our pandemonium,
And also the pretty neighbor he's not up to.

Rhoda loves your locks, Telephus.
She thinks they glisten like the evening star.
As for me, I'm stuck on Glycera:
With a love that smolders in me like slow fire.

This poem is written in a meter modeled on a Greek poet, Ascle-
piades, who lived about two hundred years before Horace's time. It
seems to be a song meter, and he uses it in several of the odes when
he wants to evoke the idea of a wild party. People who could read his
poems at the time when Latin was a living language always comment on the combination of freedom and restraint in his poems,
or spontaneity and elegance, thought to be incompatible qualities,
because elegance takes time and care. The formal radiance of this
poem, one has to assume, comes from that paradoxical mix. And it's
there thematically. The formal development of the poem involves

several turns. There is in the first stanza the rejection of Roman gravitas and of the solemn genealogies that characterize the Pindaric ode. And in the second stanza the turn instead to preparations for the party, and in the third stanza, the elaboration of that theme in a more galloping rhythm, an address to his friend and an intensifying of the theme. And in the next stanza—in the middle of the poem—the debate between license and restraint. Horace is famously the poet of sensible restraint as a kind of practical hedonism. And so the next two stanzas are the next turn, lines for which he is famous possibly because centuries of schoolboys had to translate them under strict supervision. He wants to rave. He wants roses scattered. And then the social turn again to his friend, not to a declaration of erotic desire exactly, as in the address to a lover, but to a more sociable and conspiratorial relation to it, so that the poem doesn't so much model eros as it does friendship. And it ends with a kind of confession. He wants to rave because he's been driven wild. That fire does not represent freedom. A complicated and grown-up poem in which the expressiveness of the prosody and the formal development of the themes work together strikingly.

10 . For posterity a mix of casualness, elegance, and moderation came to characterize what people thought of as the "lesser ode." Ben Jonson's "Inviting a Friend to Supper" is the illustrious example of the English Horatian mode. Horace, in fact, shows up in the poem, which scholars say borrows a few lines from the epigrams of Martial. It connects to the ode as a praise poem because it models sociability and because it contains a petition. It's an invitation. I won't reproduce all of it here. You can find it easily. But look at the beginning:

> Tonight, grave sir, both my poor house and I
> Do equally desire your company.

Not that we think us worthy such a guest,
    But that your worth will dignify our feast
With those that come, whose grace may make that seem
    Something, which else could hope for no esteem.
It is the fair acceptance, sir, creates
    The entertainment perfect, not the cates.

Casual elegance. Jonson does it with iambic pentameter couplet, rhymed. The pentameter gives a kind of suavity to what sounds like spoken English, the couplet form gives a kind of complementarity to the address—"grave sir" and "my poor house and I" are the antitheses—and Jonson is able to tune up or tune down the effect of the rhyme by enjambing it or not. The rhymes get particularly strong just when Horace and wine show up:

Digestive cheese, and fruit there sure will be,
    But that which most doth take my Muse and me
Is a pure cup of rich Canary wine,
    Which is the Mermaid's now, but shall be mine;
Of which had Horace or Anacreon tasted,
    Their lives, as do their lines, till now have lasted.

These poems, you could almost call them anti-ode odes, have been a model for many kinds of poetry that praise poetry and the private life by not being about important subjects. It is work very much like the sensibility of Frank O'Hara and other poets of the New York School, like—in general—the informality of American poets in the postwar generation as they responded to and against the solemnity of high modernism.

The middle of Jonson's poem treats a menu as a litany, and, having begun with a petition, it ends with a promise:

Nor shall our cups make any guilty men,
    But at our parting we will be as when
We innocently met. No simple word
    That shall be uttered at our mirthful board
Shall make us sad next morning, or affright
    The liberty that we'll enjoy tonight.

Jonson's liberty and Horace's slow-burning fire. Mirroring opposites of the way the small ode establishes value.

EDMUND SPENSER AND THE HIGH RENAISSANCE

11 . *Ornamental form in the Renaissance:* Let's look at fertility and the ode from another angle. Edmund Spenser's "Epithalamion" is a particular kind of ode—a wedding song. I don't know what his models were. The great classical epithalamion is Catullus's, which was apparently an imitation of one by Sappho, but Catullus wasn't available to Spenser. The formal imagination in the Elizabethan period—think of their love of intricate designs. The epithalamion is twenty-four stanzas long, with a gorgeous, echoing rhyme scheme. Its form mimes a wedding ceremony. It begins with a processional and the classic praising of and calling down blessings from the appropriate gods and goddesses. Here's the interesting thing about the structure. The bride's arrival at the altar occurs in the exact center of the poem. The last eleven stanzas follow her away from that moment—so that the first stanza echoes the last, the second stanza the second to last, and so on. It's organized as a series of concentric circles around the central event, vibrations that mimic the sound motif in the repeated refrain: "that all the woods may answer and your echo ring." An example of making a spatial form out of the temporal form of the poem.

JOHN DONNE AND
THE MEDITATIVE LYRIC

12 . *Form and the meditative lyric:* Probably these seventeenth-century devotional poems—rooted in English Christian prayer, in what I've come to think of as Protestant interiority (the need to examine the condition of one's soul to see if one is saved or damned, to know the presence or the absence of God's blessing)—are the implicit models for the entire development of English and American poetry. I think the romantic ode and much of the interiority of twentieth-century English language poetry begins here. There is a famous study of the origins of structure—of the work of the formal imagination—in the poetry of these years. Partly—famously—it begins with the transfer of subject from the Italianate love sonnet to the devotional sonnet. In a lot of the sonnets there is a certain amount of bravado play with rhetoric and with argument. In others, as in the great dramatic soliloquies of the same era, there is something like the invention of a profound and complex interiority, a fully rounded psychology of the person. But that new interiority is married in these poems to traditions of Christian prayer or prayer-behavior, which took the form of meditation. The classic study of this tradition is Louis Martz, *The Poetry of Meditation.*

13 . First of all, the aims of meditation.

> "Meditation, which we treat of, is nothing els but a diligent and forcible application of the understanding, to seeke, and knowe, and as it were to taste some divine matter."
>
> *(Richard Gibbons, 1611)*

> "Meditation: in which our mynd, not as a flie, by a simple musing, nor yet as a locust, to eat and be filled, but as a sacred Bee

flies amongst the flowres of the holy mysteries, to extract from them the honie of Divine Love."

(St. Francis De Sales, 1616)

14. These come from the numerous treatises in the period on how to meditate, and they all propose in various ways a formal order for the practice that, as Martz points out, is reflected in the organization of devotional poetry. Not surprising, when you think about it. They were all priests. They were educated in this spiritual tradition. The method entailed "a regular sequence of beginning, middle, and end: preparatory steps; meditation proper, divided into 'points'; followed by 'colloquies,' in which the soul speaks intimately with God and expresses its affections, resolutions, thanksgivings and petitions." The preparatory prayer—like the addresses to the muse or to memory or to gods and goddesses in classical poetry—is "a short simple prayer for grace in the proper performance of the exercise."

15. Brief aside. What if there is no one or nothing to pray to? Consider Rilke, at the beginning of the *Duino Elegies:* "Who, if I cried out, would hear me among the host of angels?"

16. Aside on the aside. Rilke's elegies are one of the great modernist suites of odes. The term *elegy* in German literature refers to the meter in which the poems were written—the classical elegiac meter of alternating ten and twelve syllable lines. Studying beginning, middle, and ending in this tradition would be another way into the work of the formal imagination in romantic and modernist odes. A place to start would be one of Goethe's *Roman Elegies* and then a couple of poems by Hölderlin, his "Bread and Wine" or "Homecoming," and then one of the *Duino Elegies.* What they aim at, how they propose beginning, middle, and end. Useful book: Theodore Ziolkowski, *The Classical German Elegy.*

17. Back to the seventeenth century. After the introductory prayer, the meditator was asked to perform—here's Martz: "the famous 'composition of place, seeing the spot'—a practice of enormous importance for religious poetry." And he quotes the English Jesuit Gibbons on the need to see "the places where the things we meditate on were wrought, by imagining our selves to be really present at those places; which we must endeavor to represent so lively, as though we saw them indeed with our corporeal eyes; which to performe well, it will help us much to behould before-hande some Image wherein that myistery is represented."

18. This is the work of imagination. Martz tracks it from the spiritual practice of the metaphysical poets to Coleridge. Here is Coleridge in the *Literaria Biographia:* "The poet, described in *ideal* perfection, brings the whole soul of man into the activity, with the subordination of its faculties to each other, according to their relative worth and dignity. He diffuses a tone and spirit of unity, that blends and, as it were, *fuses,* each into each, by that synthetic and magical power, to which we have exclusively appropriated the name of imagination." And from Coleridge to Wallace Stevens, in this passage from "Credences of Summer":

> Three times the concentrated self takes hold, three times
> The thrice concentrated self, having possessed
>
> The object, grips it in savage scrutiny.
> Once to make captive, once to subjugate,
> Or yield to subjugation, once to proclaim

The meaning of the capture, this hard prize,
Fully made, fully apparent, fully found.

19. The treatises track the form of meditation to their understanding of what they called the three powers of the soul: memory, or imagemaking power; understanding; and will. They even argued "that the three powers of the soul were analogous to the Trinity, and that through the integration of this trinity within man he might come to know and feel in himself the operation of the higher Trinity." It made a kind of map or guide to the inward journey toward communion with the good.

20. An instance:

Good Friday, 1613. Riding Westward
Let man's soul be a sphere, and then, in this,
Th' intelligence that moves, devotion is,
And as the other spheres, by being grown
Subject to foreign motions, lose their own,
And being by others hurried every day,
Scarce in a year their natural form obey;
Pleasure or business, so, our souls admit
For their first mover and are whirled by it,
Hence is't, that I am carried toward the West
This day, when my soul's form bends towards the East.

Martz notices this careful ten-line setup and the way it corresponds to "composition of place" at the outset of meditation. From our point of view, it seems to mix the two initiating motives of this kind of poem—desire and discrepancy. It's about wanting to be in right relation to the suffering god and the holy day and it's about heading in the wrong direction, which initiates one of Donne's most famous metaphors as the dramatic awakening of thought. In the Ptolemaic universe, subspheres and retrograde motion were required to maintain that all movements in the heaven's consisted of perfect circles.

And there is something poignant in the connection between this theme and the poem's form—the way couplet rhyme, which should express unison, harmony, feels jarring since the speaker feels that he, whether the heavens are or not, is out of tune. Next comes the powerful middle:

> There I should see a Sun, by rising, set,
> And by that setting endless day beget;
> But that Christ on this cross did rise and fall,
> Sin had eternally benighted all.
> Yet dare I almost be glad I do not see
> That spectacle of too much weight for me.
> Who sees God's face, that is self-life, must die,
> What a death were it then to see God die;
> It made his own lieutenant, Nature, shrink;
> It made his footstool crack, and the sun wink,
> Could I behold those hands that span the poles,
> And tune all spheres at once, pierced with those holes?
> Could I behold the endless height which is
> Zenith to us, and to our antipodes,
> Humbled below us? Or that blood which is
> The seat of all our souls, if not of His,
> Make dirt of dust, or that flesh which was worn
> By God, for his apparel, ragg'd and torn?
> If on these things I durst not look, durst I
> Upon his miserable mother cast mine eye,
> Who was God's partner here, and furnished thus
> Half of that sacrifice which ransomed us?

This is the middle, where the meditation, or the praise poem, or the lyric, or for that matter the elegy does its work of transformation. It's easy to feel in this poem the movement of the three-part structure though one might want to describe it a little differently from the way Louis Martz does. Donne, it would seem, begins with his intelligence. The work of the middle of the poem is calling his mind to the story of the Crucifixion in a way that moves the heart. It's also striking that implicit in the middle of this poem, as in the Greek odes, is the story of a god, in this case the Christian man-god, and the Christian story that human behavior called God down out of heaven to submit to torture and death as a form of ransom in that age of animal sacrifice. It's a story about a transformation and vividly taking it into the understanding is the poem's work of transformation. At which point, we come to the third part, which is prayer:

> Though these things, as I ride, be from my eye,
> They're present yet unto my memory,
> For that looks towards them, and thou lookst towards me,
> O Savior, as thou hang'st upon the tree.
> I turn my back to thee but to receive
> Corrections, till they mercies bid thee leave.
> O think me worth thine anger; punish me;
> Burn off my rusts and my deformity;
> Restore thine image so much, by thy grace,
> That thou may'st know me, and I'll turn my face.

The three-part structure, the sometimes enjambed and sometimes not play of the two-line couplets, it's easy to see this as the formal work the poem is doing, and, of course, they don't account for the surprising ways the metaphors develop, or the play between the torn body and the god-face, or the arrival of the poem at the suffering mother, or—however repellent to a secular reader the theology might seem—the way the mix of intellectual invention, of wit, really, and rhythmic force, and intense feeling, give the poem such a grave beauty.

I am trying to make a sinuous, Nabokovian path through this thicket of literary history. Here is where I walk around the poets of the middle and late eighteenth century who revived the ode.

ROMANTIC ODE AND ROMANTIC LYRIC

21. Odes, Horation and Pindaric, got written throughout the seventeenth century and were revived big-time in the latter part of the eighteenth. There are books on this history, and some very good poems. I want to skip ahead to the romantic ode and to the early-nineteenth-century version of the meditative lyric. There's a critical touchstone for these poems, an essay entitled "Style and Structure in the Greater Romantic Lyric," published by M. H. Abrams a half a century ago. Abrams describes a typical movement in the poems of the period: that they often begin by setting a scene—from our point of view the initiatory stirring of desire or disturbance. "Five years have passed," Wordsworth begins "Tintern Abbey." "Thou still unravished bride of quietness," Keats begins the "Ode on a Grecian Urn." Abrams observes that the poems then move inward, taking speaker and reader on a reflective journey, "a varied but integral process," he writes, "of memory, thought, anticipation, and feeling," and that the poems tend to end where they began with some sense that, "on arrival, the place where they began has been altered." Later critics would find a pattern of conflict, dealing with the conflict, resolving the conflict way too pat. But some notion of disturbance, a turn inward to explore its source or meaning, and a reorientation toward it corresponds in interesting ways to the movement of seventeenth-century poems. It also connects to what Hölderlin described as "in-

nerlichkeit," the vast interior sea of human inwardness, to navigate which he understood to be the task of poets.

22. Thinking of Hölderlin's "Der Spaziergang." The movement of several of his poems involves taking a walk, or climbing a mountain to a place where the mind can get hold of the vista onto human life. And this connects to the topographical poems of the English seventeenth and eighteenth centuries that were said to have helped form the impulse of the romantic lyric.

23. Here's an instance of this inward journey. One of the great ones, I think, Coleridge's "Frost at Midnight":

> The Frost performs its secret ministry,
> Unhelped by any wind. The owlet's cry
> Came loud—and hark, again! loud as before.
> The inmates of my cottage, all at rest,
> Have left me to that solitude, which suits
> Abstruser musings: save that at my side
> My cradled infant slumbers peacefully.
> 'Tis calm indeed! so calm, that it disturbs
> And vexes meditation with its strange
> And extreme silentness. Sea, hill, and wood,
> This populous village! Sea, and hill, and wood,
> With all the numberless goings-on of life,
> Inaudible as dreams! the thin blue flame
> Lies on my low-burnt fire, and quivers not;
> Only that film, which fluttered on the grate,
> Still flutters there, the sole unquiet thing.
> Methinks, its motion in this hush of nature
> Gives it dim sympathies with me who live,

Making it a companionable form,
Whose puny flaps and freaks the idling Spirit
By its own moods interprets, every where
Echo or mirror seeking of itself,
And makes a toy of Thought.

               But O! how oft,
How oft, at school, with most believing mind,
Presageful, have I gazed upon the bars,
To watch that fluttering stranger ! and as oft
With unclosed lids, already had I dreamt
Of my sweet birth-place, and the old church-tower,
Whose bells, the poor man's only music, rang
From morn to evening, all the hot Fair-day,
So sweetly, that they stirred and haunted me
With a wild pleasure, falling on mine ear
Most like articulate sounds of things to come!
So gazed I, till the soothing things, I dreamt,
Lulled me to sleep, and sleep prolonged my dreams!
And so I brooded all the following morn,
Awed by the stern preceptor's face, mine eye
Fixed with mock study on my swimming book:
Save if the door half opened, and I snatched
A hasty glance, and still my heart leaped up,
For still I hoped to see the stranger's face,
Townsman, or aunt, or sister more beloved,
My play-mate when we both were clothed alike!

           Dear Babe, that sleepest cradled by my side,
Whose gentle breathings, heard in this deep calm,
Fill up the interspersèd vacancies
And momentary pauses of the thought!
My babe so beautiful! it thrills my heart
With tender gladness, thus to look at thee,

And think that thou shalt learn far other lore,
And in far other scenes! For I was reared
In the great city, pent 'mid cloisters dim,
And saw nought lovely but the sky and stars.
But thou, my babe! shalt wander like a breeze
By lakes and sandy shores, beneath the crags
Of ancient mountain, and beneath the clouds,
Which image in their bulk both lakes and shores
And mountain crags: so shalt thou see and hear
The lovely shapes and sounds intelligible
Of that eternal language, which thy God
Utters, who from eternity doth teach
Himself in all, and all things in himself.
Great universal Teacher! he shall mould
Thy spirit, and by giving make it ask.

    Therefore all seasons shall be sweet to thee,
Whether the summer clothe the general earth
With greenness, or the redbreast sit and sing
Betwixt the tufts of snow on the bare branch
Of mossy apple-tree, while the nigh thatch
Smokes in the sun-thaw; whether the eave-drops fall
Heard only in the trances of the blast,
Or if the secret ministry of frost
Shall hang them up in silent icicles,
Quietly shining to the quiet moon.

Four blank verse stanzas, and the habitual three-pulse form. The first stanza is the meditative setup, the composition of place in Louis Martz's terms. The last stanza is the conclusion. The remarkable middle stanzas—in Abrams's terms, the inward journey—is worth attending to closely.

    Think of it this way. Their culture and traditions gave the Greek writers of ode their form and the content of their form. The vocative address at the beginning of their poems comes to them from their sense of the powers that govern nature and the mind. They knew what divinities to solicit for what purpose because they'd received a mythology, which is to say a sophisticated narrative elaboration of an animist, polytheist sense of the universe. The middle parts of their poems, the storytelling that dips into the wealth of mythic lore, belong to their sense, an oral tradition's sense of the archival and genealogical function of poetry. And the conclusion, the petition, came from an understanding of power relations in their social world. You ask favors of power and give it in return the gift of praise and, if you are a poet, of the immortality that praise confers.

The Christian poets of the seventeenth century had a similar map, a monotheist (more or less) map of whom to address, a process of bringing the faculties of the mind to bear, based on medieval understandings of the functions of the mind, and a theologically appropriate form of petition.

My sense is that beginning in the late eighteenth century in European cultures, poets were beginning not to have such a map. They understood that the deities they were invoking were a literary fiction. And what exactly they were trying to get in right relation to was often not very clear to them either. What Wordsworth and Coleridge had was not the Aristotelian categories of mental activities so much, perhaps, as the developing tradition of British empiricism, the mind described by John Locke and David Hartley was some combination of constructive and impressionable, and knowledge was derived not so much from reason but from the association of ideas rising from sense experience—"the mighty world of eye and ear," Wordsworth would call it in "Tintern Abbey," "both what they half create, and what perceive." I imagine that this notion was liberating, and intended to be liberating, the tabula rasa from which a new look at things could occur.

But the poet, as a result, had no map for the interior journey for what was to be the transformative middle of the meditative lyric. Or at least this would be a place from which to look at the way the formal imagination works in the poems of this period.

To watch this work in "Frost at Midnight," you need one piece of information. Fires were the main source of heat in the house of this period, in stoves or in grates, and people must have spent a good deal of time staring into embers. And there was a tradition in English folklore—Coleridge made reference to it in a footnote to the poem—that if you looked hard into the embers of a fire, if an absent friend was going to visit you, you would see that friend. If there is a goddess invoked at the beginning of this poem, it is midnight quiet and the image of the fire at the end of the first stanza, which makes "the puny flaps and freaks" of the fire a companion spirit—even a tutelary spirit—for the mind—"the idling spirit"—which—notice—is seeking itself. It is itself, he says, the object of the hunt.

You'd have to know the poets of the late eighteenth century, especially Cowper, I imagine, to know how new this is, but it's new. Notice the transition. The flutter in the grate reminds the speaker of his childhood. Biographical note. Coleridge was born into a large boisterous family. His father was a vicar and a schoolmaster in a small town. When his father died, he was sent to school as a scholarship boy in London. This is the source of the aching homesickness that the poem evokes. By association and the work of memory the fire in the grate returns him to childhood and his village life and the fires he stared into, looking for signs of a visitor, who is called, interestingly, the "stranger." The longing for the stranger returns him to his village, and the village bells, a sound associated with a grand future. Then he tells us he remembers falling asleep in that dreamy state and waking to another schoolday and himself a boy pretending to study and yearning for, half expecting the arrival of "the stranger," who is not imagined to be a stranger, but someone known from his former world—a townsman, or closer still an aunt, and closer still a sister. This is something like what Freud called "regression in the service of the ego." Not just a sister, but "a sister more beloved, / my playmate when we both were clothed alike." He's gone back before gender.

And that makes the transition to the sleeping infant, whose breathing has been filling "the momentary pauses" in what he calls "thought," which up to this point we would probably call reverie. And that leads him—Coleridge was twenty-seven when he wrote this poem, a young man and a very new father—back to his orphaned London childhood and forward to his imagination of his son's very different childhood in close contact with the natural world, which is, he says, "that eternal language which thy God utters." And then at the end of the paragraph we get the invocation to the deity, Nature's God, the "great universal Teacher" who he says—he's addressing the baby—"shall mold / Thy spirit and by giving make it ask." So the idea of petition emerges at the end, not as an obligation but a gift.

And then comes the ending. It's interesting that the end of the poem is not about union with the great Universal teacher. That union permits the future in which the child and vicariously the speaker will be in communion with the natural world, which is evoked in a few lines of the kind that Coleridge was brilliant at and didn't write enough of—"while the nigh thatch / Smokes in the sun-thaw" is stunning and as near to union with nature as descriptive language can get. But the poem doesn't end there either. It seems intent on the return that Abrams describes to the opening situation when "the eave-drops fall" from the roof edge or "the secret ministry of frost / Shall hang them up in silent icicles, Quietly shining to the quiet moon."

All the commentators on the poem I've looked at connect the ici-cles reflecting the moonlight back to the moon to the mind seeking an "echo or mirror" of itself at the end of the first stanza. Something like Emerson's transparent eyeball (which could have come from his read-ing of this poem). But my interest isn't in interpreting the poem here, but to look at the way the ode structure is undergoing change. "Frost at Midnight" is my exemplary case, but it might have been "Tintern Abbey" or the more grand-scale odes like Wordsworth's "Intimations of Immortality" or Coleridge's "Dejection." Inspections you can make for yourself. I wanted to call attention to this rivery movement in the verse of this period because it tracks a different sense of mind that anticipates both surrealism and the representation of the mind by stream of consciousness in fiction. It represents thought as something nearer to what we think of as imagination, a proceeding by intuitions having to do with likeness, with mirroring and echoing, with an oscillation between thought and sensation, discursive and mimetic modes. The capacities of mind are here—memory, the consciousness with which we experience a present, the imagination through which we create a future, the resemblances—*"correspondences,"* Charles Baudelaire called them, by which we seem to sense meaning, but all the orderly priorities of the theologians are gone. And that opens the way to many tactics of development in the quest poems of the twentieth century and also to the tactics of a postmodern skepticism about meaning—Derrida enters here among others—that understand the movement of the mind not as something that has points of arrival, but as something that circulates through stations recurrent enough for memory to give it an identity with itself.

24. *Keats and Endings:* John Keats was twenty-five or twenty-six when he wrote his suite of six odes. They are perhaps the most studied and commented upon poems, after Shakespeare's sonnets, in the English language. Here is a small exercise. Take an afternoon and reread Wordsworth's "Tintern Abbey" and "Immortality Ode" and maybe one other Wordsworth ode or the first book of *The Prelude* and Coleridge's "Frost at Midnight" and his "Dejection: An Ode" and then read—written about twenty-two years later, the five Keats odes—"Psyche," "Melancholy," "Nightingale," "Grecian Urn," and "To Autumn." I don't know if you will share my experience of them, but I found that when reading them in that order, the striking thing

about the Keats poems was that they seemed so beautifully finished and a little old-fashioned. It struck me that he had perfected
the form of the eighteenth-century ode and—except for "Ode to
a Nightingale"—had not really absorbed the challenging experiments with the interior journey of the poem that Wordsworth and
Coleridge had been working out. I don't mean to criticize them for
not doing something they weren't trying to do. They are gorgeous
poems, of course, and formally radiant.

Look at "Psyche," the earliest to be written: six stanzas, which
divide neatly into three sets of two, beginning, middle, and end. The
first stanza is twelve lines, the second eleven, the third twelve, the
fourth fourteen, the last two eight and ten lines. They have the irregularity that the ode form licensed, a mild irregularity, and within
the stanzas are varying line lengths, mostly iambic pentameter lines
with a scattering of more songlike dimeter and trimeter lines and a
varied rhyme patterning. It could hardly be more neatly done, and
it's a poem self-conscious about the antiquity of the ode. It begins by
addressing the muse and claiming her as his audience for a description of a vision of Psyche in the arms of Eros:

> They lay calm-breathing on the bedded grass:
>   Their arms embraced, and their pinions too,
>   Their lips touched not, but had not bid adieu;
> As if disjoined by soft-handed slumber
> And ready still past kisses to outnumber

(On the subject of odes: surely the passage in Whitman's "Song
of Myself" about the poet's erotic relation to his soul is a denim-and-
flannel version of the preceding scene in Keats:

> I mind how once we lay such a transparent summer morning,
> How you settled your head athwart my hips and gently
>   turned over upon me,

And parted the shirt from my bosom-bone and plunged your
   tongue to my bare-script heart
And reached till you felt my beard, and reached till you held
   my feet.

It's the same allegorizing impulse of the eighteenth-century ode.
And on the subject of Eros and Psyche, you should take a look at
what Robert Duncan does with it and with the ode form in "Poem
Beginning with a Line from Pindar.")

Of the poems that followed "Psyche," "Ode on Melancholy" and
"Ode on a Grecian Urn" and "To Autumn," each have an even tighter
formal arrangement. "Melancholy" is three ten-line stanzas with a
fixed rhyme scheme, ababcdecde: each stanza is a curtailed sonnet.
"Grecian Urn" uses the same stanza. It's five stanzas. It begins with
ode's personification and address: "Thou still unravish'd bride."
And ends with it: "Thou, silent form dost tease us out of thought."
And the journey in the middle through the landscape of the vase is
straightforward, a focused development of its central teasing idea.
And the great "To Autumn" is three eleven-line stanzas, even more
nearly a sequence of sonnets. Compared to them, the movement of
"Ode to a Nightingale" seems much more complex. The turnings of
mind from stanza to stanza are quite complicated. Take a look:

Ode to a Nightingale

1.

My heart aches, and a drowsy numbness pains
   My sense, as though of hemlock I had drunk,
Or emptied some dull opiate to the drains
   One minute past, and Lethe-wards had sunk:
'Tis not through envy of thy happy lot,
   But being too happy in thine happiness,—

That thou, light-winged Dryad of the trees,
   In some melodious plot
Of beechen green, and shadows numberless,
   Singest of summer in full-throated ease.

2.

O, for a draught of vintage! that hath been
   Cool'd a long age in the deep-delved earth,
Tasting of Flora and the country green,
   Dance, and Provencal song, and sunburnt mirth!
O for a beaker full of the warm South,
   Full of the true, the blushful Hippocrene,
    With beaded bubbles winking at the brim,
      And purple-stained mouth;
That I might drink, and leave the world unseen,
   And with thee fade away into the forest dim:

3.

Fade far away, dissolve, and quite forget
   What thou among the leaves hast never known,
The weariness, the fever, and the fret
   Here, where men sit and hear each other groan;
Where palsy shakes a few, sad, last gray hairs,
   Where youth grows pale, and spectre-thin, and dies;
    Where but to think is to be full of sorrow
      And leaden-eyed despairs,
Where Beauty cannot keep her lustrous eyes,
   Or new Love pine at them beyond to-morrow.

4.

Away! away! for I will fly to thee,
　Not charioted by Bacchus and his pards,
But on the viewless wings of Poesy,
　Though the dull brain perplexes and retards:
Already with thee! tender is the night,
　And haply the Queen-Moon is on her throne,
　　Cluster'd around by all her starry Fays;
　　　But here there is no light,
Save what from heaven is with the breezes blown
　Through verdurous glooms and winding mossy ways.

5.

I cannot see what flowers are at my feet,
　Nor what soft incense hangs upon the boughs,
But, in embalmed darkness, guess each sweet
　Wherewith the seasonable month endows
The grass, the thicket, and the fruit-tree wild;
　White hawthorn, and the pastoral eglantine;
　　Fast fading violets cover'd up in leaves;
　　　And mid-May's eldest child,
The coming musk-rose, full of dewy wine,
　The murmurous haunt of flies on summer eves.

6.

Darkling I listen; and, for many a time
　I have been half in love with easeful Death,
Call'd him soft names in many a mused rhyme,
　To take into the air my quiet breath;

Now more than ever seems it rich to die,
  To cease upon the midnight with no pain,
    While thou art pouring forth thy soul abroad
      In such an ecstasy!
Still wouldst thou sing, and I have ears in vain—
  To thy high requiem become a sod.

7.

Thou wast not born for death, immortal Bird!
  No hungry generations tread thee down;
  The voice I hear this passing night was heard
    In ancient days by emperor and clown:
Perhaps the self-same song that found a path
  Through the sad heart of Ruth, when, sick for home,
    She stood in tears amid the alien corn;
      The same that oft-times hath
Charm'd magic casements, opening on the foam
  Of perilous seas, in faery lands forlorn.

8.

Forlorn! the very word is like a bell
  To toil me back from thee to my sole self!
Adieu! the fancy cannot cheat so well
  As she is fam'd to do, deceiving elf.
Adieu! adieu! thy plaintive anthem fades
  Past the near meadows, over the still stream,
    Up the hill-side; and now 'tis buried deep
      In the next valley-glades:
Was it a vision, or a waking dream?
  Fled is that music:—Do I wake or sleep?

There are not quite numberless readings of where the bird's song—the longing for something in the bird's song—takes the poet in this poem. I'm not going to add to them here. From our point of view—trying to understand what has been the shape and impulse of the ode—the thing to notice is that it begins with an address to the bird that has been elicited by a paradoxical mix of fullness and emptiness in the bird's song. What seems the nightingale's pure happiness makes the speaker's heart ache. One might locate the whole history of the form here in this mix of desire, prayer, a sense of lack or loss, a devotional reverence. And then the poem takes us on an interior journey in which the poet comes to inhabit the world of the bird's song—"Already with thee! Tender is the night," the famous line goes—and then in stanza six comes to understand his desire as an ecstatic longing for death, or a longing for death while experiencing ecstasy. (One of my students called it "the rock star stanza"—think Jimi Hendrix, Janis Joplin, Kurt Cobain. Check out the elision between death and paradise in the disco songs evoked by D. A. Powell in his book *Tea*.) Keats had the reputation in the nineteenth century of being a sensuous poet but not a thinker. Now it would seem that an extraordinary complexity and subtlety of thinking about the nature of desire and imagination is packed into the seventh stanza, in which he begins to end the poem by addressing the bird again, which is no longer a summer bird but an idea about the immortality of art that puts us in touch with a desire that fuses a kind of existential homesickness with an imagination of other, more magical and perilous worlds. A compression of images that might work as a definition of the sublime. (Emily Dickinson read Keats and so did Rilke and Stevens.)

And then there is the end of the poem. If Keats did not reinvent the ode, he thought very hard in April and May of 1819 when he was writing these poems about how to end one. Traditionally they ended in a prayer or a solicitation of favor. The whole weight of literary expectation, of the consciously and unconsciously absorbed ideas that a writer has about how a poem should behave, would have—I would think, without reading through the history of the late-eighteenth-century poems in which the young Keats had soaked himself—been to arrive at some kind of sententious summing up, something like a moral precept or comforting truth about the relationship to the power addressed, and that seems to be what Keats was trying to imagine his way past. "Psyche" ends with an image of the ideal the poem courted:

> And there shall be for thee all soft delight
> That shadowy thought can win,
> A bright torch, and a casement ope at night,
> To let the warm Love in!

A subjunctive, a wish fulfilled in imagination (like the wish in the little lyric "Western Wind" and in Emily Dickinson's "Wild Nights"). If "Psyche" delivers the soul to love, "Melancholy" delivers it to melancholy, also in an almost allegorical image:

> Though seen of none save him whose strenuous tongue
> Can bust joy's grape against his palate fine;
> His soul shall taste the sadness of her might
> And be among her cloudy trophies hung.

They are both in their way moral summings up. In "Grecian Urn," Keats seems to have tried to evade the impulse by distancing it:

> Thou shalt remain, in midst of other woe,
> Than ours, a friend to man, to whom thou sayest,
> "Beauty is truth, truth beauty,"—that is all
> Ye know on earth, and all ye need to know.

And in this way the ending of "Nightingale" is particularly surprising. The first line returns the poet from the voyage. The next set of lines untwines the bird as a metaphor for fancy and the bird as a bird and says good-bye to them both and ends, emptied of the music that initiated the poem, with a question.

> Fled is that music:—do I wake or sleep?

Which I am inclined to take not as a question, not even as a rhetorical question, but as a statement of fact, as in Chuang Tzu's famous remark that he didn't know whether he was Chuang Tzu dreaming he was a butterfly or a butterfly dreaming he was Chuang Tzu. It is a description of the condition of being in the world. Which is how, it would seem, William Butler Yeats understood it when he borrowed Keats's method to end his poem "Among Schoolchildren," maybe the preeminent modernist ode:

> O chestnut tree, great rooted blossomer,
> Are you the leaf, the blossom, or the bole?
> O body swayed by music, O brightening glance,
> How can we know the dancer from the dance?

(It would seem in one reading to be an image of form itself, of the fusion of movement and stillness in a work of art.) And in "To Autumn," he also ends with an image, but it is a different thing in kind from the images—eighteenth-century allegorical images—that end "Pysche" and "Melancholy." It's like watching the symbolist image from Coleridge's "Frost at Midnight" passed into his hands as it gets passed on to the modernists:

> Hedge-crickets sing; and now with treble soft
> The red-breast whistles from a garden-croft;
>   And gathering swallows twitter in the skies.

Lines, as many critics have remarked, that Wallace Stevens used as a model for the end of "Sunday Morning":

And in the isolation of the sky,
At evening, casual flocks of pigeons make
Ambiguous undulations as they sink
Downward to darkness on extended wings.

25. *Mid-nineteenth Century:* Walt Whitman is the great model in midcentury, in "Crossing Brooklyn Ferry" and "Out of the Cradle Endlessly Rocking." And—for that matter—the great explosion of the ode form, "Song of Myself." Helen Vendler in her very rich book on the odes of Keats proposed to read them—all six of them; she includes "Ode on Indolence"—as a single long poem about mortality and imagination. And in that way the Keats odes and "Song of Myself" might be read together as a way that the ode form opened up to the modernist long poem.

26. *Elsewhere in the Nineteenth Century:* French Symbolist voyage poems and the ode. See Charles Baudelaire, "Invitation to a Voyage"; Arthur Rimbaud, "The Drunken Boat"; Stéphane Mallarmé, "A Throw of the Dice."

27. *Modernism and the Ode Form:* The first generation of twentieth-century poets in the English language were skittish about genre. Their starting place was the idea that the old forms needed to be renovated. Also the old values. So the modernist poem is often a quest form, initiated by a desire to name what it values. It's not an accident that the *Duino Elegies* begins with the question of whom or what to address:

Who, if I cried out, would hear me among the angels' orders?

And because it is a quest form, it is haunted or informed by the ode, or at least by some hybrid of the formal inheritance we have been looking at of the classical odes, the seventeenth-century meditative poem, and the romantic odes. It's clear, for example, that Wallace Stevens's "Sunday Morning" and "The Idea of Order at Key West" come out of the odes of Keats, that classical ideas of the ode hover behind many of Ezra Pound's *Cantos*. And one could see many sections of Hart Crane's *The Bridge*, and William Carlos Williams's *Paterson* and his "Asphodel, That Greeny Flower" that way, and the long poems of the war years, T. S. Eliot's *Four Quartets* and H. D.'s *Trilogy*, and study their formal shaping by asking what they address and how they develop and in what relation the endings of the poems stand to what desired goods they discover.

But let me suggest here looking at two poems, Marianne Moore's "An Octopus" and Federico Garcia Lorca's "Ode to Walt Whitman" from his *A Poet in New York*. I won't analyze their structures or their prosody. I will leave that to you. Marianne Moore hiked Mount Rainier with her brother in 1922. The title of the poem refers in a weird way to the glacier that grips the peak and the poem belongs to the genre of mountain odes—poems trying to get sublimity in their sights—that include the ascent of Mount Snowdon at the end of Wordsworth's *The Prelude*, Shelley's "Mont Blanc," Friederich Schiller's "The Walk," and perhaps more specifically Hölderlin's "Bread and Wine" and "The Rhine" in which the German poet associates the view from mountain heights with the sensibility of ancient Greece and its gods. It is a view with which the Scots-Irish and Presbyterian Moore seems to be in polemic at the end of "An Octopus." One of the delicious things about this delicious poem is the way she comes to the subject of Greece. The poem is too expensive to reprint here (though it first appeared almost a hundred years ago) and readers should, ideally, consult *Becoming Marianne Moore: The Early Poems, 1907–1924*, where you will be able find the version of the poem published in *The Dial* in 1924 and in her book *Observations* also in that

year, and compare it with the revised version in the *Complete Poems*
of 1957, which is the version that is usually reprinted, for example in
the 2003 *Poems of Marianne Moore*.

Most of the poem, as you will see, is a description, in her in-
imitably strange and beautiful patchwork of vivid description and
quotation, of her ascent up the mountain. There are many things to
marvel at in it, especially the way the poem does the ode's work of
praise by seeing what's there with her entirely fresh and unexpected
eye and also the way (1924? Was she mocking the use of allusion to
high literature in Eliot and Pound?) she borrows passages from the
National Park Service guidebook to the mountain and its trails. The
Park Service was created six years before her first visit to it. Rainier
was the fifth National Park to be designated by Congress, and the
publications she was quoting were themselves relatively new, so
she is also quite consciously framing the poem through the lens of
tourism, of the visitor looking at things, that the poem celebrates,
wonders at, and perhaps slightly mocks. So one of the first modernist odes, a praise poem about a powerfully North American subject
in dialogue with the whole history of nineteenth-century European
mountain odes. And the question of the ode form: Beyond piling up
praise in the form of description, where is it going? What values is it
getting in right relation to and how does it present or embody them?

The move toward conclusion begins about 150 lines into the poem
by moving from a description of one of the mountain's remarkable
flowers, the Calypso orchid, to one of its liveliest birds, the blue jay, a
sociable "villain," who, she remarks, "knows no Greek."

Comparing the two versions of the poem you will see how she
struggled with this transition. I love the oddness of her original impulse. The bluejay's ignorance of Greek allows her to comment—as
against the paganism of Holderlin and Shelly and Pound—on the
superficiality of the idea of happiness in classical Greek civilization,
which she contrasts with the tough-minded authors of the Park Service pamphlets she has been quoting that forbid guns, hunting, and

explosives on the mountain and let you know that if you are going to climb it you'll need hardtack and raisins. And this leads her—the first-time reader may be a bit dizzy taking it in—to Henry James who, like the mountain, isn't easy. Infinitely better to read the poem than this paraphrase and to see how she comes at the end—in the manner of the Romantic odes—to the place where she started: the icy glacier itself that she came to praise.

Federico Garcia Lorca arrived in New York City in June 1929. He was thirty-one years old. He completed his ode to Walt Whitman a year later in June 1930 when he was returning to New York from a visit to Cuba. He first published the poem in a limited edition printed in Mexico City in 1933. It was never published in Spain, a conservative culture in which his homosexuality was still a private and closely guarded matter. It's a very moving poem for that reason. The ode in Spain has a history at least as complicated as the English. There is a massive study of Horace in Spanish and there is a Pindaric tradition. In the 1920s the ode in Spain was still largely metrical, and the Lorca odes in *Poet in New York* were his first experiments in free verse, the prosody itself part of his homage to Whitman, who had shown him how to imagine a sexuality without shame and to confront the languages of shame in which he had come to understand his own erotic life. The translator has had to deal, as part of the inward journey, with the terms of sexual denigration in several Latin American cultures. Notice the way the poem wavers between ode and elegy, between a love for what Whitman represents and anguish at what seemed to him then the soul-destroying machinery of a new century (which he entangles with homophobia) and the way that the petition at the end of the ode takes the form of a wish:

Ode to Walt Whitman

By the East River and the Bronx
boys were singing, exposing their waists

with the wheel, with oil, leather, and the hammer.
Ninety thousand miners taking silver from the rocks
and children drawing stairs and perspectives.

But none of them could sleep,
none of them wanted to be the river,
none of them loved the huge leaves
or the shoreline's blue tongue.

By the East River and the Queensboro
boys were battling with industry
and the Jews sold to the river faun
the rose of circumcision,
and over bridges and rooftops, the mouth of the sky emptied
herds of bison driven by the wind.

But none of them paused,
none of them wanted to be a cloud,
none of them looked for ferns
or the yellow wheel of a tambourine.

As soon as the moon rises
the pulleys will spin to alter the sky;
a border of needles will besiege memory
and the coffins will bear away those who don't work.

New York, mire,
New York, mire and death.
What angel is hidden in your cheek?
Whose perfect voice will sing the truths of wheat?
Who, the terrible dream of your stained anemones?

Not for a moment, Walt Whitman, lovely old man,
have I failed to see your beard full of butterflies,
nor your corduroy shoulders frayed by the moon,
nor your thighs pure as Apollo's,

nor your voice like a column of ash,
old man, beautiful as the mist,
you moaned like a bird
with its sex pierced by a needle.
Enemy of the satyr,
enemy of the vine,
and lover of bodies beneath rough cloth . . .

Not for a moment, virile beauty,
who among mountains of coal, billboards, and railroads,
dreamed of becoming a river and sleeping like a river
with that comrade who would place in your breast
the small ache of an ignorant leopard.

Not for a moment, Adam of blood, Macho,
man alone at sea, Walt Whitman, lovely old man,
because on penthouse roofs,
gathered at bars,
emerging in bunches from the sewers,
trembling between the legs of chauffeurs,
or spinning on dance floors wet with absinthe,
the faggots, Walt Whitman, point you out.

He's one, too! That's right! And they land
on your luminous chaste beard,
blonds from the north, blacks from the sands,
crowds of howls and gestures,
like cats or like snakes,
the faggots, Walt Whitman, the faggots,
clouded with tears, flesh for the whip,
the boot, or the teeth of the lion tamers.

He's one, too! That's right! Stained fingers
point to the shore of your dream
when a friend eats your apple

with a slight taste of gasoline
and the sun sings in the navels
of boys who play under bridges.

But you didn't look for scratched eyes,
nor the darkest swamp where someone submerges children,
nor frozen saliva,
nor the curves slit open like a toad's belly
that the faggots wear in cars and on terraces
while the moon lashes them on the street corners of terror.

You looked for a naked body like a river.
Bull and dream who would join wheel with seaweed,
father of your agony, camellia of your death,
who would groan in the blaze of your hidden equator.

Because it's all right if a man doesn't look for his delight
in tomorrow morning's jungle of blood.
The sky has shores where life is avoided
and there are bodies that shouldn't repeat themselves in the dawn.

Agony, agony, dream, ferment, and dream.
This is the world, my friend, agony, agony.
Bodies decompose beneath the city clocks,
war passes by in tears, followed by a million gray rats,
the rich give their mistresses
small illuminated dying things,
and life is neither noble, nor good, nor sacred.

Man is able, if he wishes, to guide his desire
through a vein of coral or a heavenly naked body.
Tomorrow, loves will become stones, and Time
a breeze that drowses in the branches.

That's why I don't raise my voice, old Walt Whitman,
against the little boy who writes

the name of a girl on his pillow,
nor against the boy who dresses as a bride
in the darkness of the wardrobe,
nor against the solitary men in casinos
who drink prostitution's water with revulsion,
nor against the men with that green look in their eyes
who love other men and burn their lips in silence.

But yes against you, urban faggots,
tumescent flesh and unclean thoughts.
Mothers of mud. Harpies. Sleepless enemies
of the love that bestows crowns of joy.

Always against you, who give boys
drops of foul death with bitter poison.
Always against you,
Fairies of North America,
Pájaros of Havana,
Jotos of Mexico,
Sarasas of Cádiz,
Apios of Seville,
Cancos of Madrid,
Floras of Alicante,
Adelaidas of Portugal.

Faggots of the world, murderers of doves!
Slaves of women. Their bedroom bitches.
Opening in public squares like feverish fans
or ambushed in rigid hemlock landscapes.

No quarter given! Death
spills from your eyes
and gathers gray flowers at the mire's edge.
No quarter given! Attention!
Let the confused, the pure,

the classical, the celebrated, the supplicants
close the doors of the bacchanal to you.

And you, lovely Walt Whitman, stay asleep on the Hudson's
    banks
with your beard toward the pole, openhanded.
Soft clay or snow, your tongue calls for
comrades to keep watch over your unbodied gazelle.

Sleep on, nothing remains.
Dancing walls stir the prairies
and America drowns itself in machinery and lament.
I want the powerful air from the deepest night
to blow away flowers and inscriptions from the arch where
    you sleep,
and a black child to inform the gold-craving whites
that the kingdom of grain has arrived.

28. *Pablo Neruda—Endings:* Pablo Neruda wrote over two hundred odes; for a while he wrote one a week for a newspaper. The poems are mostly written in short, sinuous lines, though translators and scholars have noticed that they tend to fall into the seven- and twelve-syllable rhythmic units of classical Spanish poetry. And formally many of them are litanies, cascades of metaphor in praise of the objects they address; and the objects they address are the ordinary stuff of life: tomatoes and sox and ships inside glass bottles and seaweed. If the ode began as an address to divinity, these poems were an answer to the question of how a twentieth-century Marxist poet from a Catholic culture could conjure a divinity from everyday life.

A way to study them formally—to see what Neruda was up to—is to look at how he ends the poems. Where in the classical ode came the request addressed to a god or a patron and in the romantic ode to nature or a creator-imagination, it is interesting to think about

what Neruda does with the final turn. Here are five instances, in the
translation of Margaret Sayers Peden.

"Ode to an Artichoke" begins by allegorizing it as a soldier, then
sends a cook out to buy one in a market, and ends like this:

> Once home
> and in the kitchen
> she drowns it in a pot.
> And thus ends
> in peace
> the saga
> of the armored vegetable
> we call the artichoke,
> as
> leaf by leaf
> we unsheathe
> its delights
> and eat
> the peaceable flesh
> of its green heart.

"Ode to a Dictionary" traces a fairly complicated relation to the
dictionary, seen in the arrogance of youth as an unimaginative beast
of burden and at other times as the grave of language. The poem
takes several turns and ends like this:

> From the depths of your
> dense and reverberating jungle
> grant me,
> at the moment it is needed,
> a single bird song, the luxury
> of one bee,

one splinter
of your ancient wood perfumed
by an eternity of jasmine,
one
syllable,
one tremor, one sound,
one seed:
I am of the earth and with words I sing.

"Ode to a Hummingbird" begins by speculating on the evolutionary origins of this creature and ends like this:

Seed
of sunlight,
feathered
fire,
smallest
flying flag,
petals of silenced peoples,
syllable
of buried blood,
feathered crest
of our ancient
subterranean
heart.

(The adjective *antigua* and the noun *corazon* show up often toward the end of these poems.)

"Ode to Seaweed" contains a strange richness of associations. They are the funeral gloves of the ocean, flags, nipples, plunder, coin, a marine version almost of Walt Whitman's catalog of metaphors for grass. The poem ends like this:

Orange, rusted spatulate
shapes, eggs
of date palms,
drifting
fans
flailed
by the
eternal
flux
of a marine
heart,
islands of Sargasso
that reach
my door
with the plunder
of
the rainbow,
let me
wear around my neck, on my head,
the wet vine tendrils
of the ocean,
the spent comet
of the wave.

The often-translated "Ode to My Socks" begins with a description of the gift of a pair of hand-woven socks so beautiful it makes the speaker think less of his feet, makes him reluctant to encase them in merely utilitarian shoes. The ending is interesting because it suggests, playfully, that Neruda did think of odes as ending, at least implicitly, with a moral:

So this is
the moral of my ode:

twice beautiful
is beauty
and what is good doubly
good
when it is a case of two
woolen socks
in wintertime.

POSTMODERN PRACTICE

29. There is a poem by Robert Pinsky entitled "Poem With Lines in Any Order":

Sonny said, Then he shouldn't have given Molly the two
    more babies.
Dave's sister and her husband adopted the baby, and that was
    Babe.
You can't live in the past.
Sure he was a tough guy but he was no hero.
Sonny and Toots went to live awhile with the Braegers.
It was a time when it seemed like everybody had a nickname.
Nobody can live in the future.
When Rose died having Babe, Dave came after the doctor
    with a gun.
Toots said, What would you expect? He was a young man
    and there she was.
Sonny still a kid himself when Dave moved out on Molly.
The family gave him Rose's cousin Molly to marry so she
    could raise the children.
There's no way to just live in the present.
In their eighties Toots and Sonny still arguing about their father.
Dave living above the bar with Della and half the family.

The proposition seems to be that this is a poem without a begin-ning, a middle, and an end because a family and a family's stories are a kind of echo chamber that exists in space rather than time. So that the first and last lines, for example, could just as well be each in the other's place. It's not causality or the narrative that the poet is after, but that sound of old stories getting rehashed through the generations that is itself one definition of family. And in that way it is a sort of ode to this idea of family. The sentences of more general comment—at least the first one—*You can't live in the past*—sound like part of the family noise, a thing these people said to get through their lives. So the poem belongs to the formal impulse in contemporary poetry to resist or qualify the idea of beginnings and middles and ends. It wants to be more like a mobile than an arrow shot at a target.

And yet it does presuppose certain formal constraints. It wouldn't work, or would work very differently, if the three or four (if you count the remark about nicknames) more general remarks were bunched together at the beginning or the end of the poem. It probably doesn't matter in what order the lines about the past, present, and future appear, but it does matter that they are scattered through the poem. A certain poise is involved in turning these overheard stories and gossip-over-coffee fragments of talk—you can invent your own—*I don't think your aunt Claire ever got over Curt Berndt; the truth is Nell and Winnie never got along*—into poetry.

A similar version of the desire not to subordinate one element in a series to another lies behind C. D. Wright's "The Ozark Odes," I think. This is a longish poem, or suite of poems, but it is interesting to take the time to study the order of the parts. It matters that it feels a little desultory, but there is a pulse that orders it—the three poems or sections entitled "Lake Return"—connecting the sense of place to sexuality, or the memories stored in sexuality, the erotic pulse of memory and lived life:

The Ozark Odes

Lake Return

Maybe you have to be from there to hear it sing:
Give me your waterweeds, your nipples,
your shoehorn and your four-year letter jacket,
the molded leftovers from the singed pot.
Now let me see your underside, white as fishes.
I lower my gaze against your clitoral light.

Rent House

O the hours I lay on the bed
looking at the knotted pine
in the added-on room
where he kept his old Corona,
the poet with the big lips—
where we slept together.

Somebody's Mother

Flour rose from her shoulders
as she walked out of her kitchen,
The report of the screendoor,
the scrapdog unperturbed.
Afternoon sky pinking up.

Table Grace

Bless Lou Vindie, Bless Truman
bless the fields

of rocks, the brown recluse
behind the wallpaper,
chink in the plaster,
bless cowchips, bless brambles
and the copperhead, the honey locusts
shedding their frilly flower
on waxed cars, bless them
the loudmouths and goiters
and dogs with mange,
bless each and every one
for doing their utmost.
Yea, for they have done
their naturally suspicious part.

Girlhood

Mother had one. She and Bernice racing for the river
to play with their paperdolls
because they did not want any big ears
to hear what their paperdolls were fixing to say.

Judge

Had a boyhood. Had his own rooster. Name of Andy.
Andy liked to ride in Judge's overall bib.
Made him bald. This really vexed Judge's old daddy.

Arkansas Towns

Acorn
Back Gate

Bald Knob
Ben Hur
Biggers
Blue Ball
Congo
Delight
Ebony
Eros
Fifty-Six
Figure Five
Flippin
Four Sisters
Goshen
Greasy Corner
Havana
Hector
Hogeye
Ink
Jenny Lind
Little Flock
Marked Tree
Mist
Monkey Run
Moscow
Nail
Okay
Ozone
Rag Town
Ratio
Seaton Dump
Self
Snowball
Snow Lake

Sweet Home
Three Brothers
Three Folks
Twist
Urbanette
Whisp
Yellville
Zent

Lake Return

Where the sharp rocks on shore
Give way to the hairy rock in the shallows,
We enlisted in the rise and fall of love.
His seed broadcast like short, sweet grass.
Nothing came up there.

Dry Country Bar

Bourbon not fit to put on a sore. No women enter,
their men collect in any kind of weather
with no shirts on whatsoever.

Café at the Junction

The way she sees him
how the rain doesn't let up

4-ever blue and vigilant
as a clock in a corner

peeling the label from his bottle
hungry but not touching food

as she turns down the wet lane
where oaks vault the road

The Boyfriend

wakes in darkness of morning
and visits the water

lowering his glad body
onto a flat rock

the spiders rearrange
themselves underneath

Remedy

Sty sty leave my eye,
go to the next feller passing by.

Porch

I can still see Cuddihy's sisters
trimming the red tufts
under one another's arms

Bait Shop

Total sales today: 3 doz. minnows, ½ doz. crawdaddies, 4 lead
    lures,

loaf of light bread, pack of Raleighs, 3 bags of barbecued pork
    skins.

Fred

One of your more irascible poets from the hill country.
Retired to his mother's staunch house
in Little Rock after her death; began to build
a desk for Arthur. Beautiful piece
of work. For a friend. Beautiful.
Drinking less, putting on a few pounds.

Lake Return

Why I come here: need for a bottom, something to refer to;
where all things visible and invisible commence to swim.

And the final couplet does seem conclusive, though one can
imagine the first poem, or section of the poem, reversed to create
a slightly different set of thematic emphases. Likewise the other
sections that give us snippets of glimpses of the rural Arkansas she
aims to celebrate. One might want to make an argument for this
particular sequencing of the poem—and compare it to Lorine Niedecker's "Paean to Place," from which it may have derived, but a
certain looseness is part of its formal force. Compare both Niedecker
and Wright to the place poems of the English seventeenth century—
Ben Jonson's "To Penshurst" and Andrew Marvell's "Upon Appleton
House"—with their ambulatory manner and sense of hierarchy.

Lyn Hejinian has pursued this impulse in a more formally rigor-
ous way in some of her work. Her essay "The Rejection of Closure" is
an argument against the formal notion of arrival and her determina-

tion to make poems in which the lines might occur in no particular order (and paradoxically, of course in *this particular version* of no particular order) is reflected in the title of a recent book, *The Unfollowing*. Which is to say, the formal principle in operation is the non sequitur. *The Unfollowing* is either a book of fourteen-line poems or a serial poem made of fourteen-line poems, so it is sonnetish. And the author describes it in an introductory note as having its impulse in elegy but its formal principle is continuous invention, the conversation with no beginning and no end between consciousness and the world that time and our senses—and here the verb is the issue—immerses us in? bombards us with? makes us a part of? It's the question the form itself interrogates as it fuses sonnet, ode, and elegy. Here is a sample, the second and fourth poems in the book:

> Every minute proves that reality is conditional
> Sounds paddle the air, echoing as I speak my mind
> The door opens, I rise naked from the tub
> It's strange to return from Abyssinia by train from my bed
> I hear a demographer singing below
> Sleep?—yes I sleep almost in fear of the lovely night before I slept
> Boom—one—one—one, boom one and boom one and one
>   and one
> Only one
> A woman appears carrying a pink bag
> You stay, okay with the sheets, we'll get a suit, you're in the story
> When love can't be composed any better, love can't be
>   postponed any longer
> Things predicted are always restricted
> Go, smoking pan, with your bacon to window
> This afternoon there will be "une grand séance" and everyone
>   will nap
>   *

One spring the wise guys booming *one* paraded: boom: I
The next thing they knew it was a warm day in spring, and
    each had several deaths to mourn
Is this another sphinx trick, a hole, a minus-device like a mad
    wave
Up go the shades but there is no light outside to be let in
She concentrated for, she identified in, she told to
They who accomplished banging gather, they who diminish
    do so proudly
Half is done with a quarter to spend for a worrywart wearing
    sunglasses
The sun is too coherent, the egg in the glacier hatches out mice
Mother!
As generous as a caterpillar she has given her very body away
Now we witness with the senses and materiality is singled out
Mad manifest squares, the semantics of an evil activity
The phrase, this stream, among wolves
How vulgar the vulnerability of the earholes, the armholes, of
    anything that serves as a window of the body to the world

30 . *The takeaway:* Out of litany and prayer came the praise poem and endless lyric variations on the praise poem. In their formal development these poems have a beginning, middle, and end; an inescapable (unless you are Gertrude Stein) three-part structure. The beginning part is often initiated by desire or dissent. The middle section is almost infinitely variable. It can proceed by narrative, by argument, by association, by the elaboration of a metaphor, by a mix of these. In postmodern practice development often proceeds by braiding and disparity, by disruption and non sequitur. An ode can have few or many parts. It can attempt to name, or possess, or stand at the right distance from, in the right relation to, even veer away, from the spoken or unspoken object of desire or imagination of value that initiates it, and its third and final section is apt to get to, or point toward, or try to instantiate, or ask a favor from that object or power. (Which is apt to be, at least implicitly, the power of poetry, or the action of the imagination of which poetry is an instance.)

31. And the prosodic form in which a poem is cast can intensify or qualify the formal development of the content in any number of ways. See Horace's Cleopatra ode again: the irony implicit in treating epic material in a lyric stanza that undercuts it or Neruda's rivery simplification of classical prosody. This is the work that craft consciousness and the unconscious shaping power of imagination are doing all the time in the making of a poem.

ELEGY

1 . From the Greek *elegos*, lament. A formal lament for the dead. Lament, or dirge, or *planh*, must have begun as a sorrow song. The opposite of litany. The elegy originates, as a form, in Alexandria in the third century BCE. It is associated with Theocritus—and so with the curious history of pastoral poetry in Europe. Curious because from this time to the time of Shelley, the basis of European economies was agriculture and herding and from the time of the rise of the first great imperial urban center, Alexandria, it became customary for poets, once they had arrived in the city—Theocritus, for example, was from Sicily—to write in the personae of idealized sheepherders, the agricultural workers and animal tenders on whose labor the great cities depended.

The *pastoral elegy* that Theocritus is said to have invented was adapted from ritual laments for Adonis (a year god; a male Persephone figure, the object of a divine ritual accident—killed by a wild boar in one version—or slaying at the center of our myth-life in the dream-time; cognate of Osiris, prefigurement of Christ) common in the Mediterranean countryside. The central convention of the form is that the author is a shepherd mourning the death of another shepherd. Deeply odd, in one way, and a Marxist or poststructuralist take on it would certainly have to do with economics and displacement.

But an immediate sense that it makes is a way of connecting personal loss to very ancient funerary folk beliefs and practices that connect death as a central fact of existence with seasonal death and rebirth and also with the funerary origins of art. An old connection between loss, figuration, and renewal. There is a brilliant book on this subject, *The English Elegy*, by Peter Sacks.

Note: the first glimpse archaeology has given us of the emergence of human culture from hominid development is an ancient gravesite in what is now the Ukraine, perhaps thirty thousand years ago—the skeletal remains of a child around which were placed in a symmetrical pattern the curved horns of sheep.

2. From there to the early evidence of classical archaeology and literature. Sacks: "*Elegy* itself derives from the Greek elegiac verses, traditionally accompanied by the flute, or more precisely by the oboelike double pipe called *aulos* . . . The *aulos* was related to the Phoenician *giggras*, flutes played at the funeral rites of Adonis, and descended from an Egyptian wind instrument associated with mourning and with its divine inventor, Osiris, god of the dead. The Greeks themselves mythologized the invention of the wind instrument, clinching its association with loss and consolation in the legend of Pan and Syrinx . . ."

3. *Survivals:* Auden, in his great elegy on the death of Yeats, is very much aware that the classical lute has been replaced by the weather gauge:

> What instruments we have agree
> The day of his death was a dark cold day

and Robert Lowell, in "The Quaker Graveyard," looking out at the turbulent Atlantic where his cousin died during World War II, has the classical elegy in mind:

> Ask for no Orphean lute
> To pluck life back. The guns recoil and then repeat
> Their harsh salute.

and see James Merrill's "Syrinx."

4 . Peter Sacks, *The English Elegy:* "The elegy, as a poem of mourning and consolation, has its roots in a dense matrix of rites and ceremonies, in the light of which many elegiac conventions should be recognized as being not only aesthetically interesting forms but also the literary versions of specific social and psychological practices. Among those conventions are pastoral contextualization, the myth of the vegetation deity (particularly the sexual elements of such myths), the use of repetition and refrain, the reiterated questions, the outbreak of vengeful anger and cursing, the procession of mourners, the movement from grief to consolation, the traditional images of resurrection."

Sacks notes the recurrence in Greek myth of stories connecting mourning with the origin of poetry: "Orpheus's introduction of song in mourning for the dead Linus, Orpheus who could not sing Eurydice into the world, the blinded love-torn Daphnis's invention of pastoral poetry, Apollo's frustrated derivation of the laurel, sign of poethood, from the loss of Daphne, the invention of the flute or pipe by Pan, patron god of pastoral and elegy." See H.D.'s *Trilogy* and Brenda Hillman's *Death Tractates* for interrogations of the relation of women's mourning to this complex.

5. A note on form: the English elegy, like the ode, is formally various, mimicking spontaneity, but elegy was originally associated with the elegiac couplet, one line of hexameter and one of pentameter, and the term passed into Latin meaning any poem using the elegiac distich. Hence Donne's erotic poems in couplets are "elegies," and in Germany Hölderlin's ode "To Bread and Wine" is an elegy, but it is in the pastoral form—Spenser, Milton—that the elegy as lament enters the English tradition.

Sacks: "Daphne's 'turning' into a tree matches Apollo's 'turning' from the object of his love to a sign of her, the laurel bough. It is the substitutive turn or act of troping that any mourner—perhaps that language—must perform." And here is Ovid on Pan and Syrinx:

> The nymph had no use for the god's prayer:
> It was desire; it had designs on her.
> She fled him through pathless wastes and came
> To Ladon's stream where it flowed peacefully
> Along its sandy banks, and there the waters
> Checked her flight. Frantic, she begged her sister
> Of the stream to change her form, and Pan,
> Who thought at that moment to have caught her,
> Instead held only marsh reeds in his arms.
> He sighed his disappointment. The soft air,
> Stirring in the reeds, made a low, mournful note,
> And, touched by wonder, charmed by the sweet sound,
> The god cried, "This, at least, I'll have of thee."
> And so the pipes, made of cut, unequal reeds
> He fit together with a joint of wax, and played
> A ravishment that took and kept the maiden's name.

The Sacks thesis: "Although it is crucial for the mourner to assert a continued sexual impulse, that assertion must be qualified, even repressively transformed or rendered metaphorical, by the awareness of loss and mortality. Indeed, our consoling images are most often figures for an immortal but metamorphosized sexual force."

6. So the territory of death and its sign is the sign and territory of all thwarted desire. To mourn one is to mourn the other. Often this is the father's territory, the territory of the given order of things. Emily Dickinson:

> I never lost as much but twice
> And that was in the sod.
> Twice have I stood a beggar
> Before the door of God.
>
> Angels, twice descending,
> Reimbursed my store.
> Burglar! Banker! Father!
> I am poor once more.

And the traditional structure of elegy, the template of Theocritus's pastoral—adapted by Milton in "Lycidas" and Shelley in "Adonais"—is implicated in this history. Cut flowers: Milton's painful plucking of berries and leaves, the mounds of broken lilacs Whitman heaps on Lincoln's funeral car. Tokens of renewal but also of brokenness. Hence also the importance of anger in elegy—Milton's lashing out at the bad fathers, Shelley's rage against the critics, the bankers in Auden's elegy for Yeats "roaring like beasts on the floor of the Bourse."

7. The best way to study the elegy, perhaps, is to study the big poems in the pastoral tradition that work out forms for mourning and for large, ambitious efforts to understand and include death in

the order the poem makes. This might include hunting up translations of Theocritus, Bion, and Moschus, and after getting a sense of the big poem to look at the whole tradition of poems of death and mourning. "Lycidas" is central. It was written when the pastoral tradition already seemed entirely played out. Elegy both before and after it in the seventeenth century had swung toward other styles, the complicated conceit or some version of restrained rational stoicism. Then Shelley revived the form, Matthew Arnold followed in Shelley's tracks, and that was the end of the large-scale pastoral in English. Lowell's "The Quaker Graveyard" is interesting among other reasons for its effort to entirely appropriate and redefine the genre. For a study of this, see Hugh B. Staples, *Robert Lowell: The First Twenty Years*. Interesting, I think, though it is not strictly a pastoral, to look at *In Memoriam* in this context and Auden's elegy for Yeats. And to compare Brenda Hillman's *Death Tractates* with *In Memoriam*, especially in terms of how the deepest conventions of pastoral can survive in the contemporary world.

8 . An essay that might be useful is Freud's "Mourning and Melancholia." It's about the problem of surviving grief, of not becoming dead by identifying with the dead one, or lost by identifying with the lost thing, and how to do this without disloyalty to what one has loved. See Wordsworth, "Surprised by Joy." So the work of transformation inside the elegy is that. So if the ode is about getting in right relation to the powers that make us feel alive, elegy is about warding off, or transforming, the powers that want to kill us.

9 . Interesting from that perspective to look at what happens inside short poems about grief and loss, Ben Jonson's "To His Son," Elizabeth Bishop's "One Art."

Some readings:

PASTORAL ELEGY

Edmund Spenser: "Astrophil"
John Milton: "Lycidas"
Percy Shelley: "Adonais"
Walt Whitman: "When Lilacs Last in the Dooryard Bloom'd"
Matthew Arnold: "Thyrsis"
Robert Lowell: "The Quaker Graveyard in Nantucket"

THE ELEGY TRADITION

Chidiock Tichborne: "Tichborne's Elegy"
Ben Jonson: "On My First Daughter"
    "On My First Son"
    "To the Immortal Memory and Friendship of That Noble
        Pair, Sir Lucius Clay and Sir Henry Morrison" (a Pindaric
        ode)
    "To the Memory of My Beloved, the Author Mr. William
        Shakespeare"
Thomas Carew: "An Elegy upon the Death of the Dean of
    Paul's, Dr. John Donne"
John Dryden: "To the Memory of Mr. Oldham"
Jonathan Swift: "A Satirical Elegy on the Death of a Late
    Famous General"
Thomas Gray: "Sonnet (on the death of Mr. Richard West)"
William Wordsworth: "Elegiac Stanzas"
Alfred Tennyson: "In Memoriam A.H.H." (a crucial poem:
    Tennyson knew both "Adonais" and "Lycidas" quite well and
    thought of calling his work "Fragments of an Elegy," the title
    itself a refiguring of modern mourning)
Emily Brontë: "Remembrance"

Emily Dickinson: "I could not Live with Thee—" (a preemptive anti-elegy)

Algernon Swinburne: "Ave Atque Vale" (Swinburne's elegy for Baudelaire)

Thomas Hardy: "A Singer Asleep" (Hardy's elegy for Swinburne; see also Sacks for a study of Hardy's remarkable series of elegies to his first wife, the poem of 1912–1913)

William Butler Yeats: "In Memory of Major Robert Gregory" (Yeats took his stanzaic form from Cowley's "On the Death of William Hervey.")

SOME MODERN INSTANCES

T. S. Eliot: "The Wasteland"
   "The Hollow Men"
Wallace Stevens: "The Owl in the Sarcophagus"
W. H. Auden: "In Memory of W. B. Yeats"
Theodore Roethke: "Elegy for Jane"
William Everson: "The Poet Is Dead"
Robert Hayden: "Mourning Poem for the Queen of Sunday"
John Berryman: "Dream Song #324: An Elegy for W.C.W., the Lovely Man"
Robert Lowell: "My Last Afternoon with Uncle Devereux Winslow"
   "In Memory of Arthur Winslow"
   "For the Union Dead"
Robert Duncan: "An African Elegy"
Amy Clampitt: "A Procession at Candlemas"
Allen Ginsberg: "Howl"
   "Kaddish"
   "To Aunt Rose"
Donald Justice: "In Memory of the Unknown Poet, Robert Boardman Vaughn"

Geoffrey Hill: "In Memory of Jane Fraser"

Frank O'Hara: "The Day Lady Died"

Sylvia Plath: "Daddy"

Seamus Heaney: "In Memoriam Sean O'Riada"

   "In Memoriam Francis Ledwidge"

   "Elegy (for Robert Lowell)"

Norman Dubie: "Elegy for Wright & Hugo"

Jorie Graham: "On Form for Berryman" (in *Erosion*)

Lyn Hejinian: "Gesualdo"

Bob Perelman: "Chronic Meanings" (An elegy for an acquaintance,
   dead from AIDS at age twenty-five, the poem consists of twenty-
   five stanzas, each line consisting of a five-word phrase cut off
   without completion.)

RECENT SEQUENCES TO BE CONSIDERED IN RELATION TO
ELEGY

Sharon Olds: *The Father*

Louise Gluck: *Wild Iris*

Brenda Hillman: *Death Tractates*

Jorie Graham: *Materialism*

Carolyn Forche: *The Angel of History*

C. D. Wright: *Deepstep Come Shining*

Harryette Mullen: *Muse and Drudge*

READING THE ELEGY

The study of the elegy—to get a sense of what the genre is as it was received and transformed by poets in the English language—can be accomplished by looking at the structure of a few poems. Here the reader is asked to get out a copy of Milton's "Lycidas" and Shelley's "Adonais" and to pay attention to the ways that they adapt the form of the Alexandrian pastoral elegy. Useful to have at hand is something like the *Norton Anthology of Poetry* for annotation of the poems. And, having taken in these classic loci of the elegy, then to look briefly at Eliot's "The Wasteland," Robert Lowell's "The Quaker Graveyard in Nantucket," and Allen Ginsberg's "Howl" and "Kaddish." Remarkable poems all and worth the time.

Partly I will be tracking Peter Sacks's reading of the poems in his *The English Elegy.* We are tracking old, inherited formal structures for surviving and transforming the kinds of devastating loss that can sicken the roots of life. To begin . . .

THE STRUCTURE OF LYCIDAS

1-14 YET ONCE MORE, O YE LAURELS

Invocation: laurel, myrtle, and ivy are anciently associated with poetry. Apostrophe: grief and an animate universe. "yet once more": he's writing another elegy, and the tradition is receiving another one; echo as a feature of the genre. Grief is haunted, echoic. Allusion: the verse echoes directly Virgil's "Eclogue II": "Et vos, o lauri, carpam, et te, proxima myrte" and Spenser's elegy for Sydney in which he complains of the death and of his poem as "a flower untimely cropt." Milton was twenty-nine years old. The fall into language: the "forced fingers" and the shattered leaves underscore the death as violation and the poem as violation of grief's silence. "For Lycidas is dead": echoes this repeated cry of the name of the dead one in earlier elegies and also, probably, the crying of the name of the dead and to-be-resurrected year-god in very ancient rituals: see the cry "Tamuz! Tamuz!" in Pound's *Cantos*.

15-36 BEGIN THEN, SISTERS OF THE SACRED WELL

Calling on the muses: this is of course deeply traditional, in this case echoing the opening of Hesiod's *Theogony:*

> With the Helicon muses let us start
> Our song: they hold the great and godly mount
> Of Helicon, and on their delicate feet
> They dance around the darkly bubbling spring
> And round the altar of the mighty Zeus

It may also refer to what Sacks calls the "barely Christianized" version of this image of a seminal patriarchal source of life-energy in *Revelations:* "And he showed me a pure river of water of life, clear as crystal, proceeding out of the throne of Gog and of the Lamb."

"Hence with denial vain and coy excuse": strangely sexual courting, seducing of the female muses. "For we were nursed on the selfsame hill" etc.: to mourn another is to mourn one's own death. "Together both": this is the convention of the young poets as fellow shepherds; it was to be understood as referring to their schooldays together— the "high lawn" is Cambridge—but it also calls up the vivid natural world of childhood; it mourns growing up, versions of a lost self. "old Damoetas": probably meant to call up some idea of a tutor at school in the person of an old shepherd; his kindliness about their early verse contrasts with the anxiety about judgment in taking on this big poem; the time of writing before workshop-judgment miseries and self-consciousness. This mild figure concludes the idyll.

37-49 BUT O THE HEAVY CHANGE

Now Lycidas is addressed, and his loss is treated as absolute and based, curiously, on a prohibition: "Now thou art gone, and never *must* return." "The willows and the hazel copses": all of nature is sickened by the loss—this is the myth that also underlies Eliot's *The Wasteland* as an elegy in search of its subject/victim. Cf. Berryman's *Dream Songs:* "Often he reckons, in the dawn, them up. Nobody is ever missing," which suggests what happened to the modern elegy: when the cosmology collapsed, the form became diagnostic. Thus, Eliot's Phlebas the Phoenician may echo the drowned Lycidas, a possibilty that seems to have occurred to Robert Lowell in "The Quaker Graveyard." And consider Carl Solomon who is imagined to show up wet—as if emerged from the sea—at the door of the cottage at the end of Ginsberg's "Howl." "Such, Lycidas, thy loss to shepherd's ear." So the deep loss is the loss of the poems Henry King might have written. And more deeply the ability to hear. Here the Christian trope of the poem, shepherd = priest, is first adumbrated. Perhaps an echo of the gospel of John: "He that hath an ear let him hear what the spirit saith."

50–63 WHERE WERE YE, NYMPHS,

The complaint to local gods—the complaint against nature for not preserving the life of the beloved—is a convention of the elegy and accurate to the psychology of grief. "Druids": Milton mixes the British and the mythic landscapes. "What could the Muse": Here for the first time the efficacy of poetry is questioned—a problem that persists in the elegies for poets. Auden on Yeats: "Poetry makes nothing happen." Hence "Ay me! I fondly dream" could be written over the entrance to schools of creative writing. "For her inchanting son": Even Calliope could not save Orpheus—and perhaps poetry isn't going to save anybody. Critics have pointed out that Milton's mother died five months before he wrote the poem. Hence Lycidas as a shadow elegy for the loss of his mother as "Howl" is a shadow elegy for the mad Naomi Ginsberg.

64–84 ALAS! WHAT BOOTS IT

The response to the crisis sponsored by poetry-gloom. And Apollo's rebuke, telling him that he is not to court success but the "perfect witness of all-judging Jove," is probably the least useful thing in the poem for modern readers. For Milton, the Puritan reformer, it involves a larger idea of sonhood. See Paul's Epistle to the Hebrews: "If ye endure chastening, God dealeth with you as sons; for what son is he whom the father chasteneth not. Furthermore, we have had fathers of our flesh who corrected us; and we gave them reverence: shall we not much rather be under subjection to the Father of spirits, and live?" Sacks points out that this passage marks a transition in the poem from the addressing of female figures to the addressing of male figures, a movement, he says, "that is itself part of the work of mourning: the movement from the primary object of desire associated with the mother and an identification with the father and his symbols of power." Which more or less echoes Jacques Lacan's account of how we resolve the Oedipus complex and acquire language (the *non* of the father is the *nom* of things) and the ensuing lifelong pursuit in language of what language displaces and can't recover. Which considerably intensifies doubt about the efficacy of language and hence of elegy and would seem to be a point of crisis in the contemporary use of the form.

85-100 O FOUNTAIN ARETHUSE

The creakiest transition in the poem: having leapt past the pastoral mode in his consideration of the problem of poetry, he announces his return to it, evoking Theocritus (the fountain Arethuse in Sicily) and Virgil's Mincius, and asks the next question—not Why, Mom, didn't you save him? but Why, Dad, did this happen? Triton pleads Neptune's innocence and also that of Aeolus, the storm god, and says the cause was "that fatal and perfidious bark, built in the eclipse, and rigged with curses dark." How this works figuratively—bad ship? human error? original sin?—I'm really not sure, but it is this issue that seems to lead to the next passage, in which the flaring of anger, and the denunciation of the world, another convention of the elegy, occurs.

101-31 NEXT CAMUS, REVEREND SIRE

After Triton—what Nature has to say—comes Camus—or Cambridge—what classical learning has to say: it says "alas! alas!"—and after that comes St. Peter who simply unleashes a vengeful denunciation of the corrupt clergy of England. This makes more psychological than logical sense. It doesn't answer the question, why death? or why this death? It asks the question that anger asks: why this death when the world is so full of assholes we would have been well rid of? In a larger scheme, anger and justice are closely allied. Because the fundamental unfairness of death is in the world, we hate all the other kinds of unfairness, and one power of language is to speak against them. Thus, one of the fruits of death is that it makes us hate injustice. This is the root of this tradition of denunciation in the classical elegy. And this is where Milton unites the classical and Christian traditions through the figure of the Lamb. The Church is a bad shepherd. It is a shifting of the burden of pain, and a retaking of sexual energy from grief through totemic anger. In some contemporary version, I suppose, the Cam would be replaced by the Iowa River or the Mississippi and bad teacher-poets might be denounced for producing young artists whose "lean and flashy songs grate on their scrannel pipes of wretched straw."

132-53 RETURN, ALPHEUS

The second return to the classical mode after it had been outleapt. This time the return seems to signal the return of poetry, of a kind of erotic confidence. For this the evocation of the river god Alpheus and the nymph Arethusa, associated with the springs of poetry, seems a figure. And the flowers—symbols of sacrifice, but also resurrection—cf. Gluck's *The Wild Iris*—get heaped on the "laureate hearse" in a passage beloved by English poets and imitated for two hundred years.

154-64 AY ME! WHILST THEE THE SHORE

Milton is careful—as a Christian in a culture that was still quite interested in ghosts—to define as fictive this bringing home to England as spirit the body of Lycidas. It's another thing we do with grief: marry it to local earth. And the angel who looks homeward is not just the patron saint of mariners, but a figure for Justice, indeed a figure for revolutionary Justice, which was to sweep England in a few years and lead to regicide and a new social order. Michael is also protecting Protestant England from Catholic Spain, so the political subtext here is large.

165-85 WEEP NO MORE, WOEFUL SHEPHERDS

The apotheosis. After the purging of anger, the return of sexual energy, restored confidence in imagination, which brings the lost one home and plants him there, Milton invokes Christian resurrection, mixed with pagan nuptial feast, in a language of which African American Protestantism—"When the Saints Come Ma'ching In"—is an echo. Lycidas as "Genius" of the shore seems a reinscribing of the possibility of poetry in terms that blends pagan, Christian, and English elements.

186-93 THUS SANG THE UNCOUTH SWAIN

As Sacks says, the mourner's act of self-distancing is taken one step further in this little coda written in *ottava rima*. "Sun" here puns on "son" in ways that have both Christian and psychological bearings. For those of us who don't have a use for the Christian mythos of the poem, it is interesting to think about what Shelley would do with the form and to think of what his contemporary John Ruskin wrote: "Man is the sun of the world; more than the real sun. The fire of his heart is the only light and heat worth gauge or measure. Where he is are the tropics; where he is not, the ice-world." Something else we have trouble believing.

THE STRUCTURE OF ADONAIS

The best-known scholarly reading of the poem is to be found in Earl Wasserman, *The Subtler Language*, Johns Hopkins, 1959. The poem is written in Spenserian stanzas, the opening passage very closely resembles Bion's "Lament for Adonis," one of the most important Alexandrian elegies, which Shelley had also translated. Keats died in 1821 at the age of twenty-six. Shelley is twenty-nine. He died the following year.

Wordsworth, Coleridge, Byron, Keats, and other romantic poets avoided what they thought of as the artificial conventions of pastoral, and Wordsworth wrote against them by portraying the actual lives of the rural poor in the Napoleonic era. Shelley picks up the convention to write this strange, allegorical rather than pastoral poem that nevertheless observes many conventions of pastoral elegy, some of them ironically. Twice as long as "Lycidas," it shares a subject—the untimely death of a young poet—and some of the same issues—what poetry is in the face of death, how to overcome grief, what to feel in the face of the trivialization of poetry by the culture (this much stronger in Shelley, a central anxiety), and how to come to terms with one's own work and one's own death in relation to all of the above. Critics have commented on Shelley's idealizing Neoplatonism, the way this makes the whole problem of representation in poetry acute, and on what seems to be the intense death wish in the poem. So it has gotten a lot of attention as a psychological document. Whether it is a successful poem or not, whether you can submit to Shelley's way with language and imagery or not, it's worth looking at how he frames these issues in this elegy, where the forms of very ancient funerary ritual are put to use in a struggle with a sense of the uselessness of poetry.

STANZA 1

> I weep for Adonais—he is dead!

Echoes Bion and the tradition of vegetation myth directly. By giving Keats the name of both Adonis and Adonai—Hebrew for "Lord"— see Lowell: "The Lord survives the rainbow of his will" and Ginsberg: "Lord lord lord caw caw caw"—Shelley at the outset splits (or joins) the earthly and the spiritual symbolism of the dead poet. The phrase—

> though our tears thaw not

—questions the efficacy of poetry immediately, and the phrase—

> And thou, Sad Hour

—immediately turns the task of mourning over to the first of a long series of delegated mourners. That it takes Shelley so long to present himself as mourner has been much commented on.

> his fate and fame shall be an echo and a light unto eternity

This makes the claim for transcendence immediately, most critics have said very prematurely.

STANZAS 2-7

> Where wert thou, mighty Mother

Invokes the convention—"Where were ye, nymphs . . . what could the Muse herself . . ."—of questioning the female figures, including the mother, who failed to offer protection. In Shelley's allegory the mother of the poet is Urania, the goddess of astronomy. Here she is Venus, so like the split Adonis/Adonai there is the earthly-heavenly maternal figure Venus/Urania. And she seems not to be listening. Shelley is trying to wake her up, to make her mourn.

> With veiled eyes, mid listening Echoes, in her Paradise she
> sate,

She seems to be listening to some bad poet instead—Wordsworth, whom Shelley thought had sold out his earlier radicalism?—who "rekindled all the fading melodies with which, like flowers that mock the corse beneath, . . . he hid the coming bulk of death."

Yet wherefore (line 21)

After asking her to weep, he somewhat spasmodically withdraws the request. Why bother? These lines echo a passage in Keats's "Endymion," which Shelley had been reading: "Saturn, look up—though herefore, poor old King?"

Lament anew, Urania (line 29)

These lines appeal to her as the mother of a line of poets—Homer, Dante, Milton. Sacks: "Shelley is trying to compel a certain recognition" and "would have Urania admit the poet Keats to a grand genealogy, one that would perhaps include himself . . ." These poets are (see stanza one) "the sons of light."

The broken lily (line 55)

Sacks comments that the broken flower image "by some sad maiden cherished" emphasizes a poet not come into his sexual force. He calls this image "castrative" and connects it to the introduction of the father, "kingly Death" in the next line in which he brings the reader and Urania to Keats's grave in Rome. Here the dark father must be faced.

STANZAS 8-17

Shelley now presents a profusion of allegorical delegate-mourners, all of whose mourning is inadequate—they are the "pageantry of mist on an autumnal stream." Even Hyacinth and Narcissus, traditional figures of consolation and renewal, are impotent, and Spring, Milton's trope of the sexual renewal of the earth, throws "down her kindling buds as if she Autumn were." This passage evokes the elegiac convention of the procession, and it ends, surprisingly and abruptly, with a curse against the critic whose review of *Endymion,* Shelley believed, had broken Keats's spirit and contributed to his death. This belongs to the convention in which the poet must find a focus for his anger and express it in order to mourn successfully.

STANZAS 18-21

Ah, woe is me!

The first expression of personal grief. Sacks: "By expressing anger, Shelley has begun to undo the repression of his grief." These stanzas express anguish at the meaningless renewal of nature and desire that he doesn't feel—"The amorous birds now pair in every brake"—and come to the anguish of human consciousness, which, alone in creation, knows that it must die: "Nought we know, dies. Shall that alone be as a sword consumed before the sheath by sightless lightning?" and leads past that to anguish that "grief itself is mortal" and then leads to ultimate questions: "Whence are we and why are we? of what scene the actors or spectators?" Why this life in which "month follow month with woe and year wake year to sorrow"? Note: What Shelley wants connected to immortality in humans is that "which knows," a sword, the intense atom.

STANZAS 22-29

As if the poet can't bear the questions, the poem veers back to the mother figure Urania. Misery wakes her from her paradise, "swift as a thought by the snake Memory stung." And Mother Poetry walks into the tomb and confronts Father Death. She shames Death at first and almost brings her son back to life—"breath revisited those lips"—and she makes her speech of mourning.

STANZAS 30-38

Which brings forth a procession of poet-mourners, Byron, Moore, Shelley himself (described in the third person), and Leigh Hunt. The central passage is Shelley's self-portrait in 31–34. It ends with another denunciation of the critic in 36–37. This curse makes for a complex turning point, because what Shelley curses him with is life: "Live! fear no heavier chastisement from me." So what elegy and mourning traditionally seek the recovery of has become the object of contempt.

STANZAS 39-52

And with that, grief is defiantly transformed:

> Nor let us weep that our delight is fled
> Far from these carrion kites that scream below

and spirit and the unembodied purity of poetry exalted:

> Dust to the dust! but the pure spirit shall flow
> Back to the burning fountain whence it came

and again:

> He hath awakened from the dream of life

STANZAS 53-55

Lots of readers have found these last stanzas profoundly disturbing not only because they seem to contain intense suicidal yearning, but because they are so prophetic of Shelley's death the following year. *My spirit's bark is driven, Far from the shore, far from the trembling throng.* When Shelley—who could not swim—was sailing in a storm, a passing crew warned him to strike his sail. He ignored them and drowned. The question of whether his death was an accident or not has never been answered and some biographers have looked to the end of "Adonais" for evidence.

ELIOT'S "THE WASTELAND" AND THE ELEGY TRADITION

If you've studied "Lycidas," it's interesting to look at "The Wasteland" again in terms of the number of elegiac conventions it contains: the underlying vegetation myth, the failure of sexual energy, the intensive use of allusion, the chorus of mourning voices, the drowned sailor, and, in the last section, the reaching for some principle of transformation. Makes it possible to see how much it has been read as an elegy for an entire culture.

THE STRUCTURE OF "THE QUAKER GRAVEYARD AT NANTUCKET"

Marjorie Perloff: "'The Quaker Graveyard at Nantucket' has frequently been compared to 'Lycidas.'" Hugh Staples lists the following parallels: the death of a young man to whom the poet has a more than casual yet less than intimate relationship, death by drowning, the unrecovered body, the movement beyond the lament to a larger consideration of contemporary and universal issues, the attempt to answer the apparent futility of the young man's death (but in terms of Catholic mysticism rather than Protestant militancy). Both Lowell and Milton draw upon classical and biblical sources for their patterns of imagery; both pay homage to individual figures in their native traditions—Thoreau and Melville in Lowell's case and Theocritus, Bion, and Virgil in Milton's. Both use place names to invoke the *genius loci:* for the Hebrides, Namancos, and Bayona, Lowell substitutes Nantucket, Martha's Vineyard, and Walsingham. Even the verse form of "Quaker Graveyard" resembles "Lycidas": its 194 lines are divided like the 193 lines of "Lycidas" into a loose structure of pentameter lines varied by an occasional trimeter. Each stanza has its own highly intricate rhyme scheme, repeated in only two cases (stanza II and stanza VII), yet differing from each other only slightly. Like Milton, Lowell adapts the canzone for his own purposes. Hugh Staples: "Lowell has made only one radical departure from the old tradition: he has omitted any expression of personal grief and he has made no allusion to his personal career as a poet."

The most striking transformation, perhaps, is that Lowell has abandoned the conventional decor of the pastoral elegy, the shepherd, nymphs, and personified beings, the echoes of classical poetry, and replaced them explicitly with echoes of New England writers. For example,

> The sea was still breaking violently and night (line 2)

Thoreau, *Cape Cod:* "The brig *St. John*, from Galway, Ireland, laden with immigrants, was wrecked on Sunday morning; it was now Tuesday morning, and the sea was still breaking violently on the rocks."

> ### Light
> Flashed from his matted head and marble feet, (lines 4–5)

Thoreau, *Cape Cod:* "I saw many marble feet and matted heads as the clothes were raised, and one livid, swollen, and mangled body of a drowned girl . . ."

> The corpse was bloodless, a botch of reds and whites,
> Its open, staring eyes
> Were lusterless dead-lights

> Or cabin windows on a stranded hulk
> Heavy with sand (lines 8–12)

Thoreau, *Cape Cod:* ". . . the bone and muscle were exposed, but quite bloodless—merely red and white,—with wide-open and staring eyes, yet lustreless, dead-lights; or like the cabin windows of a stranded vessel, filled with sand."

And, of course, there are references to *Moby-Dick* throughout. For the biblical echoes and for the source of "Our Lady of Walsingham," see the notes in an anthology like the *Norton*.

PART 1

The description of the drowned sailor, rifted with echoes of Thoreau, is the equivalent to the elegy's opening cry: "Adonis is dead!" Notice that the speaker is subsumed among the other sailors: "We weight the body . . ." The most conventional elegiac move, the direct vocative, "Sailors . . ." seems to end in a rejection of the convention—the one clear signal of the pastoral ancestry of the poem: ". . . ask for no Orphean lute to pluck life back." So—a lot of the rhetoric of the poem seems at the very outset to deny poetry as an agency of renewal. Also nature: the body gets heaved "seaward whence it came," where the sharks—the heel-headed dogfish—are feeding on Ahab. This seems to pick up on "Lycidas":

> Where thou perhaps under the whelming tide
> Visit'st the bottom of the monstrous world

And there are elements of elegiac animism—the "hell-bent deity" (I'm not sure of the grammar here, of the corpse? of the sea?), the sea as "earth-shaker, green, unwearied, chaste," that word *chaste* important perhaps to the usual fertility-ritual underpinnings of elegy, since the stanza ends not with the phallic lute of Orpheus, but the dreadnaughts' guns. Lowell was a conscientious objector to World War II. The phallic guns have in them something of Hamlet's disgust with sexual appetite. Much darker opening than in either "Lycidas" or "Adonais," as if the tradition had been soaked in "The Wasteland" or Hart Crane's "The Tunnel."

PART 2

Eighteen lines, sonnetlike. No line-end periods, which is part of what gives it its intensity. In this section, Warren Winslow is addressed directly, and the convention of animate sorrow evoked: "terns and gulls tremble at your death in these home waters." First, the cousin is asked if he hears the presence of the Pequod; then, he is told that the sea cries out at his death in just the way the bones of the Quakers cry at the cruelty and violence of the old whaling industry. Moby Dick has, of course, and Warren Winslow begins to acquire, emblematic, sacrificial, and Christlike motifs. Compared to both Milton and Shelley, though, it would seem that the violence and futility of this death is merely intensified.

PART 3

"All you recovered from Poseidon" picks up on the body "heaved seaward whence it came" in the first stanza. The address to WW is continued and at the end of the section, the poet introduces himself not as a person in the historical present but as a witnessing memory and conscience. He sees the Quakers drowning, hears the fantastic hubris of their cries.

The thought, or dense image-packing, here is complex. It seems that passing time wears away, forgives suffering and evil: "time's contrition blues whatever it was these Quaker sailors lost in the mad scramble of their lives." But that kind of wearing away is also seen as sterile: "the harrowed brine is fruitless on the blue beard of the god . . ." (As if Emily Dickinson's New England ferocity were being evoked: "They say that time assuages. / Time never did assuage.")

Innocence: the only kind is that of the figureheads on the old sailing ships: "They died when time was open-eyed, wooden, and childish."

Unlike the attacks on the clergy and the critics in Milton and Shelley, the whole of this poem is, from the beginning, permeated with Lowell's rage against the greed and violence of his ancestral New England and there seems to be no escape from it.

"Of IS, the whited monster": Exodus, iii, 14: "And God said to Moses, I AM THAT AM: and he said, Thus shalt thou say unto the children of Israel, I AM hath sent me to you." Also in much Roman Catholic symbolism Jesus is *Iesus Salvator*. Lowell borrows all the symbolic glintings and ambiguities that Melville gave the white whale.

PART 4

Clamavimus, O depths:
Psalm cxxx, Out of the depths have I cried unto thee, O Lord

            Let the sea-gulls wail
For water, for the deep where the high tide
Mutters to its hurt self, mutters and ebbs.

    Thoreau, *Cape Cod*: "I sympathized rather with the wind and waves, as if toss and mangle these poor creatures was the order of the day. If this was the law of Nature, why waste any time with awe and pity?"

            Who will dance
The mast-lashed master of Leviathans
Up from this field of Quakers in their unstoned graves?

Ahab is the mast-lashed master, but Odysseus, lashed to the mast to resist the Sirens, is probably also evoked. And the question of poetry gets raised again: Who will be an Orpheus to resurrect Ahab? And there is probably also an echo of Christ as a dancing-master in the English folk tradition. And a pun on "let him who is without sin cast the first stone."

The poem seems to come to a kind of turn here. "This is the end of the whale-road" and again "This is the end of running on the waves" may mean: this graveyard is where it all ends. But it also seems to supply historical distance—the distance that mourning requires if it is to be transformed into something else—to say: this is where it all ended. But the sea itself remains a ferocious emblem of the restless meaninglessness of human endeavor:

> Waves wallow in their wash, go out and out,
> Leave only the death-rattle of the crabs,
> The beach increasing, its enormous snout
> Sucking the ocean's side.
> This is the end of running on the waves;
> We are poured out like water.

PART 5

This is a culmination of the theme of violence. After saying in the last part that we have come to the end of the whale road, he imagines the gutting and disemboweling of the whales and the corruption overrunning the earth. This passage seems particularly to echo Milton—

> Beyond treeswept Nantucket, and Wood's Hole
> And Martha's Vineyard, Sailor, will your sword

but instead of imagining Warren Winslow being brought home from "beyond the stormy Hebrides," as Lycidas is, he is imagined as being complicit in the whale killing—the description is adapted from the "Stubbs Kills a Whale" chapter of *Moby-Dick*—and the killing is made to seem at once like torture, like the wounding of Christ, and like a kind of sexual violence: "the death-lance churns into the sanctuary." And here the violence, real, imagined, historic, present, nightmarish, a metaphor for human greed, for the food chain, for sexuality, has become so intense that the poem utters its first prayer because it needs some place to put the violence: "Hide our steel, Jonas Messias, in Thy side."

PART 6

See the Norton notes for Lowell's source, Watkin's *Catholic Art and Culture*. This is the startling passage in the poem. It, in effect, reverses the pastoral convention. Where the pastoral had been located in a mourning but idyllic landscape, from which it spoke out in anger against some social evil, Lowell's elegy speaks from the middle of loss, suffering, violence, and evil and then pauses to invoke a pastoral alternative.

Again the sailor is addressed, but by now "sailor" has acquired a symbolic resonance that clearly includes the speaker and the reader. It has come to mean something like "pilgrim" and Walsingham was a place of pilgrimage where the "dragging pain" of the poem can be put down.

Commentators have focused on the relative emptiness of the symbol. It "expressionless, expresses God." It goes past "castled Sion," that is, Zion, that is, any imagination of a political state that could reflect divine justice. It even goes beyond the cross at Calvary and the crib at Bethlehem.

In "Lycidas" there was the trinity of judging father, nourishing but limited mother, and lost son, which seems to get picked up in different ways throughout the elegiac tradition. Hence Sacks's idea that successful mourning duplicates the resolution of the Oedipus complex. Here is a mother to think about.

And what about the question of poetry? Does this passage answer the question, "Who will dance the mast-lashed master of Leviathans up . . . ?" This seems a place to leave pain and the Virgin seems a representation that is utterly simple and plain and points past representation.

Perloff: "Although 'Our Lady of Walsingham' is meant to provide a positive alternative to the sins the poet has been denouncing so vehemently, it fails to cohere with the rest of the poem . . . Within the larger context of the whole elegy, the shrine of Our Lady of Walsingham stands in sharp opposition to the Quaker Graveyard in Nantucket, and it is hard to see how these two symbolic locales can be fused."

Hass: "I imagine for a lot of young writers this was the place where they learned how far you could go away from the poem and still be in it . . . Lowell is not after sacramental mediation but a contemplative peace beyond any manifestation in the flesh, so there is no resolution of the conflict between Nantucket and Walsingham; there is irresolvable tension, and it's in this way that 'Quaker Graveyard' is finally a Manichean poem."

PART 7

In this last section, the Atlantic is addressed. In the beginning of the poem, the ocean is the earth-shaker, green, unwearied, chaste. He is also from whence we came. In the third section he is associated with Poseidon and with blue: "harrowed brine is fruitless on the blue beard of the god." Also warships rock "in the hand of the great God, where time's contritions blue . . ." So there are two gods: god and God, Poseidon and Jonathan Edwards's Jehovah. Here the Atlantic is "fouled with the blue sailors," who are "sea monsters, upward angel, downward fish"—echo of Milton. And the Lord God is something else and it is what Lowell ends up identifying with. As in a lot of cosmologies, he's had to split off the good God from the bad one.

Here the Creator Spirit is one thing and the blue killer of the Atlantic another:

> When the Lord God formed man from the sea's slime
> And breathed into his face the breath of life.
> And blue-lunged combers lumbered to the kill.
> The Lord survives the rainbow of His will.

This split between some kind of naturalism and some longing for a transcendent principle to identify with is an old imagination of the structure of things. The Gnostics imagined creator-monsters, archons, and an unembodied God of pure light, Blake called the creator-God Nobadaddy, and so on. Lowell's imagination of the split between the way we can imagine nature and spirit, good and evil, seems to be the same one that Ginsberg represents at the end of "Kaddish," where there is an unresolved debate between the voices of scavenging crows and the voice of praise for the (male) principle of the holy:

> Caw caw caw caw caw caw
> Lord Lord Lord Lord Lord Lord
> Caw caw caw Lord Lord Lord

"HOWL" AND "KADDISH"

Carl Solomon is not dead—and "Howl" has often been read as a shadow elegy for Ginsberg's mother, Naomi, a subject he finally broached directly in "Kaddish"—he is merely incarcerated, but "Howl" has many elements of pastoral elegy. And for all the ways in which Lowell looks back to Milton, there are a number of ways in which Ginsberg looks back to Shelley. The "angel-headed hipsters" in part one are, in a strikingly modernized Shelleyan language, "burning for the ancient heavenly connection to the starry dynamo in the machinery of the night." They are a procession of mourners, violent seekers of transcendence. As in the classical elegy, Ginsberg turns, in the Moloch section, to denunciation before he can reconnect to his art, and at the end of the poem Carl Solomon shows up at his door, as if emerged from the sea.

SATIRE

Shame on you! you who make unjust laws and publish
 burdensome decrees,
Depriving the poor of justice,
Robbing the weakest of my people of their rights,
Despoiling the widow and plundering the orphan.

—*Isaiah, 10:1–2*

Volusius, who does not know what monsters lunatic Egypt
Chooses to cherish? One part goes in for crocodile worship;
One bows down to the ibis that feeds upon serpents;
 elsewhere
A golden effigy shines, of a long-tailed monkey!
Where the magic chords resound from Memnon, half-broken,
Where with her hundred gates old Thebes lies buried in
 ruins,
Whole towns revere a dog, or cats, or a fish from the river.
No one worships Diana. But they have a taboo about biting
Into a leek or an onion; this, they think, is unseemly.

Oh what holy folk! whose gardens give birth to such gods!
Lamb and the flesh of kids are forbidden at the table;
Feeding on human flesh, however, is perfectly proper.

—*Juvenal, "Satire XV"*

Bring me my Bow of burning gold:
Bring me my Arrows of desire:
Bring me my Spear: O clouds unfold!
Bring me my Chariot of fire!

—*William Blake, "Milton"*

America I've given you all and now I'm nothing.
America two dollars and twentyseven cents January 17, 1956.
I can't stand my own mind.
America when will we end the human war?
Go fuck yourself with your atom bomb.

—*Allen Ginsberg, "America"*

1. Satire, from *satura*, a dish of mixed fruits. Supposedly because early Latin satire involved a medley of prose and verse. From the beginning satire implied cultural criticism—realistic portrayal of the evils, or annoyances, of the time with the aim of correcting them, though one could also argue that its roots are in anger and that it means to do damage.

2. According to one theory, satire originates in the curse, in the idea that denunciation or excommunication or disavowal had, like blessing, magical efficacy—the father's power to disown a child, the shaman's power to hex. Another source in shame cultures was

the power of ridicule as a way of enforcing social norms. (See Robert Elliott, *The Power of Satire: Magic, Ritual, Art,* 1966.)

3. But as a literary genre, it begins with the Roman poets. The typical metrical form in satire was the epic meter, dactylic hexameter, and so, when it was brought into English, it was often written in blank verse, though it came to be written in any of the typical period meters, in the eighteenth century the heroic couplet.

4. The two orienting Latin poets were Horace and Juvenal. Horace was associated with urbane poems, written with a light touch; Juvenal, with fury and invective. Though particular poems by each were imitated—Samuel Johnson's "The Vanity of Human Wishes" is modeled on a poem by Juvenal, for example—the classical satires were not formal models in the sense that they suggested particular patterns of development. What they did suggest was an intention (moral or political correction), a tone and diction appropriate to the subjects (demotic, realistic, down-to-earth), and a milieu (the satire was urban).

5. The other model for a satiric tradition is the Old Testament prophets: visionary, moral, and denunciatory. The rhythmic model, of course, was the English of the King James Bible. Many passages in Jeremiah, Ezekiel, and the late Minor Prophets were written in prose. Some of this prose (cf. Robert Alter, *The Art of Biblical Poetry*) loosely employs the semantic and syntactical parallelism that is the main metrical feature of Hebrew verse. But most of the prophetic writing in early Hebrew literature (before 586 BCE) was composed in verse. The verse, according to Alter, has the overarching purpose of reproof and uses three basic strategies—direct vocative accusation of a specific historical audience; satire, in the sense of mocking

hyperbolic criticism; and the monitory evocation of disaster. In this way satire and prophecy are connected to apocalypse. One can speak of it as a two-part tradition: a poetics of destruction and a poetics of restoration.

6 . So there are these two traditions. The Roman satiric modes tends to combine some formal metrical manner with the basic trope of realism, metonymy. And it was often funny, or at least witty. The prophetic mode in English echoes the rhythmic flow of the King James, its anaphora and parallel constructions, and tends to be heavily metaphorical. And it isn't a tradition notable for its sense of humor, though that probably needs to be looked at.

One would have to do more study of Horace and Juvenal and the Hebrew prophets than I've done to answer the question of whether or not there is a pattern of development, an inner logic to the shape of satire and prophecy like the ones one can make out in the ode and the elegy. It would seem that satire's natural form would be the list, the bill of particulars.

Most helpful is Thomas Jemielity's *Satire and the Hebrew Prophets*. Jemielity quotes from the biblical scholars who tend to confirm one's sense that the prophetic books are, well, a fruit stew. Johannes Lindblom on their literary qualities: "sermons and admonitory addresses, announcements of doom and punishment, lyric poems, prayers, hymns, parables, dialogues, monologues, short oracles, didactic sentences, predictions, letters, etc." Gene M. Tucker, *Form Criticism in the Old Testament:* ". . . a maze of sayings, speeches, and reports run together." Which is to say satire is not reasonable; it tends, in many versions, toward explosive and disorganized force; and because the powerless see power as theater, it is often theatrical: it mocks, parodies, devours literary genres that in other contexts make the world seem reasonable and orderly. So it can be formally antagonistic to form.

7. In *Anatomy of Criticism*, Northrop Frye proposes a way of looking at narrative genres based on the seasonal circle of our lives. Comedy is associated with spring and fertility ritual, tragedy with autumn and rituals for allaying the ghosts of harvest. Romance, stories that tend to flatter a culture's values, belong to high summer, and satire belongs to winter. It is the world stripped bare.

8. It was the Roman model that prevailed in the English Renaissance. Prophecy enters English poetry as a romantic mode. Northrop Frye: "Blake's *Marriage of Heaven and Hell* can be thought of as the epilogue to the Golden Age of English Satire, a vigorous Beethovenish coda, big with portents of the movements to follow."

9. Almost every literary magazine that proposes a series of questions on the current state of poetics for practicing poets to answer includes one about poetry and politics. Partly this is a question about genre. Should poems propose political ideals? For Frye, I suppose, that would be the territory of romance. Should it be in the business of analysis and protest? That would be the territory of satire.

10. But the whole idea of kinds or genre in English poetry as orienting models more or less died away by the middle of the eighteenth century—though the writing of sonnets, elegies, and odes persisted into the nineteenth century and though certain French and Italian medieval forms like the sestina, the villanelle, and the ballade were introduced into English poetry in the Victorian period. A few of these kinds—the ones with specific formal rules like the sonnet, the sestina, and the villanelle—have persisted to the present, and so have—as very adaptable ideas of kinds of poems—the elegy and the ode. And so, as orienting ideas, have a few other formal propositions, like prayer and hymn and lament. See, for example, Geoffrey Hill's "Mercian Hymns" and poems like Leslie Silko's "Prayer to the Pacific." The epistle passed into the letter poem, the eclogue into the debate poem, and so on. And some new forms—borrowed from non-European literatures—like the Japanese tanka and haiku and the Islamic ghazal have been introduced.

But the idea of a poet sitting down to write a particular kind of poem defined by a classical inheritance begins to end with the romantics, and one of the symptoms of this trend is the disappearance sometime in the 1760s of the formal satire. The deepest reason for this probably has to do with the fact that satire, as it was conceived, depended on a notion of common values. Its weapon was shame. As poetry, beginning with Blake, Wordsworth, and Coleridge, came to have a fundamentally adversarial relation to the cultural, political, and religious center, the whole stance of the urbane social critic appealing to his audience to correct social evil and excess became untenable. By the time of Baudelaire in France, the world made by capitalism and a middle class was in place, and writing poetry, or making art of any kind, had come to seem a form of social protest per se.

(Hence a hundred years later the scandal of George Oppen in Brooklyn in the 1930s putting poetry aside to do political work for twenty years, on the principle that rent control was rent control and poetry was poetry.)

11. What survived the passing of genres in English was a poetry of social criticism nearer to the tone of the Hebrew prophets—the great example is Blake's "London"—and also a poetry that comes closer to our modern sense of satire, the ironic protest poem, of which Lawrence's "How Beastly the Bourgeois Is" or Auden's "The Unknown Citizen" are examples. And so the two kinds of satire—Horatian and Juvenalian—persist as tones in our poetry of protest and social

criticism, along with prophetic rage and outrage. It's probably also the case that this adversarial feeling can't be contained so neatly, so sealed off from the "lyric," so that the kind of social criticism in the elegy and in the political sonnet—see Wordsworth, "The World Is Too Much With Us"—is nearer to our sense of wrongness and deeper than the witty satirical poem. In that way one answer to the question of poetry and politics has to do with the work it does in the way poetry wrestles with its own value when it addresses the public world—in poems like Auden's elegy for Yeats, in H.D.'s poem of the bombing of London, "The Walls Do Not Fall," in Robert Duncan's "Poem Beginning with a Line from Pindar."

12 . I'm not sure, therefore, that there are usable forms in the history of satire or in the great examples. One would want to attend to the turn they take at the end. One form might be just to list evils, one worse than the last. The tendency of that form is apocalypse. Another is analysis. That is the way of Blake's "London." The city as systematic injustice and cruelty in the last line "blasts with plague the marriage hearse." It has made sex death. It's Blake's insistence that the streets are "charter'd," that the manacles that imprison its inhabitants are "mind-forged" that gives the poem its force. The poem doesn't draw the moral, but it is implicit: this is a human order; it can be changed. Neruda's "United Fruit Company" is another instance. He begins with a mock-biblical narrative. In the beginning the U.S. corporations created the Banana Republics that attracted fruit flies in the form of vicious dictators and led to the dropping into the harbors of Central America, like rotten fruit, the native peoples of that place. Four stanzas of short-lined free verse, intended, I think, like Blake's quatrains, to carry a sense of contained force.

Another formal shape comes from doing what the ode does with litany: it makes the indictment—legal language is another feature of satire—and turns to prayer for relief or release: "Great God!"

Wordsworth writes of his London. "I'd rather be a pagan suckled on a creed outworn, so might I, standing on this pleasant lea, have glimpses that would make me less forlorn, have sight of Proteus rising from the sea, or hear old Triton blow his wreathed horn."

13 . Laughter is important to the satiric tradition; its source is discrepancy between value and fact. The world stripped bare: the exhilaration of plain speaking. Its work is tearing down, not building. The Moloch section of "Howl" is terrific, the conclusion that "everything is holy!" not so great.

14 . Formally the most interesting idea here may be *satura*, that the old, lost Latin satires were mixes of verse and prose, a form we'll be looking at later.

Some readings:

CLASSICAL SOURCES

Horace, Satire, I, 9: "The Bore"
Juvenal, Satire 3: "The City of Rome"

BIBLICAL SOURCES

Isaiah, Jeremias

COMPLEYNT: EARLIER ENGLISH POEMS IN THE NATIVE
TRADITION

William Langland: *Piers Plowman*
John Skelton: "Speke, Parrot"
"Why Come Ye Not to Court?"

ENGLISH SATIRE

Thomas Wyatt: *from* Satire 1
Henry Howard: *from* A Satire of London
John Donne: "Satire III"
Ben Jonson: "An Execration Upon Vulcan"
John Dryden: "Mac Flecknoe"
John Wilmot: "A Satire Against Mankind"
Jonathan Swift: "A Description of the Morning"
                "A Description of a City Shower"
These are not satiric poems but interesting to think about for
the connection between satire and the emergence of literary
realism.
                "The Lady's Dressing Room"
Alexander Pope: "The Dunciad"
                "Epistle to Dr. Arbuthnot"
Samuel Johnson: "The Vanity of Human Wishes"
Charles Churchill: "The Rosciad"
                "The Candidate"
(Churchill is usually thought of as the last poet in the tradition
of formal satire.)

AFTER SATIRE

William Blake: "London"
                "Let the Brothels of Paris Be Opened"
                "The Marriage of Heaven and Hell"
William Wordsworth: "Composed on Westminster Bridge"
John Clare: "The Parish"
D. H. Lawrence: "The English Are So Nice!"
Ezra Pound: "Mr. Nixon" *from* Hugh Selwyn Mauberly
Robinson Jeffers: "Shine, Perishing Republic"
ee cummings: "I sing of Olaf"
Hart Crane: "The Tunnel" *from The Bridge*

W. H. Auden: "The Unknown Citizen (x)"
Gwendolyn Brooks: "We Real Cool"
Frank O'Hara: "Ave Maria"
Amiri Baraka: many poems
Robert Bly: "The Teeth Mother Naked at Last"
Claudia Rankine: *Citizen*

Further reading: Thomas Jemielity, *Satire and the Hebrew Prophets*, Westminster/John Knox Press, 1992.

To think about ode, elegy, and satire mixed, Federico Garcia Lorca, *A Poet in New York*.

GEORGIC

I've sung the tillage of the earth, the lore of heaven,
Now it's the turn of wine, and with it the trees that crowd
in woody copse, and the produce of the gradual-growing
   olive.
Come, Lord of the Wine-press—everything here is lavish
By your largesse, for you the field's a-flower and laden
With vines of autumn, the vintage foams in vats
   overflowing—
Come then, Lord of the Wine-press, pull off your boots and
   paddle
Bare-legged with me and dye your shins purple in the grape
   juice.

—*Virgil, Georgics, II, 1–8*

Neither needed men of so excellent parts to have despaired of
a fortune which the poet Virgil promised himself (and indeed
obtained) who got as much glory of eloquence, wit, and learning in the expressing of the observations of husbandry, as of
the heroical acts of Aeneas.

Surely if the purpose be in good earnest not to write at leisure that which men may read at leisure, but really to instruct
and suborn action and active life, these Georgics of the mind
concerning the husbandry and tillage thereof, are no less worth
than the heroical descriptions of Virtue, Duty, and Felicity.

—*Francis Bacon, The Advancement of Learning*

Almost all the great works of antiquity were done on request.
The *Georgics* are propaganda for the farming of the Roman
countryside.

—*Pablo Neruda*

I'll spend three thousand years writing it, it'll be packed full
of information on soil conservation, the Tennessee Valley
Authority, astronomy, geology, Hsuan Tsung's travels, Chinese painting theory, reforestation, Oceanic ecology and food
chains.

—*Japhy Ryder, in Jack Kerouac's* The Dharma Bums,
describing a long poem he imagines writing

1. We don't have a useful vocabulary for poems of information and
instruction or the way the formal imagination might work in them,
partly because, beginning with the romantics, poets came to feel
that poetry had different work to do from the work of the expository, idea-synthesizing intelligence, and they stopped writing didactic or instructive poems. By the time of Baudelaire and Whitman,
however, poetry had come to have an oppositional relation to its
dominant cultures and could come to seem, among other things,
a tradition of alternative information. So Ezra Pound could refer to

his *Cantos* as "the Ezra-versity" and his young friend Louis Zukofsky could have a go at explaining Leninist economics in a long poem called *A*. So Japhy Ryder—Jack Kerouac's portrait of the young Gary Snyder—could imagine a poem containing all the practical and spiritual information not on the curriculum of Cold War America in the 1950s, and by the 2010s a book of literary theory called *Ecocriticism* could have a chapter called "Georgic."

2. The georgic got its name from Virgil's *Georgics*, a set of four long poems in dactylic hexameter about farming.

3. From the introduction to a 2005 translation: "*The Georgics* is a poem for our time. Though written more than two thousand years ago, it speaks to us just as it spoke to Virgil's contemporaries. The poem not only gave specific instruction to Italian farmers but also passionately advocated caring without cease for the land and for the crops and animals it sustained. A message inhabits the instructions: only at our gravest peril do we fail to husband the resources on which our lives depend" (Janet Lembke, *Virgil's Georgics*, Yale University Press, 2005). See also *The Georgics: A Poem of the Land*, translated by Kimberly Johnson, Penguin Classics; *Georgics*, translated by David Ferry; and a recent translation by an Irish poet, Peter Fallon, *Georgics*.

4. They were translated by John Dryden at the end of the seventeenth century—his versions are still very readable, if you have a taste for their sound—and for a period there was a vogue in English for a poem of instruction and information. It corresponded roughly with the rise of the new science and an appetite for practical knowledge. Readers, at least some readers, seemed to feel that it was more

pleasant—it was the age of the rhymed couplet—to get one's information from poetry than prose. Joseph Addison wrote an essay praising the georgic, and Dryden wrote about the form in his prefaces to
the translations. They both said, in effect, that maybe it was time
that poetry actually do something of practical use.

5 . The first book of practical and theoretical instruction about
farming by an American writer was Samuel Deane's *The New-England
Farmer, or Georgical Dictionary,* and it is possible to think of Thomas
Jefferson's *Notes on the State of Virginia* (1785) as prose in the georgic
tradition. In the twentieth century, Wendell Berry's *Farming: A Hand-
book* (1970) is in this tradition, though it is book of poems nearer to
ode and satire. Maybe the distinction is that poems in the territory of
ode are toward-which poems, ones in search of value or a right relation to values. In the georgic the values are in place.

6 . When I was first compiling these notes for the forms class, it
didn't occur to me to include the georgic because it seemed both out
of the way and extinct. Three things made the form suddenly interesting to think about. One was the emergence of an environmental poetry and efforts toward a critical ecopoetics, reflected in Janet
Lembke's sense of the contemporaneity of the poem. Another was
the emergence of a documentary poetics. And another was the work
of my Berkeley colleague Kevis Goodman, a scholar of eighteenth-
century poetry, who has had interesting things to say about the
genre and why it disappeared in her book, *Georgic Modernity and British Romanticism.*

Her basic argument is that when the romantics redefined the nature of poetry by claiming that it was not a pretty and musical way
of dressing up knowledge, but itself a form of knowledge, it made
poetry seem the opposite of practical instruction, and the georgic

disappeared, or rather the role of information and practical instruction in poetry went underground.

7. Didn't Ezra Pound describe the *Cantos* as "sailing after knowledge"? This is me now, not Goodman. Mightn't it make sense to regard those poems—or parts of them, the stuff on Italian banking, and Chinese history, and the friendship of Adams and Jefferson—as georgics?

8. And thinking about genre, about the elegy and the ode, might it not make sense to say that satire is to the elegy, as georgic is to the ode? If the formal elegy contains an element of social criticism, uses public anger at social evils as a way to find a channel from private grief back to life-giving feeling, perhaps in the work done by the ode to connect its speakers to the creative imagination and notions of the good, there have been poems that work to tell you, in a practical way, how to get there.

9. There aren't many sharp boundaries in nature, and ecologists have a word to describe the transition zones between grassland and forest, sea and shore. They call them ecotones. And it strikes me that a lot of poems inhabit the ecotone between elegy and satire, ode and georgic. The ecotone between elegy and satire: Aimé Césaire's *Notebook of a Return to a Native Place* comes to mind, also interestingly, an experiment in mixing verse and prose.

10. Another interest of Goodman's work is that she writes about what was for Virgil and his readers in the English Augustan age, the problem of language. He was writing in a heroic meter, the meter of the *Iliad*, which raised the issue of what level of diction one used to write about fertilizing fields and the mechanics of stock-breeding. To use a language of instruction raised the usual formal questions familiar to writers of expository prose about what order to present materials in—Do you take up tillage first? Or the cultivation of fruit trees? And in what order do you present the orchardist's tasks?— but it also raised questions about what kind of language to use, and, more complexly, what aesthetic energy and what sense of the nature of the world came from the formal effects created by trying to know something. Wasn't this, more or less, the subject of Wallace Stevens's *Notes Toward a Supreme Fiction*?

11. That is, the philosophical poem, if it takes up the question of what the proper work of poetry is, and what kinds of language, what uses of metaphor constitute it, is doing a sort of exploration of poetic husbandry. Interestingly, like Virgil's poem *Notes Toward a Supreme Fiction* is written in four parts, each taking up a proposed aspect of its subject.

12. So it seemed suddenly useful to think about the georgic as a literary form. And to think about the ways in which some of the typical formal devices of modernist and postmodernist poetics—collage, fragmentation, braiding, and juxtaposition—have been put to work by contemporary poets doing expository work in verse. This turn in the twentieth century begins with Pound, who evokes Hesiod in Canto 47: "Begin thy plowing / when the Pleiades go to their rest, / Begin thy plowing, / forty days are they under seabord" and initiated *The Cantos* partly from an instinct (which was his ruin) that a poem ought to do useful work. This sense deepened in the years of the Great Depression and produced the two documentary sets of poems, *The Chinese Cantos* and *The Adams Cantos*, both published in 1940. The

formal problem of this kind of work is the same in prose or verse, how to organize and present the material. Pound, using the method of the earlier parts of the poem (or earlier poems, depending on how you think of *The Cantos*), experimented with "piths and gists," trying to make ideograms from fragmentary quotation. Though the case, as he said in another context, "presents no adjunct to the Muse's diadem," it suggested a way for what was to become a documentary poetics. The poet to take it up immediately was Louis Zukofsky, in the first eleven books of *A*, written mostly in the early 1930s.

It's interesting that the other books that begin to make a documentary tradition were published in those years, Charles Reznikoff's *Testimony* in 1934 and Muriel Rukeyser's *Book of the Dead* in 1938. As the aesthetic of the English georgic was connected to the rise of the empirical sciences as a rational response to a sclerotic social system, the Depression in the United States altered for some poets their sense of the work that poetry might do.

13. *Doc-po:* The twinned concerns with environmental crisis and evident social injustice has had some similar effect in the last decade. Documentary poetry—common enough to have gotten a nickname—and ecopoetics have both, in a range of ways, taken up the tasks of being an alternative history and a place to present useful ideas. Almost all this work mixes genres: now georgic, now elegiac, now satiric, now lyric. And maybe amounting to a vast ode, as in the case of Pablo Neruda's *Canto General* or Ernesto Cardenal's *Homenaje a los indios Americanos*, in which he uses Pound's method to evoke the native peoples of Central America. See also his *Zero Hour: Documentary Poems*.

14. For our purposes the thing to attend to is what work the shaping imagination is doing in this range of work.

READINGS:

Hesiod: *Works and Days*

Lucretius: *On the Nature of Things*

Virgil: *Georgics*

Anne Bradstreet: *The Quaternions*—This is the young Anne
  Bradstreet, writing sometime before *The Tenth Muse* was published in 1650: a set of five four-part poems on the seasons,
  the ages of man, four kinds of monarchy, etc. I don't know
  that she thought of them as Virgilian georgics, but they are
  poems of information and the first American long poems.
  The four-part structure is like Virgil's and seems to have
  conveyed a sense of completeness.

John Dryden: *The Georgics* 1697—This is his Virgil translation.

I doubt many contemporary poets will want to read through the
history of the georgics boom in the English eighteenth century, but
here is some of the scholarship on the subject: John Chalker, *The
English Georgic*, 1969; Rachel Crawford, *Poetry, Enclosure, and the Vernacular Landscape, 1700–1830*, 2002; Kevis Goodman, *Georgic Modernity and British Romanticism*, 2004. The poems the scholars place in
this tradition: John Philips, *Cyder*, 1708; John Gay, *Rural Sports*, 1713;
Christopher Smart, *The Hop-Garden*, 1752; John Dyer, *The Fleece*,
1757; James Grainger, *The Sugar Cane*, 1764; and Henry Jago, *Edge-
Hill*, 1767. Nearer to a science treatise: Erasmus Darwin, *The Love of
Plants*, 1789, also a poem in four books.

Both Chalker and Goodman trace the history of the landscape
poem, a track that might be interesting to poets working in an
emerging ecopoetics. Chalker begins with John Denham, *Cooper's
Hill*, 1642, and Alexander Pope, *Windsor Forest*, 1713, and proceeds to
James Thomson's *The Seasons*, 1726–1730, a poem I still find readable,
and William Cowper's *The Task*, which is perhaps to eighteenth-
century poetry what *Tristram Shandy* is to the eighteenth-century
novel. It's in six books of what Coleridge called "divine chitchat" and

invents a conversational blank verse to make a poem of sublimely disorganized meanderings. Goodman ends with Wordsworth's *The Excursion*, 1814, a blank verse poem in nine books.

Ezra Pound, *The Chinese Cantos, The Adams Cantos;* Louis Zukofsky, *A 1–11;* Charles Reznikoff, *Testimony;* Muriel Rukeyser, *The Book of the Dead.*

A SAMPLING OF MORE RECENT WORK:

Peter Scott: *Coming to Jakarta* (1989)

Gary Snyder: *Mountains and Rivers Without End* (1996)

Lisa Robertson: *The Weather* (2001)

Juliana Spahr: *The Connection of Everything with Lungs* (2005)

C. D. Wright: *One Big Self* (2007)

Mark Nowak: *Coal Mountain Elementary* (2009)

Claudia Rankine: *Don't Let Me Be Lonely* (2004), and *Citizen* (2014)

Evelyn Reilly: *Styrofoam* (2009)

Craig Santos Perez: *Guma: from Unincorporated Territory* (2014)

And there is work clearly in the lyric tradition, for our purposes the ode or quest tradition, whose work contains georgic and documentary elements: Jorie Graham's look at the Second World War in *Overlord* and at the environment in *Sea Change;* Brenda Hillman's tetralogy of books on the elements.

VARIABLE STANZAS
AND ORGANIC FORM

So much for genre. Let's return to the subjects of shaping and of formal means.

1. The most common free verse stanza is variable.

The reasons for this are pretty obvious—if one is going to get rid of meter under the theory that the poem should find its own rhythm, it seems to follow that it should also find its own stanza pattern. Equally important was the fact that fixed stanza lengths in metrical poetry were tied to rhyme schemes, so that, when end rhyme was not used, the main technical reason for uniform stanzas disappeared.

Both rhyme and meter in short poems were connected, of course, to their origin as lyrics—words to accompany music, which was also a reason for the repeated formal patterns. The first divergence of lyric from music in English occurred with the invention of printing, and from the 1550s to the 1850s the short poem for the most part continued to be organized, fundamentally, on the metaphor of song. The departure from fixed stanzas was the second divergence.

2. That is why—outside the ode forms—Walt Whitman was, as far as I know, the first poet in the English language to experiment with the variable stanza, and "Song of Myself" is the first fruit of those experiments. It's strange, reading the poem, to realize that hardly anyone had ever done before what Whitman was doing with the stanza. His explicit notion of what he was doing was based on analogy to nature:

> Urge and urge and urge,
> Always the procreant urge of the world.

> Out of the dimness opposite equals advance, always
>   substance and increase, always sex,
> Always a knit of identity, always distinction, always a breed
>   of life.

> To elaborate is no avail, learn'd and unlearn'd feel that it is so.
> Sure as the most certain sure, plumb in the uprights, well
>   entretied, braced in the beams,
> Stout as a horse, affectionate, haughty, electrical,
> I and this mystery here we stand.

3. A decade later French *vers libre* was launched, and its early practitioners, also free to vary stanza length, were more inclined to use that possibility to startle, to abruptly shift subjects or tones. The appeal was not so much to nature but to mind, to the creative freedom of the artist, or to the creative compulsion of the artist whose loyalty was to something other than formal regularity. This came into English most dramatically in Eliot's imitation of Jules Laforgue in "The Love Song of J. Alfred Prufrock" in 1917:

> Shall I say, I have gone at dusk through narrow streets
> And watched the smoke that rises from the pipes
> Of lonely men in shirt-sleeves, leaning out of windows?

I should have been a pair of ragged claws
Scuttling across the floor of silent seas.

And the afternoon, the evening, sleeps so peacefully!
Smoothed by long fingers,
Asleep . . . tired . . . or it malingers,
Stretched on the floor, here beside you and me.
Should I, after tea and cakes and ices,
Have the strength to force the moment to its crisis?
But though I have wept and fasted . . .

4 . It is an interesting fact about the development of Wallace Stevens that there are eighteen poems in *Harmonium* (1923) in the variable free verse stanza, and after that he only wrote three or four in the next thirty years. It was for him a thing of the 1910s, of *vers libre* as the new poets were trying to adapt it. Here is H.D., the first poem in her first volume *Sea Garden* in 1916:

Rose, harsh rose,
marred and with stint of petals,
meager flower, thin,
sparse of leaf,

more precious
than a wet rose
single on a stem—
you are caught in the drift.

Stunted, with small leaf,
you are flung on the sand,
you are lifted
in the crisp sand
that drives in the wind.

Can the spice rose
drip such acrid fragrance
hardened in a leaf?

She tends to vary stanza length all through her early work from 1912 to 1944 and then returned to fixed stanzas for *Trilogy* and *Helen in Egypt*. Here is D. H. Lawrence in 1917:

When she rises in the morning
I linger to watch her;
She spreads the bath-cloth underneath the window
And the sunbeams catch her
Glistening white on the shoulders,
While down her sides the mellow
Golden shadow glows as
She stoops to the sponge, and her swung breasts
Sway like full-blown yellow
Gloire de Dijon roses.

She drips herself with water, and her shoulders
Glisten as silver, they crumple up
Like wet and falling roses, and I listen
For the sluicing of their rain-disheveled petals.
In the window full of sunlight
Concentrates her golden shadow
Fold on fold, until it glows as
Mellow as the glory roses.

This is the Lawrence who wrote in 1918: "Free verse toes no melodic line, no matter what drill-sergeant . . . We can get rid of the stereotyped movements and the hackneyed associations of sound and sense. We can break the stiff neck of habit . . . free verse has its own *nature*, that . . . is neither star nor pearl, but instantaneous like plasm . . . It has no finish. It has no satisfying stability, satisfying to those who like the immutable. None of this."

Here is Williams in 1920:

> By the road to the contagious hospital
> under the surge of the blue
> mottled clouds driven from the
> northeast—a cold wind. Beyond, the
> waste of broad, muddy fields
> brown with dried weeds, standing and fallen
>
> patches of standing water
> the scattering of tall trees
>
> All along the road the reddish
> purplish, forked, upstanding, twiggy
> stuff of bushes and small trees
> with dead, brown leaves under them
> leafless vines—
>
> Lifeless in appearance, sluggish
> dazed spring approaches—
>
> They enter the new world naked,
> cold, uncertain of all
> save that they enter. All about them
> the cold, familiar wind—
>
> Now the grass, tomorrow
> the stiff curl of wildcarrot leaf
> One by one objects are defined—
> It quickens: clarity, outline of leaf
>
> But now the stark dignity of
> entrance—Still, the profound change

> has come upon them: rooted, they
> grip down and begin to waken

It's interesting to wonder whether the impulse of Whitman or of Laforgue applies to this poem with its last processional quatrains.

5. Both of these ideas would get articulated in one way or another during the free verse revival of the '50s and '60s in the notions of "organic form" and "projective verse." The modernist architect's credo applies and was applied: "Form follows function." Very close to Robert Creeley's remark that "Form is always an extension of content." But it is often not so simple. There are poems like W. S. Merwin's "December Night" in which the stanza functions like a paragraph:

> The cold slope is standing in darkness.
> But the south of the trees is dry to the touch.
>
> The heavy limbs climb into the moonlight bearing
>   feathers
> I came to watch these
> White plants older at night
> The oldest
> Comes first to the ruins
>
> And I hear magpies kept awake by the moon
> The water flows through its
> Own fingers without end
>
> Tonight once more
> I find a single prayer and it is not for men

There is also a careful mix, or what appears to be a careful mix, that exists somewhere between a proposed order and a discovered one, as in Robert Duncan's "Often I Am Permitted to Return to a Meadow":

> as if it were a scene made up by the mind,
> that is not mine, but a made place,
>
> that is mine, it is so near to the heart,
> an eternal pasture folded in all thought
> so that there is a hall therein
>
> that is a made place, created by light
> wherefrom the shadows, that are forms fall.
>
> Wherefrom fall all architectures I am
> I say are likenesses of the First Beloved
> whose flowers are flames lit to the Lady.
>
> She it is Queen Under The Hill
> whose hosts are a disturbance of words within words
> that is a field folded.
>
> It is only a dream of the grass blowing
> east against the source of the sun
> in an hour before the sun's going down
>
> whose secret we see in a children's game
> of ring a round of roses told.
>
> Often I am permitted to return to a meadow
> as if it were a given property of the mind
> that certain bounds hold against chaos,
>
> that is a place of first permission,
> everlasting omen of what is.

This could hardly be more delicately patterned. And a place to observe that one of the typical procedures of the poem with variable stanza length is to establish a base—here the couplet—and depart from it and return to it. The pattern here is 2-3-2-3-3-3-2-3-2. And it seems to merge the idea of form as a following of the contour of a thought with the idea of form as a made thing.

6 . —so that in the variable stanza of the free verse poem there is an expressive spectrum—from poems whose order is intended to seem natural and invisible to ones in which an order asserts itself in such a way that it seems not simply a function of subject matter, but of perception or made rhythm, implies the poet as maker rather than the poet as acolyte to some natural order in things.

7 . On this subject I often think of Barbara Hepworth, the English sculptor. Her early work, like her friend Henry Moore's, is a celebration of natural forms; the wood has beautifully the shape of wood reaching toward light, its stone the contour of worn stone. In the midst of this work, in St. Ives, on the Cornwall coast, she became pregnant by the painter Ben Nicholson, who let her know that he had no interest in becoming a father. She continued to work, understanding the child would be hers, and she had triplets. Which altered her attitude toward nature. And her work—that I've seen—is immediately much more abstract, as if she had shifted allegiances from Stephen Dedalus to Samuel Beckett. To put a thing, a pillar, a stone, next to another pillar, or stone, proposes a form. To put three objects of any kind next to one another is to propose a relation and is a form. The whole idea of this-in-relation-to-that seems suddenly and profoundly mysterious.

See Denise Levertov, "Some Notes on Organic Form" and Lynn Hejinian: "The Rejection of Closure" and also Marjorie Perloff: "The Return of the (Numerical) Repressed."

DIFFICULT FORMS

1 . After about 1540 or so the English accentual syllabic metrical system was in place—worked out first, as we've seen, by Thomas Wyatt and Henry Howard, who drew on Italian and classical as well as native models, and a remarkable explosion of poetry followed—the sonnet sequences, the pastorals, the satires, the songs, odes and elegies and epigrams, the elaborate dream-allegory of the *Faerie Queen*, and the blank verse of the Elizabethan theater. Some of the verse is extremely elaborate and inventive, but almost all of it aims for effects that the smoothness of the new meter makes possible. So in 1610 or so, seventy years after Wyatt's first translations from the Italian, something new begins to happen in the verse of John Donne. It shows up in the stanza and the metrics of "The Sun Rising":

> Busy old fool, unruly Sun,
> Why dost thou thus,
> Through windows, and through curtains, call on us?
> Must to thy motions lovers' seasons run?
> Saucy pedantic wretch, go chide
> Late school-boys and sour prentices,

> Go tell court-huntsmen that the king will ride,
>   Call country ants to harvest offices;
> Love, all alike, no season knows nor clime,
>   Nor hours, days, months, which are the rags of time.

If you look at the rhyme scheme, it's rather neatly worked out: abba cdcd ee—two quatrains, they don't repeat their pattern—followed by a couplet. But the indentations—that altered rhyme pattern, and the changing line length, and the contrast between the vivid naturalness of the speech and the willfulness of the stanza pattern—give the poem terrific energy and made it somewhat disconcerting to the ear of Donne's audience, and later audiences. It's well known that Ben Jonson said Donne should be hanged for his not keeping the meter. Clearly, without going into the details of the scansion, Donne was aiming for something else. In another early poem, this tendency was more pronounced:

> Let me pour forth
> My tears before thy face whilst I stay here,
> For thy face coins them, and thy stamp they bare,
> And by this mintage they are something worth,
>   For thus they be
>   Pregnant of thee;
> Fruits of much grief they are, emblems of more;
> When a tear falls, that Thou falls which it bore,
> So thou and I are nothing then, when on a diverse shore.

A quatrain made from lines of different lengths, followed by a dimeter couplet, followed by a triplet that ends with a fourteen-syllable line. And the intricacy is intensified by the difficulty of the thought and the strange intimacy of the voice. This also nettled—even a hundred and fifty years later when Samuel Johnson gave this kind of poem a name by complaining that Donne had no business "perplexing the wits of the fairer sex with metaphysics." Shakespeare's plays, some of the sonnets, are, of course, full of difficult thought, difficult feeling, but these poems had for the first time made the unexpectedness of the form a gesture of that difficulty. It's this I mean by the term *difficult form*.

2 . Looking at kinds, fixed forms, genres, stanza patterns, we have been using the term *form* as if it meant the set of preconditions that made a kind of container for the writing. In this sense the sonnet is "a form." But in the deeper meaning of the term, every sonnet has its own form. Every poem is its own form. When we speak about form as a container, it is as if the stanza pattern and the rhyme scheme and perhaps the meter, if it has one, are the form, and the sentences of the poem are the content, and formal imagination is therefore a matter of (1) deciding what preconditions are going to obtain, and then (2) making the matter fit those preconditions. But of course that isn't how it works. Our experience of the relation of the sentence to the pattern is just where we experience form:

Shall I compare thee to a summer's day?

is graceful; it sounds like a sentence born to be uttered in iambic pentameter. This line:

Savage, extreme, rude, cruel, not to trust,

seems awkwardly, furiously trying to strain against it. And look at these lines by George Herbert. As we enter the poem, he is explaining the attitude dissolution, dust, and earth take toward handsome gravestones:

These laugh at jet and marble put for signs,

To sever the good fellowship of dust,
And spoil the meeting. What shall point out them,
When they shall bow, and kneel, and fall down flat
To kiss those heaps, which now they have in trust?
Dear flesh, while I do pray, learn here thy stem
And true descent, that when thou shalt grow fat

And wanton in thy cravings, thou mayest know
That flesh is but a glass which holds the dust
That measures all our time, which also shall
Be crumbled into dust.

To say the form is a six-line stanza of pentameter with an abcabc rhyme scheme hardly does it. And of course the poem is about—among other things—the stupidity of that idea of form.

3 . The sentences of the poem, their shape, their relation to line and stanza pattern, are at the heart of the formal experience of the poem, its particular gesture, and its expressive force. Probably one could work out a kind of grammar of possible, or at least typical, expressive relations between the sentence and the line. Easy fit:

I read much of the night, and go south in the winter.

Overflow:

Because the Holy Ghost over the bent
    World broods with warm breast and with ah! bright wings.

This is actually a complicated example because the latter part of the second line is what I mean. Hopkins could have written "with warm breast and ah! bright wings" and gotten a magical fit; it is the

second "with" that gives the feeling of overmuch. But the enjambment "bent/World" that scandalized Robert Bridges and opened the
way to all those adjective-noun enjambments in twentieth-century
verse, repeated until a hundred years later it has worn down the
sense of the line so that it has no power to scandalize anyone, is an
example of what I mean by difficult form, form strained against and
toward. Which would be another type in our grammar: uneasy fit.
Another would be inevitable arrival:

I am too dumbly in my being pent.

Perfect iambs. The meter mimics entrapment. And so on. I don't
want to work out such a grammar. Only to make the point that it is
one of the things, perhaps the main thing, in play when we speak
about formal imagination.

4 . Difficult forms got invented and elaborated by the metaphysical
poets in the seventeenth century and they were buried by the desire for classical smoothness, intricacy, regularity, and subtlety in the
style of the eighteenth century. That style came to seem so affected
that in the beginning of the nineteenth century there was a return
to "naturalness," to easy and magical fit. Toward the end of the century, with Hopkins, with some of Browning, with Hardy, difficulty
reemerged and it was the characteristic formal gesture of some of the
modernists. Nothing expresses it as well as the invention of syllabics,
particularly the syllabics of Marianne Moore, a reader of Herbert:

"No water so still as the
   dead fountains of Versailles." No swan,
with swart blind look askance
and gondoliering legs, so fine
   as the chintz china one with fawn-

brown eyes and toothed gold
collar on to show whose bird it was.

And the impulse has continued to assert itself, alongside others,
all through the century. Look at the beginning of Jorie Graham's
"Self-Portrait As the Gesture Between Them":

1.
The gesture like a fruit torn from a limb, torn swiftly.

2.
The whole bough bending then springing back as if from
    sudden sight.

3.
The rip in the fabric where the action begins, the opening of
    the narrow passage.

4.
The passage along the arc of denouement once the plot has
    begun, like a limb,
the buds in it clinched and numbered,
outside the true story really, outside of improvisation,
moving along day by day into the sweet appointment.

And at the beginning of—the appropriately titled—"On Difficulty":

It's that they want to know *whose* they are,
seen from above in the half burnt-out half blossomed-out
woods, late April, unsure as to whether to
turn back.
The blossoming is not their home. Whatever's back there
is not . . .

5 . There seem to be two formal qualities of difficult form. One is that the form is invented, or, if received, resisted. How does resistance to received form show itself?

> There's a certain slant of light
> Winter Afternoons—
> That oppresses, like the Heft
> Of Cathedral Tunes—
>
> Heavenly Hurt, it gives us—
> We can find no scar,
> But internal difference
> Where the Meanings, are—

Dickinson is writing in the most conventional and popular form of her age—for the small magazine poem written by women. The common meter, 8-6-8-6, with an abcb rhyme scheme. And she is picking her way through it like a blind person feeling for rifts in a wall. The dashes do this, but the commas do it even more, especially the last one, placed where no grammar would put a comma.

The second characteristic seems to be that the sentence is usually, or crucially, out of sync with the line and/or the stanza pattern. Robert Creeley:

> What I took in my hand
> grew in weight. You must
> understand it
> was not obscene.

These two devices make the form difficult; of course, they don't by themselves make the poem interesting. And, in a way, these two propositions are inconsistent. If you are going to invent a form, why invent one that doesn't fit? There is an expressive answer to this question that would square it with theories of organic form—that it enacts the matter of the poem. But there are also other kinds of answers. Philosophical, even theological ones. In any case, there is perhaps a third characteristic of interesting poems in difficult forms: that they do not seem ingenious, that something in the voice or the matter of the poem has to render this way. It has to seem willed, but it also has to seem necessary. Or—in the case of someone like John Ashbery in some of his work—to take up the whole arbitrary activity in some earnest, even if it's a determination to play.

FURTHER READING:

John Donne: "The Sun Rising"
    "The Canonization"
    "A Valediction: Of Weeping"
    "A Nocturnal Upon St. Lucy's Day"
    "The Funeral"
    "The Relic"
    "Good Friday, 1613. Riding Westward"
George Herbert: "Easter Wings"
    "Affliction I"
    "Church Monuments"
    "Denial"
    "The Temper"
    "Life"
    "The Collar"
    "The Pulley"
    "The Flower"
    "Death"
    "Love III"
Richard Crashaw: "The Weeper"
    "On the Name of Jesus"
    "A Hymn for the Epiphanie"

"On the Assumption"
"*Caritas Nimia*"
"An Ode Prefixed to a Prayerbook Given to a Young
Gentlewoman"—which ends with the following stanza:

O let the blissfull heart hold fast
Her heavnly arm-full, she shall tast
At once ten thousand paradises;
　　She shall have power
　　To rifle and deflour
The rich and roseall spring of those rare sweets
Which with a swelling bosome there she meets
　　Boundles and infinite
　　Bottomles treasures
Of pure inebriating pleasures
Happy proof! she shal discover
　　What ioy, what blisse,
How many Heav'ns at once it is
To have her God become her Lover.

"A Hymn to the Name and Honor of the Admirable Saint
Theresa"—the Norton Anthology misprints the first two lines.
They should read:

Love, thou are absolute sole lord
Of life and death. To prove the word,

Andrew Marvell: "On a Drop of Dew"
　　　　　　　"The Coronet"
　　　　　　　"Eyes and Tears"
　　　　　　　"A Dialogue between the Soul and the Body"
　　　　　　　"A Picture of Little T. C. in a Prospect of Flowers"

Henry Vaughan: "Regeneration"

        "Resurrection and Immortality"

        "The Waterfall"

        "The Night"

        "The Shower"

        "The Morning Watch"

        "The Evening Watch"

        "The Passion"

        "The Relapse"

        "The Resolve"

        "The Match"

Thomas Traherne: "The Salutation"

        "Wonder"

        "Eden"

        "The Preparative"

        "On News"

Edward Taylor: "Meditations Before My Approach to the Lord's Supper" (He wrote hundreds of them in the Connecticut Valley while serving as pastor and surgeon to a little frontier town in the middle of King Philip's War.)

        "Upon a Spider Catching a Fly"

Robert Browning: "Fra Lippo Lippi"

        "The Bishop Orders His Tomb"

Emily Dickinson: 216, 258, 280, 305, 341, 640, 754

Thomas Hardy: "Thoughts of Phena"

        "In Tenebris"

        "The Convergence of the Twain"

Gerard Manley Hopkins: "The Windhover"

        "Binsey Poplar"

        "The Wreck of the Deutschland"

        "As Kingfishers Catch Fire"

        "That Nature Is a Heraclitean Fire"

Gertrude Stein: "Susie Asado" for starters

Ezra Pound: *Cantos*
Marianne Moore: "Poetry"
   "The Steeple-Jack" for starters
T.S. Eliot: "The Wasteland" for starters

—and this can be tracked through the Objectivists, particularly Zu-kofsky's *A*, then Olson's *Maximus* through Creeley, Robert Duncan—the Ashbery of *The Tennis Court Oath*; Barbara Guest, May Swenson, some of Elizabeth Bishop, the early Robert Lowell up to Jorie Graham's *The End of Beauty*; Michael Palmer's *Notes for Echo Lake*, much of Mei-mei Berssenbrugge, much of Brenda Hillman, and some of the work of the language poets. See *The Norton Anthology of Post Modern American Poetry*.

COLLAGE, ABSTRACTION, OULIPO, AND PROCEDURAL POETICS

And there is the repertoire of formal impulses and procedures associated with a postmodern aesthetic—

COLLAGE

1. Robert Rauschenberg: "Collage is the twentieth century's greatest innovation."

2. The term comes from the French verb *coller*, "to glue." And as an art form it was thought to begin with the cubist experiments of Picasso and Braque. One source says that Wyndham Lewis was the first writer to use the term in English, in 1913. One definition—a work of art made by attaching a variety of materials to a flat surface—is a minimal description of what Braque and Picasso did with bits of newspaper and theater and metro tickets.

3 . So collage in poetry could mean the inclusion of the verbal equivalents in poems. Williams experiments with this in *Spring and All*, 1923, in a 1930 poem called "Della Primavera Transportata al Morale," and, of course, in *Paterson*. "Della Primavera" includes street signs and a restaurant menu. And one could, presumably, make a verbal collage of entirely found elements to evoke a world or a state of mind, that is, use collage for the purposes of representation.

4 . The other definition of collage leaves out the idea of found materials. "An artistic work that is an assemblage of diverse elements." Which comes nearer to its literary use, but leaves out the experience of heterodox materials put to a surprising use, and it leaves out the sense in some cubist work of something having been broken analytically and reassembled.

5 . And assembled on what formal principle? Which brings us to what is involved in using techniques or metaphors from the visual arts to describe literary practices. The difference between them is that form in the visual arts is spatial and in literature it is temporal. A poem has a beginning, a middle, and an end. A work of art—whether sculpture or painting—has edges. (Not speaking of video or event-based conceptual pieces, which are in this way nearer to poetry than to painting.)

A way to come at this formally is to think about poems about works of art. The classic starting point for this subject is Gotthold Lessing's *Laocoon: An Essay on the Limits of Painting and Poetry*. The classic text for thinking about it is what may be the first ekphrastic poem, Book 18, lines 478–608 of Homer's *Iliad*, the passage that describes the forging of the shield of Achilles. It's a staggering piece of writing (if it is a piece of writing; it may be the record of an oral performance) and you might want to stop whatever you are doing and go read it in the Richmond Lattimore or Robert Fagles translation.

Spatial form and temporal form. Years ago, I heard a Chaucer scholar give a lecture on *Troilus and Criseyde*. It's a narrative poem about these lovers, the first part of which is about the way Criseyde's uncle Pandarus arranges the business of getting the two awkward young people together. In the second part, in the midst of war, they get together secretly, twine around each other, in Chaucer's metaphor, like woodbine, their hearts, in his metaphor, singing like birds in spring. In the last part, the relationship falls apart and there is an epilogue in which Troilus in heaven repents his sin of passion. The lecturer remarked that temporal forms privilege endings and spatial forms privilege middles, so literary critics wrote as if the point of the poem was Troilus's repentence. But medieval people, he said, thought spatially. They would have felt that they were standing in the middle of a triptych, and from that point of view Chaucer's point might be that, though there may have been comedy before and recantation after, there was at the center singing.

In the account of the shield of Achilles, Homer evokes the entire living world in a 120 lines, and he rounds that world, along the outer edge of the round shield, with ocean. The argument—Lessing's argument—would seem to be that the circle is poetry's way of making temporal forms spatial. As an exercise, describe a painting or a sculpture. Where do you begin? Homer begins in the center of Achilles's shield and moves outward in concentric circles. Auden's "Musée des Beaux Arts" begins inside the observer and takes its time moving to the painting, which it begins by seeing panoramically. Rilke begins with the head in "Archaic Torso of Apollo," proceeds to the loins, and ends inside the observer.

6. One of the formal moves among modernist poets toward turning the temporal form of the poem into a spatial one was nearer

to the mobile than collage, or mixed the ideas of assemblage with the idea of the kinetic movement of detached or semidetached elements. Alexander Calder produced his first mobile around 1930. He had spent some time fashioning circus toys, so the playfulness of these new three-dimensional moving sculptures was a natural evolution. The story is that he showed one to Marcel Duchamps and remarked that he didn't know what to call it. Duchamps shrugged and said, "*Mobile.*" Wallace Stevens's "Thirteen Ways of Looking at a Blackbird" anticipated this idea by some fifteen years. The trick was, in what he called a series of "impressions," to connect a series of images through the reappearance in each of a single element—the blackbird—in such a way that it didn't create an evident narrative or discursive development of that element. All the parts of the poem hovered and related to one another until the last image, which, to make the point, collapsed time: "It was evening all afternoon. / It was snowing / and it was going to snow. / The blackbird sat / in the cedar limbs." He had invented a form—the poem in parts in which the relation of the parts to each other, because there is no narrative or discursive development, is a little mysterious.

7. Some instances:

Louis Zukofsky: "The Old Poet Moves to a New Apartment
    Fourteen Times"
Lorine Niedecker: "Paean to Place"
James Wright: "Fear Is What Quickens Me"
Robert Bly: "Three Kinds of Pleasure"
Louise Gluck: "Dedication to Hunger" (though there is a kind
    of analytic development, an implied narrative about stasis)
Jorie Graham: "The Magic of Numbers"
Further reading: Peter Balakian, "Collage and Its Discontents"
    in *Vise and Shadow*, 2015

ABSTRACTION AND DISLOCATION

8 . *Abstraction:* It must be that Gertrude Stein saw the way Picasso and Braque treated the canvas as a flat surface in their cubist work, the way that they had tossed perspective, and proposed to herself to do the same thing in writing. To say to herself, or discover by experiment, that syntax was the formal principle that organized language in the way that perspective organized painting—and—a very rapid second thought—that having a subject matter at all organized both painting and writing. And in that way she got to abstraction, the experiment of abstraction, well before anyone else.

9 . So much of what we say about the experience of form in poems is based on or assumes the work done by syntax; syntax is the red wheelbarrow glazed with rainwater beside the white chickens. It does both the deep and the surface work of organizing words into expressive meanings. The perception of a pattern in a poem sets up one kind of expectation. This is going to be a sonnet, this is going to be in free verse with about four strong beats to a line, and so on. Syntax sets up another. If a poem begins with a dependent clause—

> When to the sessions of sweet silent thought,

or

> Well, if the bard were weatherwise
> Who made the grand old ballad of Sir Patrick Spence,

—you know that a main clause is coming and that it is apt to be coming in a rhythmic pattern proposed by those first lines. And there are ways in which content often creates another strand of expectation. In Michael Drayton's sonnet that begins "Three kinds of serpent do resemble thee," we not only expect those three snakes, we expect them to be enumerated in iambic pentameter and with a certain grammatical coherence.

1O. Abstraction in poetry honors and subverts syntax. Teases it or removes it altogether. The implicit analogy is painting. If you remove represented objects from the painting, you get colors and shapes and the textures that the gestures that apply the paint make. It's almost impossible to remove representation from language, because it is representation. The sound and script "apple" means "apple," the concept we've acquired from experiences of the fruit and from the culture at large.

The color magenta has an expressive range, but that's not the same thing, because words are located (1) in the phrases through which we learn language—children don't learn "I," "do," "not," "want," and "to," they learn "I don't want to" and (2) in a particular language's system of syntax. So abstraction in poetry happens by disrupting the work of syntax and/or disrupting the continuities between words and then between sentences that the mind supplies to writing and to spoken language. We supply the connection between the sentences when someone says, "I'm not going. It's Tuesday." Abstraction is interested in disarming that habit of the mind which is so much who we are and what we are by putting together a pair of sentences like "I'm not going. Some sentences begin with prepositional phrases."

11. So experiments with abstraction in poetry have had to do with either disrupting conventional expectations about the syntactical relations among words in a sentence—

    amber spike celibate the conduit room

Clark Coolidge writes in "Hot Dark Miles" (from *Space*, 1970)—or disrupting the conventional expectations around the relation of sentences to one another, as Lyn Hejinian does in *The Book of a Thousand Eyes* (2012)—

> As innocent as rubble in the workshop of oblivion.
> At its sunlit bench the stubborn singer holds her breath.
> Every stone you lift you owe to destruction.

and in this case one line to another. The effect (at least the effect on me) depends on first automatically thinking that the "its" in the second line has "oblivion" as its antecedent and then, because there is no evident narrative connection between the sentences, deciding it doesn't, though inside each of the three lines syntax is doing its usual, elegant formal work. Just not between them. A third variation is to create the same disjunctive relation between sentences but to enjamb the lines, creating a tighter weave, as Forrest Gander does in these lines from "Field Guide to Southern Virginia" in *Science and Steepleflower* (1998):

> Swayback, through freshly cut stalks,
> stalks the yellow cat. Can you smell
> where analyses end, the orchard
> oriole begins? Slap her breasts lightly
> to see them quiver. Delighting in this.

It's possible that the question that makes up the second sentence in these verses is addressed to the cat. Cats might very well stalk orioles. And it's quite possible, once one is used to postmodern habits, that it isn't. But there isn't a narrative way to get from the cat to the oriole to the breast.

12 . Interesting to me to notice the very different feel of these three uses of the technique. The Clark Coolidge line feels like anarchic play, someone in rubber boots splashing in the puddles of the English lexicon. Hejinian's lines, also playful, have an intellectual brightness, as if she were interested in the cognitive puzzle of the sentence. Gander's lines—maybe because the imagery has to do with nature and animals and the body—seem more psychological than cognitive, more like the disjunctions in the syntax of dream. One thinks of the difference between French surrealism, with its impulse to upend discourse, and Spanish surrealism, which wants to mine the unconscious.

13 . A further note on syntax and its miraculous presence in our lives. Early morning in summer. My children and their children are visiting. I am up early, sitting at the kitchen table, drinking coffee and reading the paper. My eldest grandson appears, in pajamas, still squinting from sleep, and climbs onto my lap. I read him the comics for a while and—he has just begun to string together whole sentences—he says "Grandpa, when my mom and dad get up, if they decide to go to the bakery, you can come, too." There are great croissants and muffins in the little town nearby. Not only does he have dependent and main clauses, he has a conditional, that he is using to enlist me as an ally in his plan. The sentence, as it unwinds, winds its way to sugar. And isn't that rhythmic conclusion perfect? "You can come, too." Frost used it in one of his early poems:

> I'm going out to clean the pasture spring;
> I'll only stop to rake the leaves away
> (And wait to watch the water clear, I may):
> I shan't be gone long—You come too.

"You come too," though, as I hear it is a bit more peremptory, or born of a more urgent prompting. "You can come too"—Dah-de-dah-dah—feels radiant with hope.

14 . Readings for a quick history of abstraction:

Gertrude Stein: "Portrait of Mabel Dodge" (1912)
"Susie Asado" (1912)
"Preciosilla" (1912)
Tender Buttons (1913)
"Lifting Belly" (1914)
Stanzas in Meditation (1932)
Louis Zukofsky: *Catullus* (1958–1969)
80 Flowers (1974–1978)
John Ashbery: *The Tennis Court Oath* (1962)
Rivers and Mountains (1966)
Clark Coolidge: *Space* (1970)
Solution Passage, Poems 1978–81 (1986)
Lyn Hejinian: *Writing Is an Aid to Memory* (1978)
My Life (1980)
The Cold of Poetry (1994)
Happily (2000)
Michael Palmer, *The Lion Bridge, Poems 1972–95* (1998)

15 . John Ashbery's sense of what Gertrude Stein accomplished: "*Stanzas in Meditation* is no doubt the most successful of her attempts to do what can't be done, to create a counterfeit reality more real than reality. And if, on laying the book aside, we feel that it is still impossible to accomplish the impossible, we are also left with the conviction that it is the only thing worth trying to do."

16. The other thing about abstraction is that it has to do with the texture of writing word by word, line by line, sentence by sentence. It tends not to be a proposal about the formal shape of the poem. A given piece of writing still has, unless one creates an alternative form through typography or vocal performance, a place where it begins, a length it continues, and a place it leaves off. "Susie Asado," Stein's early experiment, is a sonnet, roughly, about fourteen lines long, more or less a love poem, and it ends with the line it began with: an expressive and conventional shape. And in *Stanzas in Meditation* she often begins with beginnings. In Part V, "Stanza LI" begins: "Now this a long stanza / Even though weven so it has not well begin." And "Stanza LII" begins, "There and been a beginning of begun. / They can be caused." In Part 1, "Stanza V" begins, "Why can pansies be their aid or paths." And ends some twenty shape-shifting lines later, "He likes it that there is no chance to misunderstand pansies." The lyric motion: touching home at the place where you began.

One way with the issue of form is to find methods to resist the sense of an ending. Lyn Hejinian makes this argument in "The Rejection of Closure," *The Language of Inquiry*, 2000. Another way has been to roll the dice.

OULIPO AND
PROCEDURAL POETICS

17. A young poet at Berkeley brought a poem into a workshop that had been composed in the following way. He had asked a computer to produce a list of all the words in English that could be formed from the letters in the name "Ambrose Bierce" and then determined the length of his lines and the placement of the words next to one another in the lines by throwing dice, the results dependent on an arcane system that had to do with years between 1920 and 1950 when the New York Yankees did not win the World Series, with this excep-

tion: In each line the poet could choose one pair of words to put next to each other—like "sere" and "amber" because he liked the effect, so that a little fault line of expressive content ran through the otherwise impersonal display and arrangement of language. And nothing by way of title or note made reference to Ambrose Bierce and his mysterious disappearance or the pall cast over the city of New York on those fall days in the years of the Great Depression and the World War when the Yankees disappointed their fans. There was no invitation, by allusion, to read it as a sphinxlike elegy to the writer or as a melancholic tribute to the national pastime.

18. One of the sources of this aesthetic impulse was Oulipo, a group of French writers, mathematicians, professors, and practitioners of pataphysics—the send-up of metaphysics proposed by the Dadaist writer Alfred Jarry—who came together in the fall of 1960 to explore the possibility of what they called "a potential literature," using a series of arbitrary constraints on literary composition for the purposes of discovery and invention. Among the founding members were Raymond Queneau, Georges Perec, and the poet and mathematician Jacques Roubaud. A way into the movement, twenty years or so on from its origin, is Warren Motte, *Oulipo: A Primer of Potential Literature*.

19. Raymond Queneau: "What is the objective of our work? To propose new 'structures' to writers, mathematical in nature, and to invent new artificial or mechanical procedures that will contribute to literary activity, props for inspiration as it were, or rather, in a way, aids for creativity." More Queneau: "Our research is: (1) *Naïve:* I use the word 'naïve' in its perimathematical sense, as one speaks of the naïve theory of sets. We forge ahead without undue refinement. We prove motion by walking. (2) *Craftsmanlike*—but this is not essential.

We regret having no access to machines: this is a constant *lament* during our meetings. (3) *Amusing:* at least for us. Certain people find our work 'sordidly boring' which ought not to frighten you, because you are not here to amuse yourselves. I will insist, however, on the qualifier 'amusing.' Surely certain of our labors appear to be mere pleasantries, or simple witticisms, analogous to certain parlor games. Let us remember that topology and the theory of numbers sprang in art from what used to be called 'mathematical entertainments.'"

20. The famous example of an Oulipian form is the s+7 method. Queneau: "It consists in taking a text and replacing each substantive with the seventh following it in a given dictionary . . . The results are not always interesting; sometimes on the other hand, they are striking. It seems that only *good* texts give good results. The reason for the qualitative relation between the original text and the terminal text are still rather mysterious and the question remains open."

21. This tone, halfway between absurdist and earnest, is characteristic of Oulipian writing. Insofar as it is a send-up, it would seem it was a send-up of two things, related things: romantic expressiveness and the existentialist notion of freedom, or at least of the idea of self in the idea of a self-defining act.

22. Notice—from our point of view, interrogating form, that the s+7 method does not produce the constraints that determine the length of the line or the number of stanzas, if there are stanzas, nor the length of the poem. Those are given by the original text and its very likely conventionally defined set of constraints. Try the method on this line by Shakespeare:

When to the sessions of sweet, silent thought.

Some practitioners have treated adjectives and adverbs as "substantives" and some have not. Possible also to replace every verb. Here is the last line of Baudelaire's "To the Reader" as written by Raymond Queneau, Richard Howard's English translation of the poem, and the *American Heritage Dictionary:*

You, hypoglossal nerve, Reagan, my alignment, my brown bear!

Parody is also Oulipian, and Queneau distinguishes two kinds: autoparody and heteroparody.

23. American practitioners of procedural poetics mostly don't have this tone at all. Two of the most original, and earliest, were John Cage and Jackson Mac Low.

John Cage, *X: Writings '79-'82:*

From the beginning in the late 1930s I have been more interested in exemplification than in explanation, and so I have more and more written my texts in the same way I write my music, and make my prints, through the use of chance operations and by taking the asking of questions rather than the making of choices as my personal responsibility. Or you might say that I am devoted to freeing my writings from my intentions.

Jackson Mac Low on *154 Forties*, the set of 154 poems (the number of Shakespeare's sonnets, as his editor Anne Tardos points out) he wrote between 1990 and 2001:

Each of the Forties poems is written in the following "fuzzy verse-form": Eight stanzas, each comprising three rather long verse lines followed by a very long (typically occupying more than one typographical line) and then a short line. What "rather long," "very long," and "short" means varies from poem to poem and stanza to stanza. The words, phrases, etc., in the poems' first drafts were "gathered" from ones seen, heard, and thought of while I was writing the first drafts, which have been revised in many ways, lexical and prosodical.

Much of the rest of his note discusses how the poems were to be spoken, for they were intended to be performed. Mac Low began in the 1950s writing pieces based entirely on chance procedures. And then poems that his editor describes as *"mixes* of chance and choice," and then in the 154's poems of pure choice (once the stanza and line length constraints were established) in strings of language gathered by someone who formed his ear on the chance collisions that a taste for randomness and surprise had cultivated in him. The effect is ebullient, sometimes rhapsodic, an antiexpressive aesthetic brought round to a fullness of expression. Here is the last stanza of the last poem:

> Two   packages-like-Christmas presents   Martin-Luther-
>   King   the Power-Structure
> Panther   a weekend-house   the-Four-Seasons   a hillock of
>   stone   in-the-same-breath
> swatting-out-mosquitoes   luck or habit   the ending fire a
>   rainbow   the scenery
> encased in the clouds with the birds in-the-middle-distance
>   a coal-stove   existence-that-escapes-years-after-we're-gone
>   just-a-little-bit-sentimental-in-German
> beside a lake without a name

In his note to the poems, Mac Low notes that "there are two kinds of compounds" in the poems, "'normal compounds' and 'sloweddown compounds,'" which are "indicated respectively by two kinds of hyphens, spaced and unspaced." Hence the look of the poem. The hyphens indicate how slowly or quickly to read the compound words and phrases.

Like most constructivist work, I find the aesthetic pleasure here is like the pleasure of watching someone build something rather than the pleasure of having someone tell you something. Though one might well say they have something to tell the reader or listener about the sheer plentitude of both language and the world it names.

24. A few readings for Oulipo, chance operations, and the arbitrariness of constraints:

Warren Motte: *Oulipo: A Primer of Potential Literature* (University of Nebraska Press, 1986)

Raymond Queneau: "Potential Literature" in Motte

Jacques Roubaud: *Poetry, etc, Cleaning House* (Green Integer, 2006)

John Cage: *Silence and Lectures* (Wesleyan, 1961)
> *X: Writings '79–'82*

Jackson Mac Low: *154 Forties* (Counterpath, 2012)
> *Representative Works, 1935–85* (Roof Books, 1986)

MIXED FORMS

Some poems deploy different stanza shapes, even different generic kinds, within the same poem. The English ode, I think, with its varying line lengths and stanza shapes lies behind this patterning. I've assembled some examples.

1. *Different verse forms:* An example is Galway Kinnell's "Flowering Herds on Mount Monadnack," which changes stanza shape from section to section of the poem. Stevens's "Peter Quince at the Clavier" is a more complicated example, a four-part poem with four very different rhyme patterns: first tercets irregularly rhymed, almost a terza rima; then a songlike mix of tetrameter, trimeter, dimeter, and single foot lines, of varying stanza length, irregularly rhymed; then rhymed tetrameter couplets; and then a mix of pentameter and tetrameter lines richly rhymed. Eliot's "Four Quartets" is an again more complicated instance. Notice between "Burnt Norton" and "Little Gidding" the repeated formal elements, like the song stanzas beginning section II and the song in section IV. A very powerful, less well-known instance is Thom Gunn's "Misanthropos," to be set next

to Ted Hughes's *Crow* and Sylvia Plath's *Ariel*. Together they make a record of young postwar poets absorbing the news from Hiroshima and Theresienstadt.

2. *Verse and prose:* One model for the mix of verse and prose is the haibun, the headnotes to the haiku that evolved into a prose-poem form that ended with a short verse. The most famous mix of verse and prose in English poetry is probably Shakespearean comedy, but it wasn't until after the invention of the so-called prose poem that forms mixing verse and prose began to appear in twentieth-century literature. Here are a few examples. Williams's "Spring and All" is probably the best-known modernist text in this form. And after that, Jean Toomer's *Cane*. Later, Robert Duncan's "The Dance," very song-like, falls into prose for a moment as into memory or reverie. The contrast is very striking. Here's a bit of the poem:

> The dancers are gone.
> They lie in heaps exhausted,
> dead tired we say.
> They'll sleep until noon.
>
> But I returned early
> for the silence,
> for the lovely pang that is
> a flower,
> returnd to the silent dance-ground.
>
> (That was my job that summer. I'd dance until three, then up
> to get the hall swept before nine—beer bottles, cigarette
> butts, paper mementos of the night before. Writing it down
> now, it is the aftermath, the silence, I remember, part of
> the dance too, an articulation of the time of dancing.)

In "Route," George Oppen stops to tell a story that seems to require the suppression of verse for the plainest possible telling. The poem—partly a meditation on his experience as an infantryman in World War II—proceeds in his spare, slightly abstract manner through three sections. In the fourth section the verse opens up. He is thinking about the boredom of military experience, even in the face of fear, and of the problem of representation. The end of the fourth section and the beginning of the fifth look like this:

4.

The sea anemone dreamed of something, filtering the sea
    water thru its body,

Nothing more real than boredom—dreamlessness, the
    experience of time, never felt by the new arrival,
    never at the doors, the thresholds, it is the native

Native in native time . . .

The purity of the materials, not theology, but to present
    the circumstances

5.

In Alsace, during the war, we found ourselves at the Battle
of the Bulge. The front was inactive, but we were spread so
thin that the situation was eerily precarious. We hardly knew
where the next squad was, and it was not in sight—a quiet
and deserted hill in front of us. etc.

I found myself wanting that quality of contrast in my poems "The Yellow Bicycle" from *Praise* and "January" from *Human Wishes*.

Czesław Miłosz's "Separate Notebooks" makes a much more complicated instance. As does Ashbery's "Variations, Calypso and Fugue."
And there is the recent example of Mark Rudman's book-length mix
of lyric and narrative, *Rider.* And Lyn Hejinian in *The Book of a Thousand Eyes.* A great instance is Edmond Jabès's *The Book of Questions.*

PROSE POEM

1. The thing developed from the invention of writing. And print gave it its principal formal character, two justified margins. The word comes from the Latin *prosus*, which means "straightforward," and is also derived from *provertere*, which means "to turn forward." Pro + versus, so it is distantly related to the etymological root of "verse." Prose turns forward. Verse turns.

2. In 1802 Coleridge contributed a few of his journal entries to a miscellany edited by his friend Robert Southey. He gave one of them a title:

December Morning.

The giant shadows sleeping amid the wan yellow light of the December morning, looked like wrecks and scattered ruins of the long, long night.

It did not start a stampede toward a new poetic form, so prose did not get annexed to the formal possibilities of poetry until August 26,

1862, when a Paris daily newspaper *La presse* published a few of Baudelaire's *Petits poemes en prose (Le spleen de Paris)*. The entire collection of fifty prose pieces was published in 1869, two years after Baudelaire's death. He had written a preface describing his ideal as "a poetic prose, musical, without rhythm and rhyme, supple enough and rugged enough to adapt itself to the lyrical impulses of the soul, the undulations of reverie, the gibes of conscience." Baudelaire's model was a strange little prose book, *Gaspard de la Nuit*, published in 1842 by the Belgian writer Aloysius Bertrand.

3. The term "prose poem": it had the force at one time of contradiction, of breaking down categories. And there may still be great value in a term impossible to define. All you have to do is read the scholars to see that it is impossible to define. Prose using all the techniques of poetry except meter, lineation, and rhyme? But there are no techniques special to poetry except meter, lineation, and rhyme. Short prose written by poets? Then their letters are prose poems. Short prose that avoids the usual discursive uses of prose? A proscription, not a definition. Writings that the authors call "prose poems"? Short pieces of prose organized in books like poems?

4. *Conversation About the Definition of a Prose Poem on Woodpecker Trail at Coralville Lake at the End of March, the Wind Rising:*

    B: The thing is it doesn't have a definition.
    B: Sure it does. A poem without lines.
    B: Well, that includes all of prose.
    B: Right.

5. There are at least two kinds of this kind of thing: proses that are one paragraph long and proses that are more than one paragraph long.

The paragraph as a formal device differs from the stanza in that the proposition of the paragraph is unity.

The proposition of a composition of one paragraph is completeness.

A paragraph that goes on for much longer than a page breaks the basic contract of the paragraph.

These are all expressive possibilities.

Since one of the claims of poetry is brevity, the longer a prose is, the more involved it becomes with the expectations created by the existence of particular genres of prose.

This is also an expressive possibility.

What the texts for writers say is true: The four kinds of prose are narration, description, exposition, and argument.

This expectation is also an expressive possibility.

From the beginning, this kind of prose was torn between undermining its medium and appropriating it.

So a paragraph, which is a proposition of unity, full of non sequiturs is a contradiction in terms. This is, has been an expressive possibility.

The prose poem came into existence not only during the age of prose and the age of realism, but at the moment when prose and realism were just beginning to enjoy the prestige of art.

This kind of prose was sired by ambivalence and envy. The "prose poet" is either worshipping at or pissing on the altar of narration, description, exposition, and argument. Or both.

To write this kind of prose you probably have to love or hate the characteristic rhythms of prose.

The rhythms of poetry have quicker access to the unconscious than the rhythms of prose. It may be that this is one of the reasons many people prefer prose to verse. It does not make an indecent claim on the reader's person at the outset.

One of the obvious possibilities of this kind of prose was to fill it full of the devices that people identify as lyrical as a kind of alchemy to transform prose and the world of prose into poetry. This was the way of Rimbaud.

Another possibility was to thwart the expectations of prose. Cubist prose, like *Tender Buttons*, did it at the level of grammar. Surrealist prose did it at the level of representation and at the level of sequence.

In all three cases, varying in intensity, the idea was to use the medium in ways that would subvert the usual expectations of the medium.

6 . *Second Conversation at Coralville Lake:*

> B: Really, there are only two things about it, the right hand margin and the left hand margin.
>
> B: Yes, the left hand margin is the father and the right hand margin is the mother.

7. The history of this form in the nineteenth century is almost entirely French. So, for that matter, is the history of free verse. The scholarly consensus seems to be that the reason for these two developments at this time has to do with a crisis in French verse brought about by the extreme inflexibility of the French alexandrine. The other explanation is that it was a bourgeois age, and poets wanted to find a way to a medium that had acquired a glamour that used to be reserved to poetry alone, to what Hegel called "the world of ordinary life and of prose." Which may seem contradictory, so that there is a tension in the form between prose as the medium of realist representation and poetry as the medium of the transformation of the world through imagination. It was not toward newspaper realism that the form developed, but it did, from the outset, represent the world and interrogate language as a means of representing it.

Here's a reading list for the rest of the nineteenth century:

Arthur Rimbaud: *Une Saison en Enfer Les Illuminations* (1886)

Stéphane Mallarmé: some prose as early as 1864

Comte de Lautréamont: *Chant de Malador* (1892)

and for the first half of the twentieth:

Paul Claudel, *Connaissance de l'Est* (1900)

Pierre Reverdy, *Poemes en prose* (1915)

Max Jacob, *Cornet a des* (1916)

Leon-Paul Fargue, *Poemes* (1918)

St.-John Perse, *Anabase* (1924)

Henri Michaux, *Plume* (1937)

Francis Ponge, *Le Parti pris des choses* (1942)

Jean Follain, *Canisy* (1942)

Edmond *Jàbes, The Book of Questions* (1963–1965)

8 . The American prose poem in English probably begins with Gertrude Stein's *Tender Buttons* (1914). It belongs to the same moment as Max Jacob's *Cornet a des* and to the poetics of cubism. Eliot wrote "Hysteria" in 1915. Williams's *Kore in Hell* belongs to 1920. Then—I think it's not inaccurate to say—it disappears until the postwar generation.

9 . And in those years many European and Latin American poets wrote prose based on the French models. And some prose writers like Julio Cortázar and Italo Calvino wrote short prose, which belongs to this hybrid. Tomas Tranströmer and Zbigniew Herbert both did powerful work in the single paragraph form. Tranströmer's "How the Late Autumn Novel Begins" is a great example of a way the prose poem poaches on the conventions of fiction. Herbert's "A History of the Minotaur" is an example of the way it appropriates fable. The prose in *Elegy for the Departure* mimes the still life, the definition, the fable. Franz Kafka's short prose is relevant here. And see Seamus Heaney, *Stations*.

10. The form began to be used widely and extremely variously in the United States after about 1960.

Some instances:

Robert Duncan, *The Opening of the Field* (1960)
Robert Bly, *The Morning Glory* (1969)
W. S. Merwin, *The Miner's Pale Children* (1970)
John Ashbery, *Three Poems* (1973)
Russell Edson, *Clam Theater* (1973)
Robert Creeley, *Presences: A Text for Marisol* (1976)
James Wright, *Moments of the Italian Summer* (1976)
Mark Strand, *The Monument* (1978)
Lynn Hejinian, *My Life* (1980)
Ron Silliman, *Tjanting* (1981)
Robert Hass, *Human Wishes* (1989)
Charles Simic, *The World Doesn't End* (1989)

11. A note: The one great English ancestor of the prose poem may be the devotional prose of the seventeenth century, and after. And the great instance of this kind of writing is Thomas Traherne's *The Third Century*. Though it is really an instance of mixed form.

12. Also in the America grain:

Henry David Thoreau, *Journals*
Ernest Hemingway, *In Our Time* (the short interchapters)

Jean Toomer, *Cane*

Fanny Howe, *The Wedding Dress* (from prose poem to essay)

Claudia Rankine, *Citizen*

13. Useful anthologies:

Michael Benedict: *The Prose Poem: An International Anthology*
    (Dell, 1977)

David Lehmann: *The Great American Prose Poem* (Scribner, 2003)

Stuart Friebert and David Young: *Models of the Universe: An
    Anthology of the Prose Poem* (Oberlin University Press, 1995)

Charles Simic and Mark Strand: *Another Republic: 17 European
    and South American Writers* (Ecco Press, 1976)

Alan Ziegler: *Short* (Persea Books, 2014)

A NOTE ON STRESS

Rhythm: *A perceived pattern in a sequence of sounds and the plea-sure in the changes in the pattern that the existence of the pattern allows us to hear.*

Stress: *The rhythm of poetry depends on rhythmic elements present in ordinary speech. And those rhythms are based on the fact that we utter some syllables with more emphasis than others:*

Are you totally out of your mind?

Anyone saying that sentence knows that the syllable "tot" needs to be spoken more emphatically than any other syllable in the sentence.

Are you totally crazy?

In this sentence, on the other hand, "tot" and "craz" would prob-ably receive about equal emphasis and might even build from the first to the second. Distributing emphasis, making it up as we go along, is one of the main pleasures of speech.

Having a little lapse of sanity?

In this more understated sentence, *lapse* would probably get slightly more emphasis than *hav-*, *lit-*, and *san-*, but all of them would receive a certain light emphasis in relation to the other syllables in the sentence.

KINDS OF STRESS

In spoken English stress, or accent as it is also called, occurs for three reasons:

(1) Stress is used to underline the key elements of grammatical structure in English. Normally, the main syllables in the key words in a sentence, the ones that convey meaning, receive more emphasis than the words used to indicate relation like articles and prepositions. In the sentence "He went to the store," spoken in however matter-of-fact a way, *went* and *store* get more emphasis. Linguists call the words that receive stress (by some rule of speech we learn when we're learning to talk) "lexical words." The lexical words are nouns, verbs, adjectives, and adverbs. The nonlexical words are conjunctions, articles, and prepositions. Nonlexical words receive stress in normal speech if they have more than one syllable, however, so prepositions of more than one syllable do carry stress. Demonstrative pronouns—*this* and *that*—can, but don't automatically, receive stress. So their stress, when they are stressed, is rhetorical; it's a matter of contextual emphasis. Forms of the verb "to be" don't receive the same stress in speech as action verbs. Pronouns don't receive stress in ordinary speech, presumably because they are only markers for the nouns that do. Sometimes their degree of stress is a matter of contextual emphasis.

(2) In English the normal pronunciation of multisyllabic words
requires that we pronounce one, and sometimes two, syllables
in a word more emphatically than the others: *answer, rotating,*
in*def*initely, *constitutional.*

(3) What is contextual, or rhetorical emphasis? Saying is rarely
neutral, which is why the third reason for the use of stress is
rhetorical emphasis. You might want to emphasize the fact
that *he* went to the store, or the fact that he went to the *store,*
and in each case you'd make your emphasis differently. This is
where play comes into the way we use emphasis in speech. For
different reasons and in different situations one might say, "Are
you *totally* out of your *mind?*" or "Are *you* totally out of your
mind?" or "Are you totally *out* of your *mind?*" or *"Are* you *totally*
out of your *mind?,*" even *"Are* you totally *out* of *your mind?*" And
there are probably other variations.

Rhetorical stress is often hard to determine in printed language
because it has to be inferred from the context. "Who wants to
be a millionaire?" the song goes, "*I* do." Or "Do you take this
person to be your . . ." "I *do.*" One needs to know the story to
read the stress.

THE RELATIVITY OF STRESS

Notice that in the case of the pronunciation of multisyllabic words
and the enunciation of lexical words in sentences, the distribution
of stress is based on a codified rule. Notice also that there are not
only two degrees of emphasis, weak and strong; some words of more
than three syllables have a primary and a secondary stress. If you are
unsure which syllable gets the main and which gets the secondary
stress in a word like *fortification,* check a dictionary. In compound
nouns, the first syllable usually gets the stronger stress: rose-leaves,
milk-cow. In English the existence of secondary stress and of com-

pound nouns complicates the rules of stress, but the pronunciation of English is always rule governed. It isn't arbitrary.

Nor is rhetorical stress arbitrary. In our test case sentence, the main syllable in the intensifier *totally* always gets the most emphasis. After that the main syllables in the key grammatical words are emphasized, and how much they are emphasized in relation to each other depends on meaning—that is a matter of rhetorical emphasis. So not all emphases in a sentence are absolutely fixed. One thing gets a lot or a little more emphasis than another. This is why people speak of "relative stress," because it is almost always a comparative thing. It is governed by rules and is not, in that sense, relative at all, but it is also governed by context and intention. When people get to scanning metrical poetry or marking stresses in nonmetrical poetry, it's often the contextual relativity of stress and the existence of secondary stress in polysyllabic words that make them feel insecure.

To summarize, all spoken language in English is based on a mix of more and less stressed syllables, which convey meaning and from which speech gets its musical, or rhythmic, rising and falling quality.

Meter introduces a fourth kind of stress, metrical stress. One of the things that makes meter sound regular is that it introduces a rule that governs secondary stress. It also adds metrical stress to words that are not stressed in normal speech, usually prepositions, to heighten the order in speech rhythm and, often, create a kind of tension between speech rhythm and metrical pattern. Here is an example of the way that meter promotes a nonlexical syllable, giving it more stress than in speech to fulfill the expectation of the metrical pattern. The phrase:

They walked together in the woods,

in ordinary speech gets three stresses, on *walked*, *geth-*, and *woods*, according to the rules of lexical stress. But as part of a pattern of iambic stresses, an unstressed-stressed pattern, the syllable *in* also receives stress, heightening the feel of rhythmic regularity in the phrase:

They walked togeth- er in the woods.

By itself the phrase "in the woods" has a skipping anapestic feel, but it has been pulled into the orbit of iambic rhythm. "er in" is an iamb and "the woods" is an iamb.

And here is an example of its regularizing of secondary stress, from a poem by Stanley Kunitz about his World War II infantryman's rifle:

What the nymphomaniac enjoys,
Inexhaustibly, is boys.

In normal speech the polysyllabic words have syllables that carry primary and secondary stress. We know instinctively, having learned it quite young, though not that particular word, that *man* carries the primary stress in *nymphomaniac*. The rule has to do with the fact that *maniac* is the main idea and *nympho* is a modifier, but the difference in emphasis is quite slight, and if the question under consideration were which kind of maniac a rifle is, *nymph* would probably get the heavier stress. In the second line, *haust* carries the primary stress in *inexhaustibly* as a dictionary would tell you. The phrase

What the nymphomaniac enjoys

in ordinary speech carries three lexical stresses—*what*, *man*, and *joys*—and a secondary, somewhat lesser stress on *nymph*. Kunitz, however, is writing in an iambic meter—a kind called "headless pentameter" (it was a favorite meter of his master, the Irish poet William Butler Yeats) that has a pattern of a stressed initial syllable followed by four feet with the pattern unstressed-stressed. So the line scans like this:

What the nymph- ŏmán- ĭác ĕnjóys

nymph and *ac* have been promoted by metrical stress. The same thing happens in the next line:

Ín ĕxhaúst- ĭblý ĭs bóys.

In normal speech *haust* and *boys* carry the primary stress, *in* has secondary stress. Meter has promoted both *in* and *ly*.

(In my experience the word *nymphomaniac* belongs to an eighth-grade boy's terror of and curiosity about sexuality, rather than the supposedly insatiable sexual appetite of some women, so it is an awkward word to use as an example here, because it carries such sexist freight. On the other hand, it might therefore not be so inappropriate to locate that set of male dreams and terrors, as Kunitz does, in a rifle.)

HOW TO SCAN A POEM

Stress: The rhythm of poetry depends on rhythmic elements present in ordinary speech. In English, speakers give more emphasis or stress to some syllables than others. We learned what syllables to stress and what syllables to leave unstressed more or less unconsciously when we learned to speak. *Meter* is, in English, the organization of stressed and unstressed syllables.

How to Scan a Metrical Poem: Almost all English poetry from the Renaissance to the end of the nineteenth century is written in a meter.

There are four possible accentual-syllabic meters in English, based on the possible patternings of stressed and unstressed syllables. Two of them are based on rising rhythms, patterns that come to a stress at the end, and two on falling rhythms, patterns that begin with a stress. The names for them come from Greek. The Greek prosodists called each unit of the pattern a *foot*, as if the meter walked. Here are the four possible foot types in English:

Rising rhythms:

the iamb, or iambic foot ˅ ˈ

the anapest, or anapestic foot ˅ ˅ ˈ

Falling rhythms:

the trochee, or trochaic foot ′ ˘

the dactyl, or dactylic foot ′ ˘ ˘

The Greeks distinguished many other meters based on other pat-terns of syllables, but as a practical matter, the ear seems to hear all unstressed syllables as organized around one stressed syllable pre-ceding or following it—or at least that's the way writers in English have always thought about it. So there may be these four possible meters. But, in fact, *almost all metrical poetry in English is written in an iambic meter or in a meter that has an iambic base.* In practice, dactylic meters hardly exist because the unstressed syllables are subsumed by the rising rhythm of the next stressed syllable, and the anapest can be thought of as a skipping iamb.

In a line of Shakespeare's iambic pentameter:

When to/ the ses-/-sions of/ sweet si-/ lent thought

certain syllables, *when, ses-, sweet, si,* and *thought,* receive an accent, but one foot—/sions of/—doesn't contain a lexical stress. Meter sup-plies it.

How do you know which syllable to stress in /When to/ or /-sions of/? Normally the pattern imposed by the meter tells you—it tells you that /-sions of/ is a metrical foot in an iambic line and so you ap-ply the pattern. Sometimes rhetorical stress tells you. /When to/ is a metrical foot in a line of iambic verse, so you know to consider the two syllables in relation to one another. But the lexical rules tells you that in speech "when," an adverb, receives stress and "to," a mono-syllabic preposition, doesn't. What do you do? The rules of speech rhythm trump the metrical rule. The pattern is iambic, but the foot is trochaic. This way of establishing a pattern and then upending it from time to time is called *substitution.* It's very common in metrical poetry, but more common in some parts of the line than others.

RULES OF SCANSION

1. The first rule of scansion: *If you think you hear a meter in a poem, it is probably an iambic meter; the first thing to do is to test this hypothesis by dividing the line into poetic feet.*

Note: Ignore punctuation and meaning when you divide the line into feet. All you're trying to do is determine whether or not a pattern applies.

Note 2: Don't arbitrarily chop it into twos. There may be an extra syllable in the form of an anapestic substitution.

You are reading Robert Frost's "Stopping by Woods on a Snowy Evening" and it sounds metrical to you. So you try to discover the pattern by dividing the first two lines into feet:

    Whose woods these are I think I know.

    His house is in the village, though;

and then you mark the stressed and unstressed syllables to see if Frost was using an iambic meter.

2. The second rule of scansion is that, once you have determined the division into feet, *you only compare the level of stress in a syllable with the level of stress of other syllables in the same foot.* For example, in the second line, once you have separated the phrase "His house is in" into two feet, /his house/ is in/, you only compare "his" with "house" and "is" with "in." You don't compare "in" with "house." This is to make sure that you are marking the meter and not the rhythm.

Rhythmically, you may hear a line with three strong accentual stresses, followed by another line with three strong accentual stresses, but the stresses are *not* the meter. The relation of stressed and unstressed syllables is the meter. So even if the rhythm sounds like this to you:

Whose wóods these are I thínk I knów.
His hoúse is in the víllage, thoúgh;

—the meter looks like this:

/Whŏse woóds/ these aré/ Ĭ thínk/ Ĭ knów./

/Hĭs hoúse/ ĭs ín/ thĕ víl/ lăge, thoúgh;/

Often you will hear what feel like strong irregular emphases in metrical poems. The irregularities are strong, because once a pattern is established, you notice departures from the pattern. So, of course, poets learned that one of the best ways to get emphasis is to establish a meter and then vary it. You vary it by changing the iambic pattern to some other pattern. There are three kinds of substitution in iambic verse:

an anapestic foot ˘˘ˊ

a trochaic foot ˊ˘

a spondaic foot ˊˊ

Some people would add a fourth kind of substitution:

a double iamb ˘˘ˊˊ

This is to accommodate a very common conformation in English, the phrase based on preposition-article-adjective-noun, like "in a dark time" or "on a high peak." This isn't entirely necessary. You may think of

in a dark time

as a trochee—*in a*—and a spondee—*dark time*, but some poets have felt that the piling up of two strong stresses in the second pair of syllables mutes the effect of any comparative difference in the first pair of syllables and have felt, therefore, that calling this configuration a double iamb reflects something about iambic rhythm in English more accurately.

It is also not uncommon for a line of iambic verse to have a final unaccented syllable. If *all* the lines have a final unaccented syllable, you are in the presence of a rare poem written in a trochaic meter.

Prohibitions: Contrary to what you might read in some manuals of prosody, there are kinds of substitutions that don't occur in iambic verse. There are no pyrrhic feet—a pair of unaccented syllables—because the pattern will impose relatively more stress on one syllable in any pair in an iambic line. There are no dactylic feet. A three-syllable pattern of stressed-unstressed-unstressed doesn't exist in English because the rising rhythm will always assimilate the third weak syllable to the next stressed syllable rather than to the previous one.

And, though there are single accented syllables sometimes in the first position in a line or an unaccented single syllable at the end, there are no single syllable feet in the middle of a line. If you find a pattern that seems to demand one, rethink your perception of the pattern. (Yeats's "Lake Isle of Innisfree" is the notable exception.)

The most typical substitution in an iambic meter is the use of a trochaic or spondaic foot at the beginning of a line for emphasis. The first line in Yeats's "Sailing to Byzantium," for example, has a trochee in the first position:

That is\ no coun\ try for\ old men.\ The young

You can tell it's a trochee because the rhetorical emphasis of the demonstrative pronoun *that* requires it. There is a spondee in the first position in another poem by Yeats written in memory of two dead friends:

> Dear sha\ dows, now\ you know\ it all,

The substitution called a double iamb often occurs at the beginning of a line because of the usual structure of prepositional phrases in English—preposition, article, adjective, noun: "in a dark time, on a high peak." If you apply our second rule to these phrases, you would probably scan them this way—

> \ in ă\ dark time\   \ on ă\ high peak\

—because the prepositions get slightly more semantic emphasis than the articles. To an ear tuned to the phrase-rhythm and not to the meter, they sound, of course, like this—

> in ă dark time   on ă high peak

—and some poets tend to think of that pattern as a form of two-foot metrical substitution, in effect, a double iamb, so that you could, for example, scan a line from Robert Frost's "Birches"—

> He always kept his poise
> to the top branches, climbing carefully

—like this:

> \to the top bran\ ches, climb\ ing care\ fully

3. So, the third rule of scansion is to *be alert to substitution*. For example, look at these lines from Frost's "The Oven Bird":

There is a singer everyone has heard,
Loud, a mid-summer and a mid-wood bird,
Who makes the solid tree trunks sound again.
He says that leaves are old and that for flowers
Mid-summer is to spring as one to ten.

First, divide it into poetic feet; then mark the stressed and unstressed syllables. You will have done well if you divided the lines
like this:

/There is/ a sing/ er ev/ eryone/ has heard,/
/Loud, a/ mid-sum/ mer and/ a mid-/ wood bird,/
/Who makes/ the sol/ id tree/ trunks sound/ again./
/He says/ that leaves/ are old/ and that/ for flowers/
/Mid-sum/ mer is/ to spring/ as one/ to ten,/

The only word you may have puzzled over is *flowers*. It is a word,
like *heaven*, that is sometimes treated as a one-syllable word and
sometimes as a two-syllable word, depending on how you hear and
say it. Frost is either hearing it as a one-syllable word or he is leaving
an extra unstressed syllable at the end of the line, as poets sometimes do.

But when it comes to scansion there may be several feet that give
you pause. The first obvious substitution occurs in the foot /Loud,
a/, in which it's clear for both semantic and rhetorical reasons that
"Loud" is more strongly accented than "a." The pattern is stressed-
unstressed, so the foot is a trochee, and this is a trochaic substitution.
It's the most common one in English verse.

You may also be unsure about how to mark the second and fifth
feet in the same line. Is /mid-sum/ a spondee because both syllables
are emphasized equally, or an iamb because *sum* gets slightly more
emphasis than *mid*? And what about /wood bird,/? This brings us to
the fourth and fifth rules of scansion . . .

4. The fourth rule is that *a tie goes to the meter.* That is, the point of creating a metrical pattern is to draw the relation of stressed and unstressed syllables into an order. Ezra Pound had a metaphor for this order-making in art—"the rose in the steel dust." He was thinking of the rose shape made when a magnet pulls random particles of steel dust into the pattern made by lines of electromagnetic force. Meter pulls syllables into its pattern in the same way. So, if you are not sure which way a scansion should go, give the meter the benefit of the doubt. In that second line above, therefore, it's probably best to call both feet *iambs.* But if you think that the whole structure of sound is changed by those strong accents, then call them *spondees.*

5. Which leads us to the fifth rule: *The point is not to be right; the point is to listen and to train your ear into the deepest textures of the sound of a poem.* Once you notice what Frost is doing in that line, piling up strongly accented syllables—

> Loud, a *mid-*summer and a *mid-*wood bird.

—it doesn't too much matter whether you scan it

> /Lóud, a/ míd-súm/ mer ánd/ a mid-/ wóod bírd./

or

> /Lóud, a/ míd-súm/ mer ánd/ a mid-/ wóod bírd./

What matters is that you notice that Frost is trying to give you something of the energy of the bird's song.

To summarize:

1. you determine the meter by inspection—by testing your sense

of what it is until you discover what pattern the poet had in mind;

2. you mark stressed and unstressed syllables only by comparing the relative stress with other syllables in the same foot;

3. you are alert to substitution;

4. you assume, if you're not sure, that the metrical pattern predominates;

5. and you don't worry too much about whether you're right or not; you listen to the sound of the poem.

METER LENGTHS

Poems with two metrical feet are written in dimeter. If in iambic feet, iambic dimeter. And so on. Three feet is trimeter, four is tetrameter, five is pentameter, six hexameter.

The commonest meters in English are iambic tetrameter and iambic pentameter.

PAUSES IN A LINE

When talking about the meter and the rhythm of a poem, it is often useful to pay attention to the changing position of the main pause in each line. The term for this pause is *caesura*, and caesuras are often marked with a double line, //. For example:

> /There is/ a sing/ er//ev/ eryone/ has heard/
> /Loud,//a/ mid-sum/ mer and/ a mid-/ wood bird./

You can see, if you imagine that brief silence moving around in relation to the unchanging measure of the ten-syllable line, how it would have a strong, subtle effect on the overall rhythm. And you should notice also that the caesura can occur either in a foot or at the end of one.

SCANSION: AN EXERCISE

Here are four whole poems and one excerpted passage from a poem by Robert Frost to practice scansion on. Each is written in an accentual-syllabic meter. I think they are in ascending order of difficulty for most people. Divide each into feet and mark the metrical pattern and the substitutions. In the fourth passage, mark the caesuras as well.

1. *Stopping by Woods on a Snowy Evening*

Whose woods these are I think I know.
His house is in the village, though;
He will not see me stopping here
To watch his woods fill up with snow.

My little horse must think it queer
To stop without a farmhouse near
Between the woods and frozen lake
The darkest evening of the year.

He gives his harness bells a shake
To ask if there is some mistake.
The only other sound's the sweep
Of easy wind and downy flake.

The woods are lovely, dark and deep,
But I have promises to keep,
And miles to go before I sleep,
And miles to go before I sleep.

2. The Oven Bird

There is a singer everyone has heard,
Loud, a mid-summer and a mid-wood bird,
Who makes the solid tree trunks sound again.
He says that leaves are old and that for flowers
Mid-summer is to spring as one to ten.
He says the early petal-fall is past
When pear and cherry bloom went down in showers
On sunny days a moment overcast;
And comes that other fall we name the fall.
He says the highway dust is over all.
The bird would cease and be as other birds
But that he knows in singing not to sing.
The question that he frames in all but words
Is what to make of a diminished thing.

3. Neither Out Far Nor In Deep

The people along the sand
All turn and look one way.
They turn their back on the land.
They look at the sea all day.

As long as it takes to pass
A ship keeps raising its hull;
The wetter ground like glass
Reflects a standing gull.

The land may vary more;
But whatever the truth may be—
The water comes ashore,
And the people look at the sea.

They cannot look out far.
They cannot look in deep.
But when was that ever a bar
To any watch they keep?

4. Birches

When I see birches bend to left and right
Across the line of straighter darker trees,
I like to think some boy's been swinging them.
But swinging doesn't bend them down to stay
As ice storms do. Often you must have seen them
Loaded with ice a sunny winter morning
After a rain. They click upon themselves
As the breeze rises, and turn many-colored
As the stir cracks and crazes their enamel.
Soon the sun's warmth makes them shed crystal shells
Shattering and avalanching on the snow crust—
Such heaps of broken glass to sweep away
You'd think the inner dome of heaven had fallen.
They are dragged to the withered bracken by the load,
And they seem not to break; though once they are bowed
So low for long, they never right themselves:
You may see their trunks arching in the woods
Years afterwards, trailing their leaves on the ground
Like girls on hands and knees that throw their hair
Before them over their heads to dry in the sun.

5. Design

I found a dimpled spider, fat and white,
On a white heal-all, holding up a moth

Like a white piece of rigid satin cloth—
Assorted characters of death and blight
Mixed ready to begin the morning right,
Like the ingredients of a witches' broth—
A snow-drop spider, a flower like froth,
And dead wings carried like a paper kite.

What had that flower to do with being white,
The wayside blue and innocent heal-all?
What brought the kindred spider to that height,
Then steered the white moth thither in the night?
What but design of darkness to appall?—
If design govern in a thing so small.

HOW FREE VERSE WORKS

1. "Free verse" is the term that has come to be used for poems written in lines, but without a set meter, that is, without a fixed rule governing the number and position of stressed and unstressed syllables.

Some history: Anglo-Saxon verse was *accentual*. It was composed in a fixed number of stressed syllables per line. The measure was four stresses marked by a strong caesural pause for a pattern of 2/2. The historian of prosody George Saintsbury remarks that, when Norman French with its typically rising rhythm in the pronunciation of two- and three-syllable words got married to the German dialect of Anglo-Saxon with its typically falling rhythm in its two- and three-syllable words, English became what he calls "a country dance" of rising and falling rhythms out of which metrical poetry, or accentual syllabic verse, emerged.

So when nineteenth- and twentieth-century poets, after some four to five hundred years of accentual-syllabic verse, began to experiment with verse lines that did not have this fixed form, what they were doing got called free verse. It might well have been called accentual verse because its rhythms are based on the patterning of stresses (though not the position of unstressed syllables), but in practice people reserved that term for poems in which the number of accents per line was fixed.

Accentual verse in that sense—four stresses per line, three or five stresses per line—is, in my experience, relatively rare. And the poets I've talked to about it or read writing about it seem to have different notions of what constitutes a stressed syllable. Much more common is verse in which most lines have the same number of stresses mixed with other lines that have one or two more or less stresses. So there is a free verse that roughly approximates a metrical trimeter or tetrameter or pentameter.

2 . The term "free verse" began as a translation of the French phrase *vers libre*, though French *vers libre* tended, in the nineteenth century, to be loosely metrical and to rhyme, but just not in a regular pattern. "Loosely metrical" means that you can still hear the predominance of a specific meter, usually an iambic meter. Eliot's "Prufrock," for example, begins with a singsong line of headless iambic meter:

Lét/ ŭs gó/ thĕn yóu/ aňd Í

And the next line is roughly iambic:

Whĭle thĕ éve/ nĭng ís/ spréad oút/ ăgaínst/ thĕ ský

(This could be scanned as mostly anapestic if you demote the accent on "out":

Whĭle thĕ éve/ nĭng ĭs spréad/ oŭt ăgaínst/ thĕ ský

But from the point of view of "loose free verse" anapests are just skipping iambs.)

Even the notorious third line is iambic:

Lǐke ǎ pá/ tǐent eth/ ́erǐzed/ ǔpón/ ǎ táb/ le.

The first line has four feet, the next two are loose pentameter. I think Eliot thought of this as *vers libre,* in the French manner.

In the beginning of Wallace Stevens' s "Of Mere Being," written forty or fifty years later, the first line can be read as loosely iambic, that is, as an iamb and two anapests:

The palm/ at the end/ of the mind

And the next line can also be fitted, perhaps forced into a roughly metrical pattern:

Beyond/ the last/ thought ris/ es

That is, an iamb, an iamb, a spondee, an unstressed final syllable, and probably if the next line were regularly iambic, it would have reinforced this sense of pattern, but it doesn't quite:

In the bronze distance.

It could be scanned this way:

Ín the/ brónze dís/ tǎnce

as a trochee and a spondee and an unaccented final syllable, or in this way as an anapest and a trochee:

Ǐn the brónze/ dístǎnce

Or in this way as a double iamb with a final unaccented syllable:

Ǐn the brónze dís/ tǎnce,

And the fact that it can be scanned so many different ways tells you that the deep pattern hasn't been established. But it is probably this nearness to being scannable that gives the lines the feeling of orderliness, and in that way it is also almost *vers libre*, a trimeter line, another trimeter line with an extra syllable, a dimeter line with an extra syllable. But probably not. Probably we are in the territory of free verse, and to think about the rhythm we can mark the stressed syllables:

The palm at the end of the mind,

Beyond the last thought rises

In the bronze distance,

And begin to think about what kind of patterning we are hearing. There are three stresses, for example, in the first line, four in the second, two in the third. Statement, amplification, compression would be the patterning of the lines we hear, but it is more complicated than that. In the poem's second line, we are hearing a distinct pause, not just four beats, but three beats and then one more. One might mark this:

3

4 (3/1)

2

and then notice that the stanza is made of three phrases and that each phrase—"the palm at the end of the mind," "beyond the last thought," "rises in the bronze distance"—contains three stressed syllables. If Stevens had placed "rises" on the third line, the stanza would have had three stressed syllables per line. Verse that has the same number of accented syllables per line is called *accentual verse*, and so this isn't accentual verse, or it is accentual verse without the rule that there has to be the same number of stressed syllables per line, and so *free verse*.

But that doesn't mean that we don't hear the pattern of three phrases each with three accented syllables; we do. And when Stevens ends the second line on a fourth stressed syllable with "rises," he throws the balance in the first two phrases off, but then he does complete it, by giving us two stressed syllable to go with the excess stressed syllable in the previous line, which is, I am pretty sure, why the music of this stanza is so appealing.

To complicate the matter; Wallace Stevens revised the first stanza of "Of Mere Being." The final version of the poem reads:

> The palm at the end of the mind
> Beyond the last thought rises
> In the bronze décor.

This makes for a very great difference in the poem's way of thinking about our relationship to reality, and it makes a small, crucial difference in the rhythmic organization of those three lines by ending the stanza on a distinctly iambic sound. Line ends and especially stanza ends act like magnets. They organize what comes before them. "In the bronze distance" is loosely iambic. "In the bronze décor" ends with an emphatic iamb.

3. So free verse doesn't have a set rule about the number and position of stressed and unstressed syllables, but it does have stressed and unstressed syllables, and they are—as in speech—patterned more or less rhythmically, and though you can't scan the lines, you can inspect the degree and kind of patterning that's going on in them. And, as I hope these examples make clear, free verse flirts with metrical verse all the time, so that there is or can be a fluid movement from

metrical verse to *vers libre* to accentual verse to free verse in the same poem, as it discovers and expresses the kind of and level of orderliness there is in the thought and emotion of the poem. By itself "The palm at the end of the mind" could be or could not be a metrical line. We need to hear more to know what pattern is being made. But we do hear the pattern. We hear the skipping anapests of "at the end/ of the mind" whether the whole poem is metrical or not. The basic play of rising and falling rhythms goes on in free verse as it does in speech and it is full of the echoes of the patterns imposed by the structure of the spoken language and regularized by poetic meters.

4 . So, in practice:

* Lines serve best as a measure if they are predominantly end-stopped, or if they contain predominantly the same number of stressed syllables.
* To the extent that enjambment undercuts our hearing the line as a measure, we hear the phrase rather than the line as measure, and the typographical line becomes mainly a visual effect rather than an auditory one. (It's been argued that the visual experience affects the auditory one, that seeing the line break, even if we don't hear it, is enough to create a sense of measure. I'm not so sure. This is the interestingly hazy area in written poetry between the spoken-out-loud auditory experience of a poem and the heard-as-performed-in-the-mind auditory experience of the poem.)
* In free verse as in metrical verse, there is play between the line as measure and the phrase as measure. You could write *lines* of four stresses, employing *clauses*, units of sense, with three stresses, and you'd hear the interplay.
* There is usually an accentual base, and it usually gets announced in the first line, as in music:

One must have a mind of winter
To regard the frost and the boughs
Of the pine-trees crusted with snow

You can read the verb in the first line, emphasizing either *must* or *have*, depending on how you read the drama of it, but in either case only one of the two receives stress.

It establishes a base of four stresses, is followed by a line with three stresses, and (I hear *pine-trees* as two stresses, but one could hear it as one, emphasis on *pine*) returns to four in the third line.

5 . *Divigation on enjambment, pauses in normal speech, and the line end:*

Whenas in silks (pause) my Julia goes (pause)
Then, then, methinks (pause) how sweetly flows (pause)
The liquefaction (slight pause) of her clothes (pause)
And when I cast mine eyes and see (pause)
Those brave vibrations, (pause) each way free, (pause)
Oh! How that glittering (pause) taketh me. (stop)

After great pain (pause) a formal feeling comes (pause)
The nerves sit ceremonious (pause) as tombs (pause)
The stiff heart questions (pause) Was it he (pause) that bore? (pause)
And yesterday? (pause) or centuries before? (pause)

Nature's first green (pause) is gold,(pause)
Her hardest hue to hold (pause)
Her early leaf's a flower (pause)
But only so an hour. (pause)
Then leaf subsides to leaf. (pause)
So Eden sank to grief (pause)
So dawn goes down to day (pause)
Nothing gold can stay. (stop)

This is by way of reminding you that poems are made out of an exquisite play of phrases and pauses.

Pauses, stops, are determined partly by context and partly by the normal rules that govern speech rhythm. The important thing is to notice that there are places in spoken English where there are typically pauses between words and places where there aren't. We have learned to pause at the end of a noun phrase—The redheaded boy / rode his bike/ to the store. We know where the pauses are and where they aren't. Notice that in the sentence "The boy went to the store," there is not a pause between the subject and the verb, and that if you add an adjective, there is. We picked up these rules in the high chair. (And play with language the way we played with oatmeal.)

Denise Levertov had a quite specific way of thinking about pauses and the line end. A line end period was a full stop. A comma at line end was half a period. A breath pause without punctuation at line end was half a comma. A line end where there was no breath pause had no pause but threw slightly more emphasis onto whatever word began the next line. It was more for the eye than the ear.

If you listen to contemporary poets read, you find that some of them give pause to an enjambed line end when there is no breath pause, and some don't. I have the impression that it was Robert Creeley who introduced the disjunctive pause at the end of a line in his way of reading his poems aloud. "You were/*pause*/ not in/*pause*/the room." In his work it made for the sense that the poem was interrogating its own syntax. What does *in* mean, really? And what is *the*? the hesitations at line end seem to say. What are these so-called natural units of speech? It made one feel that where there was fluency, there needed to be interrogating gaps, something like the way a musician like Miles Davis interrogates the formal habits that underlie melody. I also have the impression that this technique in the hands of younger poets writing without Creeley's particular urgency descended into mannerism very quickly.

6 . *Violent, or ragged, or kinetic enjambments:* In the history of metrical poetry, there just aren't instances of enjambment, that is, of ending the line, where there is not a pause in ordinary speech. The metaphysical poets came nearest to it. They wanted thought to feel knotty and sometimes used what felt like violent enjambment to suggest it. Here is George Herbert in a poem called "Denial":

> When my devotions could not pierce
>   Thy silent eares;
> Then was my heart broken, as was my verse:
>   My breast was full of fears
>   And disorder:
>
> My bent thoughts, like a brittle bow,
>   Did flie asunder:
> Each took his way; some would to pleasures go,
>   Some to the warres and thunder
>   Of alarms
>
> As good go anywhere, they say,
>   As to benumme
> Both knees and heart, in crying night and day,
>   *Come, come, my God, O come,*
>   But no hearing.

His example was picked up in some of Hart Crane—here is the beginning of "Lachrymae Christi":

> Whitely, while benzene
> Rinsings from the moon
> Dissolve all but the windows of the mills
> (Inside the sure machinery
> Is still

> And curdled only where a sill
> Sluices its one unyielding smile)
>
> Immaculate venom binds
> The fox's teeth, and swart
> Thorns freshen on the year's
> First blood . . .

and the early poems of Robert Lowell, as in this from "Colloquy in Black Rock" (which uses the word *nigger* as an adjective at a time when a white novelist, Carl Van Vechten, could call a book about Harlem *Nigger Heaven*):

> Here the jackhammer jabs into the ocean;
> My heart, you race and stagger and demand
> More blood-gangs for your nigger-brass percussions,
> Till I, the stunned machine of your devotion,
> Clanging upon the cymbal of a hand,
> Am rattled screw and footloose. All discussions
>
> End in the mud-flat detritus of death.
> My heart, beat faster, faster. In Black Mud
> Hungarian workmen give their blood
> For the martyre Stephen, who was stoned to death

but instances are rare, and needed to be rare. If using the line and line end that way were common practice, the mild shock of the effect would be lost. It was in the early experiments with free verse that the line end where there is no breath pause become common. Here is William Carlos Williams in 1917, playing with ending lines on articles, on the space between an adjective and its noun in "Summer Song":

> Wanderer moon
> smiling a

faintly ironical smile
at this
brilliant, dew-moistened
summer morning,—
a detached
sleepily indifferent
smile, a
wanderer's smile—

(Here is the pattern of stresses per line: 2/1/3/1/3/2/1/2/1/2. Here is the pattern that a listener might hear of accent based on verbal units between natural pauses: 2/4/6/4/2. In the recordings I've heard of Williams reading, he doesn't pause—in the early poems—if there is not a natural breath pause in the syntax. So how eye and ear negotiate these two rhythms, each in its way symmetrical, is an interesting question.)

7. *Syllabics:* Another of the practices of twentieth-century poetry is composing with a fixed number of syllables per line. One can do that by having the same number of syllables in every line—here is an example from Kenneth Rexroth, a bit of an erotic poem called "Inversely As the Square of Their Distances Apart," written in eight-syllable lines:

At the wood's edge in the moonlight
We dropped our clothes and stood naked,
Swaying, shadow mottled, enclosed
In each other and together
Closed in the night. We did not hear
The whip-poor-will, nor the aspen's
Whisper; the owl flew silently
Or cried out loud, we did not know.

We could not hear beyond the heart.
We could not see the moving dark
And light, the stars that stood or moved,
The stars that fell. Did they all fall
We had not known. We were falling
Like meteors, dark through cold black,
Toward each other, and then compact,
Blazing through air into earth.

Or one can have the same number of syllables in corresponding lines of each stanza, as in Marianne Moore's "The Fish," in which the title serves as a first line. Moore was the poet who experimented most with a quirky syllabic stanzas. *Becoming Marianne Moore* (2002) is a fascinating place to watch her at work. They print a 1918 magazine version of the poem in quatrains, so that it begins, after the title, "Wade through black jade. / Of the crow-blue mussel shells, one" and the 1924 version in intricate six-line syllabic stanzas. The first two lines of that version begins simply "Wade / through black jade." The syllabic pattern in this version of the poem is 1/3/9/6/8. It makes for a jaunty, even a defiant, willfulness in the relation of the maker to the attaining. As if, to quote Sharon Olds's remark, Moore had adopted the motto of the medieval French guild of secateurs, the cutters of cloth. Their crest read, "I cut where I will." If you mark the stresses, you can see that syllabics don't typically have the same number of stresses per line. But poems that have the same number of syllables per line, like Rexroth's, tend to have a loose sort of regularity, two to four stresses, or three to five stresses per line, as does a lot of free verse, if it is composed in lines of roughly equal length.

8 . Which syllables are stressed in free verse? Answer: the same syllables that are stressed in ordinary speech—(1) all semantically important words, (2) at least one syllable in all words of more than

one syllable, and (3) other words that receive rhetorical emphasis as determined by context (or italics, or some other signal of emphasis).

> April is the cruelest month, breeding

—has four stresses on the four semantically important syllables. (It also, in the middle, has a faintly iambic lilt: ril is/ the cruel/ est month/.) The next line—

> Lilacs out of the dead earth, mixing

—has four semantically important syllables, five if you count the "out" in "out of." This is a slight swelling of the pattern in the previous line, so we are not in the territory of an accentual meter, and it doesn't quite have an iambic lilt. "Breeding" and "lilacs" and "mixing" and "out of" are all strong falling rhythms. The pattern of the two lines also shares a strong rhythmic pause: 3/1, 4/1. The next line,

> Memory and desire, stirring

—has three stressed syllables, a contraction, and it continues the pattern of strong pauses, which is now 3/1, 4/1, 2/1, a tipping and pushing forward motion that is going to make coming to the end of the sentence feel like a closing, and since it is the beginning of the poem, also a sort of opening signature:

> Dull roots with spring rain.

So one way to describe the accentual pattern the lines make is 4, 4, 3, 4; another is to notice the balancing act, 3/1, 5/1, 2/1, 2/2. Odd/odd, odd/odd, even/odd, even/even.

The imagination, Robert Duncan said, is shapely and this is cer-

tainly true, or can be true, of the aural imagination in poetry. It's
always at work.

9. "Form," Robert Creeley wrote in the 1950s, "is always an extension of content." Published among the statements on poetics
at the end of Donald Allen's anthology *The New American Poetry*, it
read at the time as a rebellion against metrical poetry and the display forms of mastery implied by fixed forms like the sonnet and
the sestina. The idea was that you didn't impose a pattern on your
thought or perception; you let the perception or the thought give
you the pattern. The other critical document in the Allen anthology
was Charles Olson's "Projective Verse," which seemed to expand on
Creeley's sentence. Olson argued that the shape of a poem ought
to track, or map, the movement of its thought or set of thoughts.
Its shape was a picture of the energy of its making. In Ezra Pound's
terms, it was an ideogram. A formed thing. A poem was, or should
be, the shape of its thought or perception, and what prosody should
do is keep the thought moving.

George Oppen, in interviews in the 1960s and in a conversation
we had, slowed down Olson's high adrenaline aesthetic. Prosody,
he said, was a moral matter, because its work was analytic. A poem
ought to reflect accurately the shape and order of a perception. Language can't correspond absolutely to the thing it names, but it can
present, in any given instance, the order of the apprehension of an
object. And of the way an object is attached to a thought. And feel-
ings come from thoughts. You have to think you are in danger to feel
fear. (George had been in the infantry in France.) You have to think
of some good to be happy. So the perception implies, stated or not,
the thought, and the thought, stated or not, implies the feeling. So I
imagine his imaginative process on what he called, quoting Martin
Heidegger, "the arduous path of appearance," went something like
this: First the brick of an American city, smudged with smoke. Then

the young girl on the street and the hand-me-downs or garish, inexpensive new clothes that define her social class and the vulnerability it implies, and then perhaps her gait, which makes her particular and gives her poignance. And then his thought of the world as a sort of container, which gave him the title of his third book, *This In Which.* So he proposes that the question of form for a poet in the realist tradition is ethical, a matter of getting the meeting place of thought and perception right.

I heard Denise Levertov elaborate on these ideas in a lecture hall in Fort Worden, Washington. You are standing at a picture window in a suburban neighborhood. It's morning. You look out the window, the big picture window in the living room (it's not your house), and you see a pool of blood, bright red, and the body, goldish, of a squirrel on the concrete driveway, which is surrounded, I think she said "embowered," by the intense green of summer trees. Apparently the owner, backing out of her garage, had run over the squirrel. She proceeded to speak about how one organized the order of the perceptions. First, the pool of blood? Or the color red seen before it resolves itself into a meaning? Or the fact of being in a stranger's house? Of being the "I," later critics would call it "the subject position," in the situation implied by a picture window? It turned out to be a complicated matter. It might involve false starts. It might be, in the end, that the music, the rhythm of the feeling, would give you the way to an appropriate ordering of the images, or lead you away from what you thought was the point, the specific perception of the dead squirrel. Might take you somewhere else altogether.

10 . And poems don't necessarily begin with perceptions: Kenneth Koch, James Tate, Dean Young. They may begin with something the imagination proposes and track thought, track association, or dream logic, or a rhythm of movement of thought or feeling that the words try to keep up with. Form then would have to do with

fidelity to that movement. Something like this gets said in Robert Duncan's series, "The Structure of Rime." The second poem in the series begins: "What of the Structure of Rime, I asked." And the poem provides this answer, which has stayed in my mind for years though I'm not sure yet that I understand it: *An absolute scale of re-semblance and disresemblance establishes measures that are music in the actual world.*

11. Conversation with Brenda Hillman. Walking on a trail in a white fir forest, summer, the Sierras, a ragged border on the trail of the wildflowers that (like certain enjambments) prefer disturbed ground: poems begin for me in one of four ways, either with a scrap of musical language, or an idea, or an image, or 80 percent of the time, from the pressure of an inchoate feeling that turns into an idea or an image or a scrap of musical language.

12. Stanley Kunitz saying there were three ways a poem moves: in a straight line from A to B, in a circle beginning with A and passing through various place and coming back to A, or by braiding two, three, even five elements in such a way that by the end their relation to each other becomes clear. And I said, "What about pointillism or a Calder mobile, where elements just hang there in relation to each other or not, the connection unstated?" And Stanley, "Yes, that would be a fourth way." "Or a list," I said, "that would just be A A A A." "Yes, yes," said Stanley, getting a little weary.

13. The work of prosody in free verse, as in metrical verse, comes once the poem is under way. The twos and threes, or the fours and threes and then fours; the choice of making stanzas or not making stanzas, what kind of line endings—that work. You are hearing a

poem that is grave and slow, or charged and relentless, or hesitant, or easy and fluid, the sense of sound, arc of development, play with un-development, image- or thought-cascade occurring and telling you what it wants to be, form and content beginning to be a body. The final form exactly right, or not—seeming just okay, adequate to the task, but not radiant, not the radiance.

ACKNOWLEDGMENTS

This set of notes would not have become a book without the encouragement, persistence, and editorial eye of Daniel Halpern. It was his thought to give the browsing reader plenty of poems to read, instances of the craft to consider. As a result, my *Little Book* is not so little as I imagined when I proposed the title. This was also a fairly complicated text to present, and I am very grateful to Bridget Read for her patient attention to it and for her encouragement. A couple of compatriots known to themselves also have my gratitude for imagining this book into existence. And I am thankful for the inestimable help I received from Kelly Gemill and Paola Vergera with formatting, proofing, tracking down fugitive references, and getting accurate texts of the poems in front of readers. Thanks to them and to the students in the University of Iowa Writers' Workshop with whom I worked on my visits there and to my students at UC Berkeley.

CREDITS

Aga Shahid Ali, excerpt from "Ghazal" from *The Country Without a Post Office*. Copyright © 1997 by Aga Shahid Ali. Used by permission of W. W. Norton & Company, Inc.

———

Craig Arnold, excerpt from "Ghazal for Garcia Lorca" from *Ravishing DisUnities: Real Ghazals in English*. Copyright © 2000 by Wesleyan University Press. Reprinted by permission of Wesleyan University Press.

———

John Ashbery, 10 haiku from "37 Haiku" from *Selected Poems*. Copyright © 1985 by John Ashbery. Excerpt from "Clepsydra" from *Rivers and Mountains: Poems*. Copyright © 1966 by John Ashbery. All reprinted by permission of George Borchardt, Inc., on behalf of the author and Carcanet Press, Ltd.. All rights reserved.

———

Bacchylides, excerpt from "To the wise my words have meaning: the sky"; and excerpts from victory ode ["Sing, O generous Clio, the praise / of fertile Sicily's queen . . ."], translated by David Mulroy from David

Mulroy, *Early Greek Lyric Poetry*. Copyright © 1992 by David Mulroy. Reprinted with the permission of the University of Michigan Press.

Basho haiku, translated by Robert Hass, from *The Essential Haiku*. Copyright © 1994 by Robert Hass. Reprinted by permission of HarperCollins Publishers and Bloodaxe Books Ltd.

Ted Berrigan, "Sonnet #2" ["Dear Margie, hello. It is 5:15 a.m."] from *The Collected Poems of Ted Berrigan*. Copyright © 2000 by by Alice Notley, Literary Executrix of the Estate of Ted Berrigan. Used by permission of Viking Books, an imprint of Penguin Publishing Group, a division of Penguin Random House, LLC.

John Berryman, #14 from *The Dream Songs*. Copyright © 1969 by John Berryman. Reprinted by permission of Farrar, Straus & Giroux, LLC.

Elizabeth Bishop, excerpts from "The Armadillo" and "Sestina" from *The Complete Poems 1927–1979*. Copyright © 1979, 1983 by Alice Helen Methfessel. Reprinted by permission of Farrar, Straus & Giroux, LLC. and Penguin Random House UK, Ltd.

Andre Breton, excerpt from "Free Union," translated by David Antin, from *The Poetry of Surrealism: An Anthology*, edited by Michael Benedikt (Boston: Little Brown, 1974). Reprinted with the permission of the translator.

Sterling Brown, "Kentucky Blues" and excerpt from "Market Street Woman" from *Southern Road*. Copyright © 1936 by Sterling Brown. Reprinted with the permission of the Sterling A. Brown Literary Estate.

———

Buson haiku, translated by Robert Hass, from *The Essential Haiku*. Copyright © 1994 by Robert Hass. Reprinted by permission of HarperCollins Publishers and Bloodaxe Books, Ltd.

———

John Cage, excerpt from "Composition in Retrospect" from *X: Writings '79–'82*. Copyright © 1983 by John Cage. Reprinted by permission of Wesleyan University Press.

Catullus, ["I hate and love. Ignorant fish, who even / wants the fly while writhing."], translated by Frank Bidart, from *The Sacrifice*. Copyright © 1983 by Frank Bidart. Used by permission of the author.

———

Hart Crane, excerpt from "Lachryme Christi" from *Complete Poems of Hart Crane*, edited by Marc Simon. 1933, © 1958, 1966 by Liveright Publishing Corporation. Copyright © 1986 by Marc Simon. Used by permission of Liveright Publishing Corporation.

Robert Creeley, excerpt from "Bolinas and Me . . ." from *The Collected Poems of Robert Creeley (1945–1975)*. Copyright © 1982 by the Regents of the University of California. Reprinted by permission of the University of California Press. Excerpt from "Song" from *The Collected Poems of Robert Creeley (1945–1975)* (Berkeley: University of California Press, 1983). Reprinted with the permission of the Permissions Company, Inc., on behalf of the Estate of Robert Creeley.

———

Arnaut Daniel, "Lo ferm voler qu'el bor m'intra / The firm desire which enters," translated by Anthony Bonner from *Songs of the Troubadours* (New York: Weird Books, 1972). Reprinted with the permission of the translator.

Dante, excerpt from "Canto 2" from *Inferno*, translated by Robert Pinsky. Copyright © 1996 by Robert Pinsky. Reprinted by permission of Farrar, Straus & Giroux, LLC.

Emily Dickinson, ["Lest they short come-is all my fear," "Trust adjusts her 'Peradventure'—," "Soft as the massacre of Suns," "Is immortality above," "Brother of Ingots—Ah Peru—," "All things swept sole away," "I cannot live with You—," "There's a certain Slant of light," and "After great pain, a formal feeling comes—" from *The Poems of Emily Dickinson*, edited by Thomas H. Johnson, Cambridge, MA: Belknap Press of Harvard University Press. Copyright 1951, © 1955 by the President and Fellows of Harvard College. Copyright renewed © 1979, 1983 by the President and Fellows of Harvard College. Copyright 1914, 1918, 1919, 1924, 1929, 1930, 1932, 1935, 1937, 1942, by Martha Dickinson Bianchi. Copyright 1952, © 1957, 1958, 1963, 1965, by Mary L. Hampson.

H. D. (Hilda Doolittle), excerpts from "The Walls Do Not Fall," "Ecce Sponsus," "Archer," and "Sea Rose" from *Collected Poems 1912–1944*. Copyright © 1982 by the Estate of Hilda Doolittle. Reprinted by permission of New Directions Publishing Corp.

Robert Duncan, excerpts from "Keeping the Rhyme," "Often I am Permitted to Return to a Meadow," and "The Dance" from *The Opening of the Field*. Copyright © 1960 by Robert Duncan. Excerpt from "The Torso:

Passages 18" from *Bending the Bow.* Copyright © 1968 by Robert Duncan. All reprinted by permission of New Directions Publishing Corp.

———

T. S. Eliot, excerpt from "Little Gidding" and excerpt from "Sweeney Among the Nightingales" from *The Complete Poems and Plays.* Copyright 1936 by Houghton Mifflin Harcourt Publishing Company, renewed © 1964 by T. S. Eliot. Copyright 1940, 1942 by T. S. Eliot, renewed © 1968, 1970 by Esme Valerie Eliot. Reprinted by permission of Houghton Mifflin Harcourt Publishing Company. All rights reserved.

———

Robert Frost, excerpt from "Provide, Provide," "Acquainted with the Night," "Stopping by Woods on a Snowy Evening," "Two Look at Two," "Neither Out Far Nor In Deep," excerpt from "Design," and "Nothing Gold Can Stay" from *The Poetry of Robert Frost*, edited by Edward Connery Lathem. Copyright 1923, 1928, © 1969 by Henry Holt and Company. Copyright 1936, 1951, © 1956 by Robert Frost. Copyright 1964 by Lesley Frost Ballantine. Reprinted by permission of Henry Holt and Company, LLC. All rights reserved.

———

Forrest Gander, excerpt from "Sensations upon Arriving" from *Ravishing DisUnities: Real Ghazals in English.* Copyright © 2000 by Wesleyan University Press. Reprinted by permission of Wesleyan University Press. Excerpt from "Field Guide to Southern Virginia" from *Science & Steepleflower.* Copyright © 1998 by Forrest Gander. Reprinted by permission of New Directions Publishing Corp.

———

Federico García Lorca, "Ode to Walt Whitman" from *A Poet in New York*, translated by Greg Simon and Steven F. White. Copyright © 1988 by

Greg Simon and Steven F. White. Reprinted by permission of the Noonday Press/Farrar, Straus & Giroux, LLC.

Allen Ginsberg, excerpts from "American Sentences" and "After Lalon" from *Cosmopolitan Greetings: Poems 1986–1992*. Copyright 1994 by Allen Ginsberg. Excerpts from "Howl" and "America" from *Collected Poems 1947–1980*. Copyright © 1955 by Allen Ginsberg. All reprinted by permission of HarperCollins Publishers and the Wylie Agency, LLC.

Jorie Graham, excerpt from "Masaccio's Expulsion" from *Erosion*, edited by Luca Sosella. Copyright © 1983 by Princeton University Press. Reprinted by permission of Princeton University Press. Excerpts from "Self-Portrait as the Gesture Between Them" and "On Difficulty" from *The End of Beauty: Poems*. Copyright © 1987 by Jorie Graham. Reprinted by permission of HarperCollins Publishers.

Jim Harrison, excerpt from ["I fell into the hidden mine shaft in Keweenaw, emerging . . ."] from *The Shape of the Journey: New and Collected Poems*. Copyright © 1971 by Jim Harrison. Reprinted with the permission of the Permissions Company, Inc., on behalf of Copper Canyon Press, www.coppercanyonpress.org.

Robert Hass, "Sad," "So," and excerpt from "Spring Rain" from *Human Wishes*. Copyright © 1989 by Robert Hass. Reprinted by permission of HarperCollins Publishers.

Seamus Heaney, excerpt from "Station Island" from *Station Island*. Copyright © 1985 by Seamus Heaney. Reprinted by permission of Farrar, Straus & Giroux, LLC, and Faber and Faber, Ltd.

Lyn Hejinian, excerpt from *The Book of a Thousand Eyes*. Copyright © 2012 by Lyn Hejinian. Excerpt from *The Unfollowing*. Copyright © 2012 by Lyn Hejinian. All reprinted with the permission of the author and Omnidawn Publishing.

Zbigniew Herbert, "Violins" from *Selected Poems*, translated by John and Bogdana Carpenter. Copyright © 1977 by John and Bogdana Carpenter. Reprinted with the permission of Oxford University Press, Ltd.

Brenda Hillman, ["(That's good, you got there; can we"], ["Sarajevo ceasefire"], ["—Nice going but you don't"], ["(And you thought"], ["(agonized"], ["and the mistake wasn't that heavy"], ["My friend called"], and "Unfinished Glimmer" from *Autumn Sojourn* (Mill Valley: Em Press, 1994). Reprinted by permission of the author.

Horace, "Cleopatra Ode" from *The Odes of Horace: Bilingual Edition*, translated by David Ferry. Copyright © 1998 by David Ferry. Reprinted with the permission of the translator.

Langston Hughes, excerpts from "Evil" and "Wake" from *The Collected Poems of Langston Hughes*, edited by Arnold Rampersad and David Roessel. Copyright © 1994 by the Estate of Langston Hughes. Used by permission of the Harold Ober Associates, Inc., and Alfred A. Knopf, an imprint of the Knopf Doubleday Publishing Group, a division of Penguin Random House, LLC. All rights reserved.

Omar Khayyam, five quatrains, translated by L. P. Elwell-Sutton, from *In Search of Omar Khayyam*. Copyright © 1971 by George Allen & Unwin, Ltd. Reprinted by permission.

———

Galway Kinnell, excerpt from "Passing the Cemetery" from "Sheffield Ghazals" in *A New Selected Poems*. Copyright © 2000 by Galway Kinnell. Reprinted by permission of Houghton Mifflin Harcourt Publishing Company. All rights reserved.

———

Kenneth Koch, excerpt from "Sleeping with Women" from *The Collected Poems of Kenneth Koch*. Copyright © 2005 by the Kenneth Koch Literary Estate. Used by permission of Alfred A. Knopf, an imprint of the Knopf Doubleday Publishing Group, a division of Penguin Random House LLC. All rights reserved.

———

Stanley Kunitz, from "Careless Love" from *Collected Poems*. Copyright © 2000 by Stanley Kunitz. Used by permission of W. W. Norton & Company, Inc.

———

Li Po, "The Jewel Stairs' Grievance," translated by Ezra Pound, in *Translations*. Copyright © 1963 by Ezra Pound. Reprinted by permission of Faber and Faber, Ltd. and New Directions Publishing Corp.

———

Robert Lowell, excerpts from "After the Surprising Conversation," "The Quaker Graveyard at Nantucket," "After the Convention," and "Colloquy in Black Rock" from *Collected Poems*. Copyright © 1976, 1977 by Robert Lowell. Reprinted by permission of Farrar, Straus & Giroux, LLC.

Jackson Mac Low, excerpt from "Finding Your Own Name" from *Thing of Beauty: New and Selected Works,* edited by Anne Tardos. Copyright © 2008 by the Estate of Jackson Mac Low. Reprinted by permission of the University of California Press.

Bernadette Mayer, "Birthday Sonnet for Grace" from *Sonnets.* Copyright © 1989 by Bernadette Mayer. Reprinted with the permission of the author and Tender Buttons Press.

Heather McHugh, excerpt from "Ghazal on the Better-Unbegun" from *The Father of the Predicaments.* Copyright © 1999 by Heather McHugh. Reprinted by permission of Wesleyan University Press.

W. S. Merwin, "December Night" from *Migration: New and Selected Poems.* Copyright © 1988, 2005 by W. S. Merwin. Reprinted with the permission of the Permissions Company, Inc., on behalf of Copper Canyon Press and the Wylie Agency, LLC.

Czesław Miłosz, excerpt from "City without a Name" and poems from "Notes" ["On the Need to Draw Boundaries," "Landscape," "Language," "Supplication," and "Aim in Life"] from *New and Collected Poems: 1931–2001.* Copyright © 1988, 1991, 1995, 2001 by Czesław Miłosz Royalties, Inc. Reprinted by permission of HarperCollins Publishers and the Wylie Agency, LLC.

Harryette Mullen, excerpt from *Recyclopedia: Trimmings, S*PeRM**K*T, and Muse & Drudge*. Copyright © 1991, 2006 by Harryette Mullen. Reprinted with the permission of the Permissions Company, Inc., on behalf of Graywolf Press, www.graywolfpress.org.

Pablo Neruda, excerpt from "The Heights of Macchu Picchu," translated by Nathaniel Tarn, from *The Heights of Macchu Picchu*. Copyright © 1967 by Nathaniel Tarn. Reprinted by permission of Farrar, Straus & Giroux, LLC. Excerpt from "Ode to the Elephant," translated by Ilan Stavans, from *I Explain a Few Things: Selected Poems* (New York: Farrar, Straus & Giroux, 2007). Originally published in *Ploughshares*, Vol 31, no. 2 (Spring 2005): 115. Copyright © 2005 by Ilan Stavans. Reprinted with the permission of Ilan Stavans. Excerpts from "Ode to an Artichoke," "Ode to a Dictionary," "Ode to a Hummingbird," "Ode to Seaweed," and "Ode to My Socks" from *Selected Odes*, translated by Margaret Sayers Peden. Copyright © 2011 by Fundacion Pablo Neruda. Copyright © 1990 by the Regents of the University of California. Reprinted by permission of the University of California Press.

Frank O'Hara, "Poem" ["The eager note on my door said, 'Call me,'"] from *The Collected Poems of Frank O'Hara*. Copyright © 1971 by Maureen Granville-Smith. Reprinted with the permission of Alfred A. Knopf, an imprint of the Knopf Doubleday Publishing Group, a division of Penguin Random House, LLC. All rights reserved.

George Oppen, excerpt from "Route" from *Collected Poems*. Copyright © 1975 by George Oppen. Reprinted by permission of New Directions Publishing Corp.

Michael Palmer, excerpts from "Notes for Echo Lake 2," "Notes for Echo Lake 10," "A Dream Called the House of Jews," "Poem," "Notes for Echo Lake 12/8," and "Purples of Barley" from *Codes Appearing: Poems 1979–1988*. Copyright © 1988 by Michael Palmer. Reprinted by permission of New Directions Publishing Corp.

Robert Pinsky, "Poem with Lines in Any Order" from *Selected Poems*. Copyright © 2011 by Robert Pinsky. Reprinted by permission of Farrar, Straus & Giroux, LLC.

Ezra Pound, "In a Station of the Metro," "Pagani's, November 8," "Coda," "Alba," "T'ai Chui," "Sestina: Altaforte," and "Hugh Selwyn Mauberly" from *The Selected Poems of Ezra Pound*. Copyright 1926 by Ezra Pound. Excerpt from "Dryad" in "Pisan Canto 83" from *The Pisan Cantos*. Copyright 1948 by Ezra Pound. "Canto II" and excerpt from "Canto 47" from *The Cantos of Ezra Pound*. Copyright 1934 by Ezra Pound. All reprinted by permission of Faber & Faber, Ltd., and New Directions Publishing Corp.

Kenneth Rexroth, excerpt from "Inversely as the Square of Their Distances Apart" from *The Collected Shorter Poems of Kenneth Rexroth*. Copyright © 1940, 1944, 1949, 1952, © 1956, 1957, 1963, 1968, 1974, 1976, 1978 by Kenneth Rexroth. Reprinted by permission of New Directions Publishing Corp.

Adrienne Rich, excerpt from "The Blue Ghazals" from *Collected Poems 1950–2012*. Copyright © 1971 by Adrienne Rich. Copyright © 2016 by the Adrienne Rich Literary Trust. Used by permission of W. W. Norton & Company, Inc.

Theodore Roethke, excerpt from "My Papa's Waltz" from *The Collected Poems of Theodore Roethke*. Copyright © 1966. Reprinted with the permission of Doubleday, an imprint of the Knopf Doubleday Publishing Group, a division of Penguin Random House, LLC. All rights reserved.

Peter Sacks, excerpts from *The English Elegy: Studies in the Genre from Spenser to Yeats*. Copyright © 1987 by Peter Sacks. Reprinted with the permission of Johns Hopkins University Press.

Tomaz Salamun, "Emptiness," translated by Charles Simic, from *The Selected Poems of Tomaz Salamun* (The Ecco Press, 1991). Copyright © 1991 by Charles Simic. Reprinted with the permission of the translator.

Shih Cheng, "Gwak! Gwak! cries the osprey" and excerpt from "We pick ferns, we pick ferns," translated by Burton Watson and adapted by Robert Hass from *Shih Cheng* in Burton Watson, *The Columbia Book of Chinese Poetry*. Copyright © 1984 by Columbia University Press. Reprinted with permission of the publisher.

Carol Snow, "For K.," *"And another,"* "In Brief," "At the Beach," "Elegy," "Breath As," ["What comfort?"], "By the Pond: *Reading*," "By the Pond: *Quiet breaths*," "By the Pond: *Watching the Goldfish*," and *"There was a moment"* from *For*. Copyright © 2000 by Carol Snow. Reprinted by permission of the University of California Press.

Gertrude Stein, excerpt from "Stanzas in Meditation" from *Stanzas in Meditation*. Copyright © 1956 by Alice B. Toklas. Copyright © 1980 by Calman A. Levin, Executor of the Estate of Gertrude Stein. Reprinted with the permission of the Permissions Company, Inc., on behalf of Green Integer, www.greeninteger.com.

Wallace Stevens, excerpts from "New England Verses," "Gallant Chateau," "Sea Surface Full of Clouds," "The Sick Man," "Credences of Summer," and "Of Mere Being" from *The Collected Poems of Wallace Stevens*. Copyright 1954 by Wallace Stevens. Used by permission of Alfred A. Knopf, an imprint of the Knopf Doubleday Publishing Group, a division of Penguin Random House, LLC. All rights reserved.

Virgil, II:1–8 from *Virgil's Georgics*, translated by C. Day Lewis. Reprinted with the permission of Oxford University Press, Ltd.

Anne Waldman, excerpt from "Makeup on Empty Space" from *Helping the Dreamer: New and Collected Poems, 1966–1980*. Copyright © by Anne Waldman. Reprinted with the permission of the Permissions Company, Inc., on behalf of Coffee House Press, www.coffeehousepress.org.

William Carlos Williams, excerpts from "Porous," "Fine Work with Pitch and Copper," "Spring and All," and "Summer Song" from *The Collected Poems of William Carlos Williams, Volume I, 1909–1939*, edited by Christopher MacGowan. Copyright 1938, 1939 by New Directions Publishing Corp. Excerpt from "The Ivy Crown" and "The Cure" from *The Collected Poems of William Carlos Williams, Volume II, 1939–1962*, edited by Christopher MacGowan. Copyright 1944, 1953 by William Carlos Williams. All reprinted by permission of New Directions Publishing Corp.

C. D. Wright, "The Ozark Odes" from *Steal Away: Selected and New Poems.* Copyright © 1991 by C. D. Wright. Reprinted with the permission of the Permissions Company, Inc., on behalf of Copper Canyon Press, www.coppercanyonpress.org.

William Butler Yeats, "Cuchulain Comforted," excerpt from "The Spur," excerpt from "Spilt Milk" "Leda and the Swan" and excerpt from "Among School Children" from *The Collected Works of W. B. Yeats, Volume I: The Poems, Revised,* edited by Richard J. Finneran. Copyright 1940 by Georgie Yeats, renewed © 1968 by Bertha Georgie Yeats, Michael Butler Yeats, and Anne Yeats. Copyright 1933 by the Macmillan Company, renewed © 1961 by Georgie Yeats. Copyright 1928 by the Macmillan Company, renewed © 1956 by Georgie Yeats. All reprinted with the permission of Simon & Schuster, Inc. All rights reserved.

Louis Zukofsky, excerpt from "A7" from *A* (New York: New Directions, 2001). All Louis Zukofsky material Copyright Paul Zukofsky; the material may not be reproduced, quoted, or used in any manner whatsoever without the explicit and specific permission of the copyright holder.

ABOUT THE AUTHOR

Robert Hass was born in San Francisco. His books of poetry include *The Apple Trees at Olema* (Ecco, 2010), Pulitzer Prize and National Book Award winner *Time and Materials* (Ecco, 2008), *Sun Under Wood* (Ecco, 1996), *Human Wishes* (1989), *Praise* (1979), and *Field Guide* (1973), which was selected by Stanley Kunitz for the Yale Younger Poets Series. Hass also co-translated many volumes of poetry with Nobel Laureate Czesław Miłosz and authored or edited several other volumes of translation, including Nobel Laureate Tomas Tranströmer's *Selected Poems* (2012) and *The Essential Haiku: Versions of Basho, Buson, and Issa* (1994). His first essay collection, *Twentieth Century Pleasures: Prose on Poetry* (1984), received the National Book Critics Circle Award; his second, *What Light Can Do*, received the PEN Diamonstein-Spielvogel Award for excellence in the art of the essay. Hass served as Poet Laureate of the United States from 1995 to 1997 and as Chancellor of the Academy of American Poets. He lives in California with his wife, poet Brenda Hillman, and teaches at the University of California, Berkeley.

"Hass is so supremely learned about and so deeply immersed in poetry, he is able to comport himself not just with incredible authority but also with casual humor. . . . Disguised as a reference book, this is actually a friendly tour of one poet's mind."
—*New York Times Book Review*

A wealth of vocabulary exists with which to talk about poetry in traditional formal terms. But the more intuitive, creative parts of a poet's work and processes are more elusive: if the most interesting aspect of the form is the shaping power of the essential, expressive gestures inside it, how do we come to language in which to speak about form as the search for the radiant shapes—the wholeness or brokenness—we experience inside powerful works of art?

In suggestive, informal "notes," former U.S. poet laureate and Pulitzer Prize and National Book Award–winner Robert Hass thinks through the idea of a poem from its barest building blocks to the grand forms of elegy and ode through which poets across human cultures have investigated the shapes of grieving and desiring. Begun as a project for students of poetry, *A Little Book on Form* is anything but—Hass investigates the ancient roots of the poetic impulse, taking a wide-ranging look at the most intense experience of human thought and feeling in language.

ROBERT HASS's books of poetry include Pulitzer Prize and National Book Award–winner *Time and Materials: Poems, 1997–2005* (2007) and *Field Guide* (1973), selected for the Yale Series of Younger Poets. His essay collection *Twentieth Century Pleasures: Prose on Poetry* (1984) won the National Book Critics Circle Award. Hass served as poet laureate of the United States from 1995 to 1997. He lives in California with his wife, poet Brenda Hillman, and teaches at the University of California, Berkeley.

DISCOVER GREAT AUTHORS, EXCLUSIVE OFFERS, AND MORE AT HC.COM.

Literary Criticism/Poetry

ISBN 978-0-06-233243-1

An Imprint of HarperCollinsPublishers

Available from HarperCollins e-books

Cover design by Sara Wood
Cover artwork © Téa Chai Beer

51899

9 780062 332431

EAN

USA $18.99 / $23.99 CAN

0318